D0629256

Praise for
THE PROMISE OF BITCOIN and Bobby C. Lee

Bobby Lee was among the earliest forward thinkers to fully recognize Bitcoin's potential as a store of value. He arrived at his conclusions not out of some whim or particular love of risk, but rather after carefully analyzing its characteristics and technological merit. *The Promise of Bitcoin* traces his thinking on the subject and explains in plainspoken language how Bitcoin works and why and how the average investor should invest in this opportunity of a lifetime.

—Tyler Winklevoss, Cofounder of Gemini

Bitcoin is starting to go mainstream, but it's still mysterious and misunderstood by many. Bobby Lee, an early Bitcoiner, has written an approachable book that demystifies Bitcoin in an easy-to-understand way and addresses people's primary fears about it head-on.

—Cameron Winklevoss, Cofounder of Gemini

This book will help quench the amazing thirst for a better understanding of the Bitcoin revolution. It should be part of the curriculum for all investors.

—Michael Novogratz, Founder of Galaxy Digital

Bobby Lee has written an important book for anyone interested in cryptocurrencies. It offers practical insights derived from Bobby's experience as a successful Bitcoin entrepreneur and informed by a global and learned perspective. Part treatise, part how-to manual, this highly accessible read is indispensable to investors, innovators, journalists, regulators, academics, and the general public alike.

—Glenn Hutchins, Chairman of North Island Ventures and Cofounder of Silver Lake

Bitcoin's big surge at the end of 2020 into 2021 reflects a growing acceptance of its infallible logic, particularly among some of the world's largest institutional investors. Bobby Lee predicted this trend years ago, even when financial institutions wouldn't touch it. In *The Promise of Bitcoin*, he explains why Bitcoin is a better form of money than traditional currencies, and offers a primer on what Bitcoin newcomers and early-stage investors need to know.

—CZ (Changpeng Zhao), CEO of Binance.com

As an entrepreneur who has built multiple businesses to help bring Bitcoin to a broader audience, Bobby is the perfect person to take readers on a journey from Bitcoin's earliest beginnings to its current state. His personal stories add a unique perspective that make this book a must-read for anyone who is interested in understanding Bitcoin and its place in our world.

—Meltem Demirors, cryptocurrency entrepreneur and investor

Much of the discussion about Bitcoin is dry and unengaging for the average investor. In this valuable book, Bobby Lee successfully interweaves his personal experiences into sound, easy-to-follow explanations about why Bitcoin is such a strong investment, and he makes the tools for investors easier to understand.

—Wences Casares, CEO of Xapo and Board Member of PayPal and DIEM

This pioneering guide captures Bobby's inspiring vision, passion for Bitcoin, and fervent desire to create a better society for us all.

—Micky Malka, Founder of Ribbit Capital

From the Ivory Coast to Silicon Valley, Bobby Lee's life experience makes him the perfect person to explain the promise of Bitcoin.

—Roger Ver, Founder of Bitcoin.com

Bitcoin is unstoppable. If you want to understand why or how it fits into the world of money or your personal financial portfolio, read *The Promise of Bitcoin*.

—Gavin Andresen, former lead developer of Bitcoin and former Chief Scientist at the Bitcoin Foundation

As an early innovator and builder of systems around Bitcoin, Bobby is an apt guide for anyone looking to go deeper on the coin.

—Chris Burniske, Cofounder of Placeholder and bestselling author of *Cryptoassets*

Bobby steadfastly follows his vision and *The Promise of Bitcoin* perfectly crafts that vision into words. Enjoy this wild ride!

—Charlie Shrem, Founder of the Bitcoin Foundation and the *Untold Stories* podcast

As an early pioneer, Bobby Lee saw the potential of Bitcoin and shared his passion for this promising new currency. This fascinating book captures the remarkable impact that Bitcoin has had on the world and Bobby's vision for its future.

—Tina Seelig, Professor of the Practice in the Department of Management Science and Engineering at Stanford University

Bobby's passion for Bitcoin is reflected in these pages. I look forward to Bitcoin's continued evolution and the public's rising awareness of this potentially transformative new system.

—Tom Byers, Entrepreneurship Professor at the School of Engineering at Stanford University

THE PROMISE OF BITCOIN

THE FUTURE OF MONEY AND HOW IT CAN WORK FOR YOU

BOBBY C. LEE

New York Chicago San Francisco Athens London Madrid
Mexico City Milan New Delhi Singapore Sydney Toronto

1 2 3 4 5 6 7 8 9 LCR 26 25 24 23 22 21

ISBN 978-1-260-46867-0
MHID 1-260-46867-4

e-ISBN 978-1-260-46868-7
e-MHID 1-260-46868-2

This publication is designed to provide accurate and authoritative information in regard to the subject matter covered. It is sold with the understanding that neither the author nor the publisher is engaged in rendering legal, accounting, securities trading, or other professional services. If legal advice or other expert assistance is required, the services of a competent professional person should be sought.

—From a Declaration of Principles Jointly Adopted by a Committee of the American Bar Association and a Committee of Publishers and Associations

Library of Congress Cataloging-in-Publication Data

Names: Lee, Bobby C., author.
Title: The promise of bitcoin : the future of money and how it can work for you / Bobby C. Lee.
Description: New York City : McGraw Hill, 2021. | Includes bibliographical references and index.
Identifiers: LCCN 2021000761 (print) | LCCN 2021000762 (ebook) | ISBN 9781260468670 (hardcover) | ISBN 9781260468687 (ebook)
Subjects: LCSH: Electronic funds transfers. | Bitcoin. | Finance—Data processing. | Financial instruments.
Classification: LCC HG1710 .L44 2021 (print) | LCC HG1710 (ebook) | DDC 332.4—dc23
LC record available at https://lccn.loc.gov/2021000761
LC ebook record available at https://lccn.loc.gov/2021000762

McGraw Hill books are available at special quantity discounts to use as premiums and sales promotions or for use in corporate training programs. To contact a representative, please visit the Contact Us pages at www.mhprofessional.com.

To my grandfather, William Sze Tsen Lee,
for always loving me and believing in me.
You were the quintessential businessman;
you gave me the confidence and
inspiration to be an entrepreneur.

CONTENTS

INTRODUCTION

MY JOURNEY INTO BITCOIN

Until they become conscious they will never rebel, and until after they have rebelled they cannot become conscious.
—George Orwell, *1984*

My name is Bobby Christopher Lee.

The cryptocurrency community knows me as one of the industry's earliest entrepreneurs and investors in Bitcoin.

I believe that any person or entity that interferes with productive individual or group enterprise is wrong. We've turned increasingly from principles of true liberty. We've allowed governments and other organizations that have mushroomed beyond their original intent to limit our activities.

Even progressive nations restrict commerce via well-meaning but ill-conceived laws. They do not fathom entrepreneurship.

For generations, my family—the Lees and Chus—built businesses and chased dreams with a singular focus that left little room for distraction or skeptics. Keep things simple and straight and financial success will follow. Complicate issues and you run into headwinds.

Central banks are a primary source of economic mischief. They wield too much power and reflect the outdated thinking of a minority that has made holding their power their raison d'être.

At their core, these institutions perpetuate themselves rather than looking critically at what they should or should not do to help people. But wasn't helping people by creating a simple, comprehensive structure for managing currency why they were created? Alexander Hamilton understood this when he pushed for a US central bank and currency that would be valued the same in every state.

Instead, the banks became political instruments, divorced from their mission. They wield too much power and are too involved with people and their money. The banks' misjudgments intertwine with nearly every economic downturn of the past two centuries and have reduced the value and purchasing power of consumers' money.

Once someone has earned money, no governing agency should have the right to take it without the individual's consent. Americans fought a revolution because their British overlords thought they could take the fruits of their industriousness at will.

Do not confuse my thinking with current brands of extremism that see evil in the slightest institutional oversight. I vote, I appreciate the free trade agreements that have opened markets in recent years and will continue to do so whatever happens post NAFTA and Brexit. My family were successful international traders. The cryptocurrency business I helped found is global. So was every company that I worked for prior to becoming an entrepreneur.

I appreciate having a passport that allows me to go pretty much anywhere in the world. And because I fly a lot, I'm grateful for the agencies that protect airports. I like owning real estate in different countries, as it diversifies my investments.

I also believe in smart regulations and products that protect our environment for future generations. I've been a gadget guy since I was a teen and have never experienced anything better than the Tesla Model 3 that I now drive. It can reach speeds up to 155 mph and cover over 300 miles without a recharge—silently, smoothly, with barely a carbon ripple. It is technology at its best, servicing a need, doing good without ruffling any government bureaucrat's feathers.

To be sure, as a Stanford-trained computer scientist and software engineer, I am biased about technology.

I was exploring computer technology long before personal computers became part of the world's DNA. I taught myself computer programming in the sixth grade, beginning with the BASIC programming language. I started the personal computer club at my US boarding school and majored in computer science at Stanford, a university at the heart of the global tech boom. During the summer of 1997, Bill Gates invited me to his home—albeit with several hundred other Microsoft summer interns.

I've worked at some of the world's most important technology and internet companies, helped kick-start a major e-commerce initiative for the world's biggest retailer, and started my own cutting-edge tech business in China in 2013. It counted over one million users before I sold it in 2018.

I am a forward-thinker with strong opinions about what tech has done for the world, and even stronger beliefs about what it will do, particularly one remarkable innovation, introduced by a developer who won't give his or her name, but who saw huge weaknesses in our monetary systems—cryptocurrency, or as most people know it, Bitcoin.

The pseudonymous Satoshi Nakamoto developed a new digital payment system that made brilliant use of disparate technological concepts. More importantly, it focused entirely on serving people worldwide—not controlling them.

Digital cryptocurrency is one of the greatest inventions of the past half-century.

Satoshi's invention has consumed me for almost a quarter of my 46-year life. It has been a surprising journey that started with a conversation that wasn't the least bit momentous at the time.

My brother, Charlie Lee, a computer scientist like me, had read about Bitcoin through online forums, and he had become interested enough to acquire his first bitcoins through trading with anonymous people online. It was early 2011 when we had one of our occasional long-distance calls. I had been living in Shanghai for about four years and was about to join Walmart, as a senior executive in charge of its technology team that was tasked with building a brand-new e-commerce unit for the China market.

Charlie was a Google engineer living in Silicon Valley. Mining, the process by which someone earns bitcoins by recording a transaction on a digital ledger, was the domain of a few dedicated computer nerds who had enough computing power to solve the algorithms required for participation. There were no Bitcoin exchanges, Medium blogs, MIT blockchain programs, or intense discussions about regulations. Any banks that were aware of Bitcoin probably brushed away the topic like a speck of dust. To outsiders, Bitcoin was no more innovative than the latest in-game virtual currency in PC and console games, where people would use in-game currency to buy virtual swords or other weaponry.

At that time, the spring of 2011, Bitcoin was selling for under $20 with a market capitalization of under $150 million. The community of enthusiasts and the curious numbered in the thousands, globally. In the course of our discussion, Charlie suggested that I check out this new electronic money called Bitcoin.

As a computer geek, I had an advantage over the average consumer in understanding the concepts that Charlie outlined. I knew about online development communities and distributed networks, which are at the heart of the blockchain system. As much as it was a digital system, in the end it relied on actual people with a deep passion. Because of my undergraduate and master's education at Stanford's prestigious computer science department, I had some training in cryptography. I also had a special interest in currencies, economics, and our monetary system. Charlie knew all that, as it was a thread that ran through our family for generations.

MY FAMILY'S LONG JOURNEY

For at least a century, the Lee family on my father's side and the Chu family on my mother's side had been prolific entrepreneurs. They acquired success through a range of business ventures in Asia, South America, Africa, and finally North America. In the early decades of the twentieth century, my paternal great-grandfather was the Regional Head of the Salt Administration of Jiangsu province, which was the largest single source of the government's tax revenue at that time. It was a chaotic time as the Republic of China sorted out its governance after years of dynastic rule. The government relied on able administrators to maintain order and govern fairly in key industries. The Salt Administration was one of the most important ministries, so only the best qualified and most honest personalities were appointed to fill such posts.

My paternal great-grandmother was a direct descendent of the imperial family from Manchuria that had ruled China for more than three centuries. She was a brilliant woman who spoke English fluently and earned a medical degree, in a profession ruled by men at the time. She enjoyed this elite education because of her upbringing. However, once the dynasty fell, she and her relatives had to assume new family names to blend into the predominantly Han-ethnic society. (Manchurian family names were all long multisyllables, whereas the Han-ethnic family names were all just one syllable.) They all took the new surname of King, the traditional spelling of the Chinese character 金, which means gold (and is now spelled as "Jin" in Chinese pinyin). Apparently, only descendants of the Manchurian imperial family could choose "gold" as their surname.

In this turbulent time, the family also developed an appreciation for accumulating wealth and holding it in what they viewed was the most widely accepted store of value: gold. It was a way to inoculate themselves against potential economic fluctuations in early twentieth-century Shanghai, which was as well known for corruption as commerce.

My grandfather, William Sze Tsen Lee, was born in Shanghai in 1925. Over the next quarter century, China experienced two pivotal events: first, the invasion by the Japanese, and second, the Communist takeover following World War II. William, who had become a successful businessman by the time he was in his early twenties, feared an end to free enterprise. He had studied law at the prestigious Fudan University in Shanghai, so he had a good grasp of what was to come.

In 1949, with Mao's forces controlling most of the country's vital operations, Sze Tsen Lee used his clout to obtain two steamer tickets to Hong Kong. The year before, he had married Julia Koo, the daughter of a local cotton trader from Pudong, Shanghai. She was pregnant with their first child (my uncle David). Because of their strong convictions about mainland China's future, they bought one-way tickets to Hong Kong, leaving the rest of their family behind.

Once in Hong Kong, he took on his new Western name William Lee. William and Julia became two of the 700,000 immigrants hoping to build a better future in the British colony, nearby but outside Communist rule. But they recognized that even receptive, democratic societies required capital to launch new ventures. They traveled with gold bars sewn into hidden pockets in their clothes. Gold was only $35 an ounce then, but it was a veritable fortune at a time when the US government made news by doubling its minimum wage to 75 cents an hour and a Hong Kong apartment rental cost the equivalent of $10 a month.

Within a year, William had created an import-export business specializing in textiles. But the couple quickly recalculated in a way that only the entrepreneurial and adventurous would consider. Alarmed by Hong Kong's population spike, they joined a small but determined group of expats who sought their fortunes not in industrialized economies with large Chinese populations but rather in developing countries with cheap labor and production costs. They spent nearly two years in Brazil, saw a business or two fail, and then later moved to Sierra

Leone, a small country in West Africa. As with many Chinese emigrants, their first business was a Chinese restaurant. A few more businesses and years later, they settled in the neighboring Ivory Coast, where William eventually founded a successful business manufacturing plastic sandals. At one point, he even dabbled in a business exporting shark fins to Hong Kong, where it was a well-loved delicacy.

Unknown to them, my mother's parents, Linning Chu and Shou Chen Pang, had followed a similar path about the same time. Linning Chu went to Hong Kong by himself in 1950 to build a pharmaceutical business. Soon after, he moved to Africa, where he built textile manufacturing businesses in Ghana, and also opened enterprises in nearby Togo and Cameroon. He was among the first Chinese people doing business in Africa.

The Chus faced an added obstacle in their odyssey to Africa. My mother and her five siblings had already been born in Shanghai, and the Chinese government was becoming increasingly restrictive about travel passes. Linning Chu sent for my grandmother, my uncle, and my mother soon after settling abroad. And over the course of the next decade, he diligently arranged exit visas for their remaining children, who had to stay back in Shanghai by themselves.

The Chu and Lee families didn't know each other, but they shared many of the same life principles. Both sides saw education, individual initiative, and hard work as keys to success. Both families insisted that their children, including my mother and father, attend good schools in Europe and the United States.

My parents met while in college, married a few years later, and then returned to the Ivory Coast, where my father also entered the family business of manufacturing. I was born in 1975, the oldest of three siblings. When people ask me about my exotic birthplace, I tell them that I didn't have a choice! The Ivory Coast is where my parents were building their lives then. Charlie followed two years later, and my sister Vivienne four years after that.

For our upbringing, my parents followed roughly the same model they had grown up with. They enrolled us in the local American School through middle school and encouraged us to study hard. The Ivory Coast had a global feel in the 1980s, as it was the most cosmopolitan of all West African countries, mostly due to its strong French influence. I grew up learning five languages: English at the American International school I attended, French with Ivorian locals, and three dialects of Chinese at home. I spoke Shanghainese with my parents and grandparents, Chinese Mandarin with local Taiwanese expats, and Cantonese with our Hong Kong relatives and nanny.

My father also believed in staying abreast of the latest tech developments and had a hunch about the potential of personal computers. He spent $10,000, a fortune in 1986, for an early Apple IIGS model, a 16-bit personal computer that generated huge buzz for its multimedia color graphics and sound, but seems medieval by today's standards.

The Apple IIGS spurred my interest in computers. I marveled at its full color display, crisp responses to typed message commands, and overall versatility. By seventh grade, Charlie and I were already teaching ourselves coding and gobbling up anything we could find on computer programming, which was minimal. Our favorites were the early personal computer magazines, which had source code listings for sample games, where we could follow along, type in, and run our own programs. (In many cases, I would politely ask Charlie to type in those long lines of computer programming from the magazine listings. He was nice about it and didn't complain.) My father nurtured our interest in computers via product upgrades and game purchases. We were always the first family in the neighborhood with the latest Apple Computer software and hardware peripherals.

When I started at Lawrenceville in 1989, I was already using a laptop computer, made by Sharp. At 20 pounds, it was heavier than the largest toaster and almost as clunky, but it was also a revelation to my classmates, who were just learning about the revolution to come. I could set up anywhere, and the device had an early LCD screen, which made for crisper fonts. It was like looking into the future, albeit through an 8-bit flickering grayscale display. From then on, I was hooked on computers and technology.

OFF TO STANFORD

My father, the MIT alum, expected me to follow his lead, but I chose Stanford instead. Twenty-five years earlier, Stanford had been among the first to create a department offering computer science degrees. Its early researchers invented the PDP-1–based timesharing system, the world's first display-oriented timesharing system, and the DEC PDP-6 program, an operating system that is the grandfather to today's Windows and macOS. Its faculty included Turing Award winners and pioneers in computer science, robotics, automation, and artificial intelligence.

Some Stanford students, I soon also learned, were as passionate about computers as I was and equally entrepreneurial. Many of them shared my experience as outliers entering uncharted territories looking for creative ways to apply the binary numbers of coding to products that could transform personal interaction and enterprise. The school had a sizable computer lab with the latest computer workstations and encouraged students to explore and invent, and I started reading snippets about a growing industry called venture capital–backed startups. In 1998, I eagerly applied for and got accepted into Stanford's entrepreneurship class, the Mayfield Fellows Program.

The tie-in between finance, tech, and entrepreneurship was already intriguing for me. I had been president of Lawrenceville's Wall Street Club, which conducted mock trading, and won the annual competition for most successful portfolio. My picks included a little-known Omaha, Nebraska-based investment company, Berkshire Hathaway, and gold mining stocks. My father was my secret stock advisor for this mock trading game, and we had many long-distance phone calls, discussing which stocks to invest in and why.

Although I didn't know this at the time, as I enjoyed my freshman year at Stanford University, Jerry Yang and David Filo had already developed the framework for Yahoo!, which would launch a year later, and for whom I would work for more than a half-decade. Google founders Sergey Brin and Larry Page had begun working toward their doctorates, Brin on a graduate fellowship from the National Science Foundation.

I had found my tribe.

MY INTRODUCTION TO BITCOIN

Fast-forward to 2011, just 13 years after graduating Stanford with bachelor's and master's degrees in computer science. Through these memorable years, I had scored internships at Microsoft, where I introduced myself to Bill Gates at the annual interns barbecue he held each summer, and at IBM, the aging lion of the modern computer industry. I had held management positions at Yahoo! and other American and Chinese technology companies, and was now about to start work on my biggest role yet: I was one of the five vice presidents managing a new e-commerce service in China for Walmart, the world's largest company by revenue.

Walmart figured it could challenge Chinese online retail powerhouses Taobao and Jingdong in the world's most populated country. Walmart called its effort Project Panda.

But it quickly became apparent that Project Panda faced an uphill struggle as much because of internal politics as outside competition. Walmart was quick to hedge its bet by investing in an established Chinese e-commerce company, Yihaodian, and pitted our newly formed division against them. We had no chance. My 150-member technology team did yeoman's work but couldn't catch up to our established in-house competitor. Within a year, we could all see the endgame for Project Panda.

During that year that I had my first conversation about Bitcoin with my brother. Charlie had graduated from MIT's five-year master's program in electrical engineering and computer science and was working as a software engineer on Google's Chrome OS team. Charlie outlined how Bitcoin worked and how it had built a small global following in its two years of existence. More importantly, Charlie made a compelling case for Satoshi's Bitcoin thesis and its potential for revolutionizing finance. I was hooked.

Just as I started my promising Walmart career, I mined my first bitcoins. The experience was addictive, and I started looking for graphics cards that would accelerate my computer's ability to solve the algorithmic problems that would reward me with more bitcoins. The global Bitcoin community was tiny, but I suspect there was at least one other hobbyist in Shanghai who always seemed to be one step ahead of me. Apparently, he bought out the local computer stores' supply of high-end graphics cards. The shelves were empty at every store I visited. Thankfully, I found supplies overseas.

I mined bitcoins from the summer through the fall of 2011. My single mining rig ran all day, every day, and it was enough to heat up that whole empty guest room in my apartment in downtown Shanghai.

In late 2012, shortly after leaving Walmart, I decided to take an early exit off the traditional technology management career path and make Bitcoin my full-time career. It was a bold step into an uncharted field. The possibilities were enormous, but the truth was I wasn't sure exactly what I would do.

Mining didn't offer enough variety: once you knew what you were doing, it wasn't mentally stimulating. But Bitcoin was just about to catch the public eye. What would consumers need to quicken the pace? I had bought additional bitcoins on a local exchange website called BTCChina.com, created by two Chinese men in their late twenties, one a computer programmer from

Nanjing and the other a businessman from Beijing. A switch turned on inside me. (This was in the days before Litecoin, Ethereum, and all of the other cryptocurrencies had launched.) The idea behind BTCChina was inspired, and it compelled me to act.

Here was an easy-to-use Bitcoin exchange platform available to everyone in China. Its functions needed work, but that's where I could apply my years of experience building consumer-facing platforms. I emailed them cold, asking via customer support to see if I could speak with the boss. A week later, I was in Beijing outlining my BTCChina vision over a Peking duck dinner, and when the three of us had closed the restaurant, we continued at a coffee shop late into the night. Our backgrounds were complementary, and our passion and vision were aligned. We would make a good team.

They were skilled entrepreneurs who had a sound foundation, but they lacked managerial know-how, vision, and a sense of how to find funding to energize the business. I could bring big-picture, corporate expertise to the mix and an understanding of how technology startups thrive. I also knew about the bumps of early-stage companies. Like startups in most new industries, BTCChina might see huge spikes and then lulls of activity. Over the ensuing weeks, I purchased shares in the company, took on the title of cofounder and CEO, and immediately began speaking with venture capitalists to raise money. When we closed the deal on my role in early 2013, bitcoin's price was just under $15.

About this time, bitcoin prices and trading volumes started climbing. We were using my Shanghai apartment as our headquarters. But after recruiting two customer service representatives and an ex-Walmart colleague, we leased our first office, a 2,000-square-foot open floor plan in the Xujiahui neighborhood, not far from Shanghai's business epicenter. It was a small office on the twenty-third floor of an office building, with brightly colored walls painted by the previous tenant, an internet content delivery network company. We were excited to get started and to build a real Bitcoin company in China.

By then, I had also secured a $5 million investment round led by venture firm Lightspeed China, an offshoot of the famed Menlo Park, California, venture firm by the same name. Lightspeed China counted some of the country's highest profile tech companies in its portfolio. We were the first cryptocurrency company in all of Asia to receive venture funding.

We adopted best practices that were drawn from the American startup world but were new to China's emerging economy. We provided free sodas and drinks at the office, handed out T-shirts and other gear with our corporate logo, and took employees to the movies to foster team building. I borrowed several traditions from Yahoo!, including one where we gave employees custom-designed coffee mugs each Christmas. Employees collected a different personalized mug for every year of service.

The hours were long. We even made Saturday a regular work day. On a memorable company retreat in the fall of 2013 at a vacation island outside Shanghai, we spent most of the time in conference rooms revamping our platform to accommodate a sudden jolt in trading volumes. Bitcoin had just passed $200.

But BTCChina also ran a lean ship. We stayed put in our small space even as we quadrupled our workforce. We mapped product designs and engineering solutions on the glass walls enclosing the conference rooms, which served as makeshift whiteboards. We felt we were part of a bold mission, the introduction of a new type of decentralized digital asset based on a technology with huge potential, called blockchain. We focused everything we did on building our business into something that the average consumer and investor could recognize.

EXITING BTCCHINA

The ride was often challenging. For every new customer, we heard from dozens of naysayers. What is this new currency? How can it be valuable? Why would anyone use it? Does it have the government's support? Who is regulating it? Isn't it more vulnerable to hacking than an online bank account?

Then there were the shocks.

After shooting over $1,100 by late 2013, bitcoin quickly lost two-thirds of its value, stoking fears that it was no better than play money. Meanwhile, two aggressive, well-supported competitors emerged, OKCoin and Huobi. They reduced the trading fees, so we started a price war by cutting trading commissions to zero. That was good for customers but drained our cash reserves. We cut staff, introduced new trading features and other new services to boost sales, and went out to seek a fresh cash infusion. A small surge in bitcoin prices and the subsequent demand for exchange services near the end of 2015 helped push us into cash positive territory. We were finally profitable!

The next obstacle arose two years later, when the Chinese government started cracking down on crypto trading and initial coin offers, a mechanism for funding blockchain projects, largely because these were activities that regulators could not control. In September 2017, we shuttered the domestic BTCChina exchange for trading. At the time, we boasted over one million registered users, a staff of 150, and four separate offices. We kept open our international business called BTCC, based in our Hong Kong office. In January 2018, we sold our business to a Hong Kong–based blockchain investment fund.

The acquisition came when the price of bitcoin was hovering over $10,000—down from a much-ballyhooed high of $20,000 a month earlier but more than 100-fold higher than the price when BTCChina opened for business.

Bitcoin was fulfilling Satoshi Nakamoto's vision that a digital currency open to anyone, controlled by no one, would find a wide following. In his 2008 paper, "Bitcoin: A Peer-to-Peer Electronic Cash System," Satoshi had outlined a system that would allow individual parties to execute financial transactions without the participation of an intermediary controlling entity.[1]

These controlling entities or centralized organizations—most prominently banks, credit card companies, or increasingly electronic payment services like PayPal—had traditionally filled an accounting role, ensuring the accuracy of every activity. Although bank loans and deposits have roots before the birth of Christ, the system upon which the modern banking model bases itself dates to the Medici family in the Italian Renaissance. The Medici recognized an ongoing need among the powerful elite for well-organized financial management services on a large scale, via one powerful entity.

Over the centuries, the public came to trust these centralized organizations as the most secure places to park their hard-earned cash. Banks ranked among society's most respected organizations. They were too big to fail—or were they?

Just three months after the economic crash of 2008, when several large financial institutions failed, Satoshi's nine-page paper offered a more streamlined, efficient alternative to the traditional system. Satoshi had recognized the greatest flaw in the traditional models: namely, that these centralized organizations controlled every activity within their networks. They could delay, stop, and even reverse transactions that they determined had not met their standards. Fairness and objectivity often did not guide their decisions. Moreover, the cost of their mediation services increased transaction costs, and perversely, the banks were financially incentivized more and more for their involvement in these financial transactions.

"The system works well enough," Satoshi wrote. But upon closer inspection, it also created obstacles to which most consumers had grown immune, such as transaction costs and lack of control.

His electronic payment system removed the impediments, allowing "two willing parties to transact directly," to move payments from one digital account to another with access based on memorizing a key of binary numbers. He described the coins as "a chain of digital signatures," or bitcoins. The now widely used term refers to bits, the zeros and ones that are the smallest units of data in computer language.

A network of computer-savvy participants, miners, used their computation power to ensure the integrity of this new currency system, by verifying and recording each transaction on a digital ledger open for public review. Each time-stamped transaction, approved by a consensus of miners, would become part of a chain of data blocks, called the blockchain. To falsify a transaction would require altering earlier entries, alerting the group and invalidating that record and all subsequent ones. The system would be safe from attack as long as miners with honorable intent outnumbered those with malicious designs. The whole system was self-healing, self-reinforcing, and self-incentivized.

The system incentivized people to participate by offering bitcoin awards for their work as miners, which required solving an algorithmic equation. Mathematical certainty was at the heart of Satoshi's system, and that would propel it forward, rather than faith in institutions that were more easily corruptible or had swung from their original intent. Its rapid growth from the idea of a singular genius to a community surpassing 50 million people globally in early 2021 (this is my rough estimate based on my tracking of the industry and discussions with other Bitcoin experts) reflected pent-up demand for a monetary system that could give everyone in the world more control of their assets.

Bitcoin was also a manifestation of a larger movement: a new scrutiny of old ways and embrace of digital innovations that had already transformed much of how we live and work. Money and currency were the last frontiers in this movement.

But for me, Bitcoin never felt completely new. It possessed a familiar quality. At first I couldn't pinpoint the feeling, but then I realized Bitcoin was the virtual equivalent of gold, the substance that my great-grandmother's family was named after; that my paternal grandparents had concealed in their clothes to start a new life in noncommunist Hong Kong; and that my family revered and collected for generations. In short, gold had given all of us a sense of security.

They knew that gold held its value—or better—because of its scarcity and its special properties that have entranced people throughout history, qualities that made it the most suitable form of natural money for thousands of years.

The shine that embodies wealth.

Perhaps more importantly, my gold-bearing ancestors had direct control over their most important asset. They didn't need bank approvals or waiting periods. It was a tumultuous, unpredictable time for them as they made their escape just years after living through one of history's most violent periods. My grandparents thought a lot about security, both in the physical sense and in the financial sense. They looked for solid ground wherever they could find it.

I'm finding similar reassurance in Bitcoin now as the world becomes more unpredictable. Political unrest fed by populist movements, environmental concerns, and a fast-changing global economy that seems to generate new winners and losers every few days have challenged much of what most of us have assumed would always be true. The next downturn seems to be lurking just out of sight. Brexit. Tariffs. Protectionism. Canyoning divides in wealth between haves and have-nots. Social inequity. Growing racial divides. And perhaps most importantly, a growing inability of people to empathize with one another.

What comes next?

Even in the current low-inflationary environment, the money I've earned does not buy me as much as it did 10 years ago, when I mined my first bitcoins. Yet untethered from the forces that determine economic policy, my cryptocurrency holdings have risen in value over 10,000 percent. I couldn't have done nearly as well investing in retail juggernaut Amazon—even over 20 years. And the great thing is, the superior performance of bitcoin continues. Figure I.1 shows how well bitcoin performed versus Amazon in late 2020.

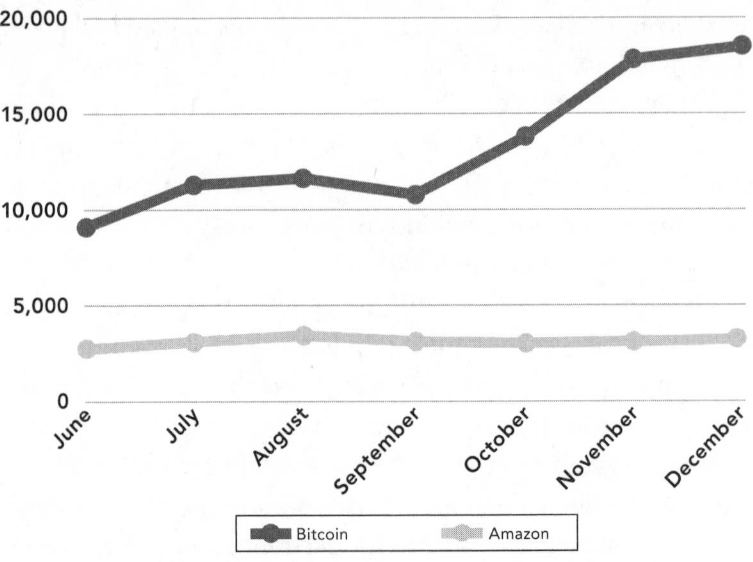

FIGURE I.1 Bitcoin Outpaced Amazon in 2020

In Satoshi's scheme, there will always be a grand total of 21 million bitcoins worldwide, so bitcoins' price should only rise as more people start using them. This asset class is a new genre, completely digital and fully decentralized, such that there is no organization controlling it or setting rules. Conceptually, Bitcoin is just information. Bitcoins are also certainly easier to transport than a gold bar. No matter the amount being transferred, bitcoins can zip around the world in just minutes.

WHY I WROTE THIS BOOK

These days, I am fortunate to be in demand as an industry speaker. I am considered an expert because of my experience and involvement early in Bitcoin's history and my board position on the Bitcoin Foundation, a nonprofit founded to build awareness of Bitcoin. The speaking invitations come not only from cryptocurrency conventions that seem to occur every week, but also from business schools and mainstream publications that want to educate their students. These are in themselves promising changes, a reflection of an industry finding acceptance. But despite becoming more well known, Bitcoin and its supporting technology are still widely misunderstood.

That is why I'm writing this book. I want to make Bitcoin less frightening. In my academic and professional career, I never considered myself the smartest person in the room. But I worked hard, excelled at distilling information until I could understand an idea, and was willing to take a few calculated risks. I treated my 2011 orientation to Bitcoin the same way.

Bitcoin never seemed like anything except a series of concepts logically arranged in the best interests of the people who bought into the system. Strip away the hash power, TXID, nodes, blockchain, and other strange-sounding technological terms that are unfamiliar to non–computer scientists, Bitcoin is a system that is conceptually easy to understand.

What could be more elemental than two parties agreeing to a payment without the need for a third officiating body? The transactions can take less time than I need to write this paragraph.

But understand that this is not a book about investment. This is a book about the promise of Bitcoin: what it is, why it's special, and where it will take the world. I'll offer a few principles based on my own harsh experience. But you will have to make your own decisions about whether or not to buy into and invest in Bitcoin.

That means understanding your tolerance for risk and investing only amounts with which you're comfortable. Skilled financial advisors say the same all the time.

I strongly believe that Bitcoin is the opportunity of our lifetime. If you work hard and proceed thoughtfully, the chances are your Bitcoin adventure will have a happy conclusion.

In that way, it's no different than exploring a new land, preferably without having to sew gold bars into your clothing.

BIRTH OF BITCOIN: SATOSHI'S GENIUS

How much does something cost? How do we pay for it?

Historically, these deceivingly complicated questions have been among Western civilization's most important concerns. They define many of our daily interactions. They raise fundamental issues about what we value and don't, our ethics, and our sense of fairness and equity.

The answers manifested themselves into the currencies and payment systems we've created over the centuries and use today. The Old Testament's Lamentations 5:4 addresses the issue of payment: "We have to pay for our drinking water, our wood comes to us at a price." So does the Koran, which sets guidelines for ethical conduct in financial matters. In his *Nicomachean Ethics*, Aristotle writes that "all things that are exchanged must be comparable, and to this end, money has been introduced as an intermediate for it measures all things."

In short, our most important religious and philosophical texts required people to define money.

Beads, shells, stone slabs, salt, spices, gold, pelts, silver, coins, bills. We've used all these objects to pay for things—sometimes unfairly. The seventeenth-century Dutch infamously snared New York for $24 in trinkets (more, say some historians when calculating inflation properly[1]) they paid the Lenape tribe. Four decades later, they received their comeuppance, ceding it to England in exchange for not being shelled by four warships.

Neither currency—the Dutch beads or English shells—endured very long. Nor have silver and gold coins and other iterations of cash that preceded and followed it in the US central bank–backed currencies. These coins, which are the foundation of our financial system, have proven to be more sustainable, but they have a number of shortcomings.

I like the latest turn in money's evolution much better: digital cryptocurrency.

The speed of its growth has been remarkable—in a little more than a decade, cryptocurrencies have achieved a total market value that has already topped $1 trillion. The rapid rise makes perfect sense, having been enabled by profound technological and social changes and addressing many of the weaknesses in traditional monetary systems.

It took tens of thousands of years, or even more, to get here. A 2018 series of articles in the journal *Science* found strong evidence that Paleolithic men, perhaps dating back as much as 300,000 years ago, were using colored crayon-like objects as currency in a trade network.[2]

More than 1,500 years before the birth of Christ, Phoenician traders operating from Mediterranean coastal towns and Babylonians on the banks of the Euphrates River developed increasingly sophisticated forms of barter, trading weaponry, spices, and other luxuries. Centuries later, the Roman Empire paid its troops in salt because it was scarce and highly valued. The use of goods as units of barter continued for millennia in Europe and throughout Asia, Europe, and North and South America.

Even after many societies opted for coins and cash, barter reemerged in Weimar, Germany, as the value of the mark plummeted to historic lows. This also happened in the United States during the Great Depression, when some hard-struck families exchanged commodities like corn for doctor's services or coal to heat their homes.[3]

This system's self-governing structure—barterers establish the rate of exchange—possessed the seeds of distributed ledger principles that are fundamental to cryptocurrency. There was no central authority refereeing the transactions or keeping track of them.

IN THE WAY OLD DAYS

The earliest currency, the Mesopotamian shekel, dates more than 6,500 years to an area in what is modern-day Iraq. Monetary systems grew increasingly sophisticated from there. As early as 1200 BC, ancient China used a form of coinage—bronze replicas of goods that later were shaped into rounded objects. But it was the sixth-century BC Lydian ruler Alyattes (in current-day Turkey) who is most widely credited with introducing the first currency, electrum coins, a largely gold-silver alloy mined from the nearby Pactolus River. The name was a Latin derivation of the Greek word *elektron* that led to the English words *electron* and *electricity*, but also referred to white gold for its pale-yellow coloring. (In the crypto world today, Electrum is also the name of a well-respected and popular desktop wallet for Bitcoin.)

The system was a drastic departure from the decentralization of bartering and earlier forms of coinage. The Lydian monarchy set the value of the stater (the Greek word for standard) coin by weight—a stater equaled 220 grams of wheat[4]—and created denominations ranging from one stater to 1/96 of a stater. The kingdom guaranteed its value by imprinting a lion's head or facing lion and bull heads on each coin. Alyattes's successor, Croesus, whose name became synonymous with wealth in Lydian culture, later issued pure gold coins.

China's seventh-century Tang dynasty often receives credit for introducing paper currency. The Tang practice of using bills of credit and exchange notes continued for 500 years, outlasting their reign and drawing the attention of the thirteenth-century explorer Marco Polo, who reported on China's paper currency upon his return to Europe. That was also the trip where he discovered the joys of spaghetti, although Sicilians also lay claim to inventing the dish.

China's early paper money system encountered the same weaknesses that have afflicted every centralized paper currency system since then. The regime had the unrestricted ability to issue new currency through printing, and no incentive to reverse course even when overprinting led to inflation, which made the currency worth less and less. Stung by an economic collapse nearly four decades before Columbus landed in America, the Chinese eliminated their paper currency and would not reintroduce a similar system until the nineteenth century.

By that time, coinage systems had flowered throughout Europe, in bronze, gold, and other alloys, often bearing the image, if not the signatures, of the rulers who minted them. Caesar's profile adorned the Roman Empire's denarii, while the deniers (currency) of Charlemagne included a monogram of his Latin name and occasionally his portrait. It is the only known portrait of Charlemagne created by his contemporaries.[5]

The Byzantine Empire's gold currency dominated European commerce for 1,000 years after Rome faded, although other cultures from the Nordic lands to the Mediterranean and parts of North Africa, Asia Minor to the Atlantic also created their own currencies. These were distinct from one another in their metallic composition but had the same goal of providing an organized system of payment.

It was Florence's powerful Medici bankers who raised currency sophistication to new levels through the introduction of florins: 54 grams of pure gold bearing the city's insignia of a lily on one side and St. John the Baptist on the other. The blending of spiritual and worldly images in one bit reflected the Medici's status as God's (the Catholic Church's) bankers. Talk about a centralized authority!

But the Medici's (and God's) presence gave the coin unparalleled respect and reflected the family's patriarch Giovanni Medici's philosophy that banking systems must win the public's embrace to succeed. The florin was used by more than 150 states and became the dominant currency in European trade.

The Medici soon pioneered letters of exchange to account for loans of high volume—an innovation that allowed successful borrowers to prosper in ways that foreshadowed modern business growth. These papers, early predecessors of today's bank notes, outlined terms of payment. (Some paper banknotes today still describe the terms of payment, saying that value promised is payable upon demand by the bearer of the note.) But they would not become more widespread until the mid-seventeenth century. Around this time, Sweden's Stockholms Banco, the precursor to Sweden's central bank, first introduced banknotes after the treasury increased the size of the country's copper coins to maintain their value against silver. Things did not progress smoothly. The bank declared bankruptcy three years later after printing too much paper money. And this wouldn't be the last mistake of this kind.

THE CENTRAL BANKS BEGIN

In 1694, the newly formed Bank of England became the first bank to launch banknotes successfully and to create a true nationally centralized banking system. The bank, which was established to raise money for the Nine Years War against France, issued handwritten notes that promised to pay the holder the exact amount it represented. King William and Queen Mary granted the bank its royal charter to "promote the public Good and Benefit of our People."[6] By the middle of the following century, the bank was printing banknotes worth up to £1,000, which was a huge sum of money in those days.

France and other European countries soon followed suit with their own centralized banking systems, again, always centered around the printing of paper money.

While novel, the idea of a central bank addressed the public's need for a reassuring voice to regulate commerce, primarily through the printing of money. In the fledgling United States, there was a major point of disagreement between the two groups vying for power. Federalists favored a strong, centralized institution, while Anti-Federalists believed this focus would erode state and individual rights.

The country's first Secretary of the Treasury, Alexander Hamilton, who spearheaded the Federalist cause, argued that a strong central bank would help the country pay its debts and establish credit lines essential for becoming part of the world economy. He spent part of 1791 lobbying George Washington for a bank, citing the newly minted Constitution's "necessary and proper" clause "to make all Laws which shall be necessary and proper for carrying into Execution the foregoing Powers, and all other Powers vested by this Constitution."

Anti-Federalists led by Thomas Jefferson saw the bank as a step toward the monarchist rule the colonies had fought to shed. Later in his life, in a letter to New York Congressman John Taylor, Jefferson would famously describe centralized "banking establishments" as "more dangerous than standing armies." These three fathers of American democracy adorn the US $1, $2, and $10 banknotes.

The first US central bank, which was formed shortly after the ratification of the Constitution, represented a compromise between the Hamiltonians and Jeffersonians. State banks controlled 80 percent of the country's currency. Yet the bank was short-lived, as Jefferson's Democratic-Republican Party, which controlled Congress and the presidency through the first quarter of the nineteenth century, allowed the bank's charter to expire.

A second national bank, launched in 1816, was fervently opposed by Andrew Jackson, who had made abolishment of what he considered elitist institutions a pillar of his populist presidential campaign in 1828. "Every monopoly, and all exclusive privileges, are granted at the expense of the public," Jackson said in an 1832 speech to Congress explaining his decision to shutter the national bank. He warned that "if any private citizen or public functionary should . . . curtail its powers, or prevent a renewal of its privileges, it cannot be doubted that he would be made to feel its influence." Jackson would have been a strong supporter of Bitcoin.

War once again played an integral role in monetary innovation. The National Bank Act of 1863, passed largely to fund the US Civil War, saw the beginnings of a renewed effort to establish a central bank. The act enabled the US government to back a single currency and issue bonds and banknotes, and it created a framework for chartering national banks. Subsequent National Banking Acts fortified the central bank and weakened state banks via tax and regulation. The Panic of 1907 spurred further interest in creating a strong central bank as a run on deposits in trust companies, which were shadow banks operating outside the United States' nationally chartered banks, created anxiety about the financial system.

The United States took a final step toward centralization with the creation in 1913 of the Federal Reserve, whose unlikely champion was a Democrat, President Woodrow Wilson. Throughout history, Democrats had continued to oppose central banks, but Wilson, whose political skills have sometimes been underestimated, understood that public sentiment had shifted in its favor. He created a plan that balanced the concerns of central bank skeptics with those of its advocates.

In his plan, passed by Congress the following year, Wilson divided the Fed into 12 regional districts, allaying fears that the central bank would ignore areas outside the banking industry's Northeastern hub and place too much power in the hands of a few. Wilson additionally tamped down the bank's power by ensuring it would serve only as an emergency backup to the

US Treasury as a source of new currency. (The Fed would not become the primary manager of the US dollar until after World War II.)

"I feel that I have had a part in completing a work which I think will be of lasting benefit to the business of the country," Wilson said upon passage of the Federal Reserve Act, although some historians insist that he later regretted the legislation.

Of course, this didn't end the debate. The yin and yang about centralization continued, with some arguing in favor of concentrating power in hands of the few and others calling for more decentralization and empowering the hands of the many.

The early twentieth century also saw the United States end a lengthy debate about whether gold or silver was more valuable, with the passage of the Gold Standard Act of 1900 during the William McKinley administration. The US government set the price of gold at $19.75 per ounce in 1792 and increased the standard to $20.67 per ounce about four decades later. The Gold Standard Act affirmed this standard. An interesting artifact of this age was the denominations of currency. If an ounce of gold equaled roughly $20, a half ounce equaled $10, a quarter equaled $5, a one-tenth ounce equaled $2, and one-twentieth of an ounce equaled $1. American paper currency dates to the first year of the Civil War, roughly a quarter of a century after the United States set its initial gold standard. These amounts were easy to correlate to a fixed gold standard. If the dollar had not been coupled to gold in these early days, we would likely not have the paper currency denominations we have today for the US dollar.

In 1934, President Franklin Roosevelt upped the price of gold to $35 per ounce and uncoupled the dollar from gold to help kick-start bank lending during the Great Depression. FDR had moved in this direction through Executive Order 6102, a nefarious directive that was designed to prevent gold hoarding, which had become a growing concern during the Great Depression. The order, which became part of FDR's New Deal legislation, allowed citizens to hold no more than $100 in gold coins, about five ounces, with exemptions for artisans and jewelers. Violators could face $10,000 fines. The effect of the ban was to make private citizen gold holdings illegal. It led to mass confiscations and the forcible exchange of private gold for dollars. The dollar lost 70 percent of its value overnight. The ban lasted over 40 years until the Gerald Ford administration lifted it.

Australia instituted a similar act more than a quarter century later, enabling its government to seize private gold. Part IV of the United States' Banking Act of 1959 was meant to protect the country's currency. The government suspended the legislation in 1976. Both events offered shining examples of the arbitrary nature of central authorities.

The Bretton Woods Agreement in 1944, named for the New Hampshire town where Allied leaders met to discuss a postwar economic future, reestablished the gold standard and made the dollar the de facto global currency. Each country pegged its currency to the US dollar at a fixed exchange rate. Countries with dollars could exchange them for gold at a fixed rate, as well. This was part of a larger effort among the Allies to ensure economic cooperation after World War II, which was nearing its end.

In 1971, the toxic combination of the Vietnam War and huge trade deficits prompted the Nixon administration to separate the dollar from the gold standard once and for all, a move with global implications. This was known as the closing of the gold window. As a result, financial markets would now determine the dollar's worth against other currencies. "The time has come for exchange rates to be set straight and for the major nations to compete as equals," the president said in his remarks at the time.

If you could pinpoint one historical event that set the path to Bitcoin, it was this decoupling, which gave the world's central banks and major financial services firms the power to print money. This decision enabled central bankers to act arbitrarily, and in my opinion, often unwisely, as they tried to solve financial crises. I believe their decisions about printing money were the equivalent of treating an infected wound with a bandage instead of more effective therapies.

A series of central banking blunders, ongoing geopolitical upheavals, and oil price spikes contributed heavily to the stagflation of the 1970s, a mild recession starting in 1991, and more severe recession in 2008. *Stagflation*, a relatively new addition to the economic lexicon, described a noxious combination of economic stagnation and high inflation. The United States reached nearly historic highs in its inflation rate in the 1970s. The 1991 recession occurred partly because of the Fed's decision to reduce inflation by tightening the money supply, a move that triggered a decline in manufacturing and increased unemployment. In 2008, the Fed was slow to address declining productivity, instead focusing on bailouts for banks that had made bad loans.[7] I believe these events helped shape wide-scale distrust in the massive agencies and financial services firms that have controlled monetary policy and previously were thought to act with integrity.

Too big to fail? Hardly, as Andrew Ross Sorkin chronicled in his book with that title.

The world was ready for something different.

But the history of Bitcoin isn't so simple. As with any great story, tangents, twists, and red herrings worthy of an Agatha Christie novel abound. It starts earlier than you might think. All the way back to the early 1980s, people in different places with different goals were developing precursor digital currencies.

LOOKING BACK, LOOKING FORWARD

The first stirrings of a virtual currency can be traced to the utopias and dystopian societies of science fiction. In his 1888 novel *Looking Backward, 2000–1887*, American writer Edward Bellamy eliminates physical money in his imagined otherworldly society. He introduces a "pasteboard" card "issued for a certain number of dollars." A clerk records the price of products that Bellamy's protagonist, a mathematician named Julian West, or other consumers purchase. "We have kept the old word [for dollar], but not the substance," one of Bellamy's characters says to the mathematician, who has awakened after a Rip Van Winkle–like 113-year sleep. "The term, as we use it, answers to no real thing, but merely serves as an algebraic symbol for comparing the values of products with one another."

Bellamy, a journalist with a deep interest in social injustice, was one of roughly a dozen writers to present alternative economic and social models following a six-year depression in the 1870s. In his 1950s Foundation series, the science fiction writer Isaac Asimov, whose work centered around futuristic, tech-enabled societies, describes electronic credits as a means of interplanetary exchange.

These authors created fictional societies that moved beyond the mundane dollars, francs, and marks and achieved higher levels of efficiency. Money was an extension of a more efficient state.

Roughly two decades later, fact met fiction in different parts of the world. Some electronic currency observers say that Dutch gas stations introduced the first electronic currency in the 1980s as a solution to a string of robberies in some of the country's more rural areas. The stations feared losing their lucrative trucking business, so they developed a cash alternative in the days before pumps accepted credit cards. About the same time, the Netherlands' largest grocery chain, Albert Heijn, a more than century-old company, contacted banks about creating point-of-sale technology that would allow consumers to pay from their bank accounts. Both systems, of course, revolved around a central organization, one that yielded absolute control and power over this new electronic currency.[8]

But the more theoretical origins of Bitcoin lie in the writings of David Chaum, a doctoral candidate in computer science at the University of California Berkeley. In a 1981 paper, Chaum introduced a so-called mix network that encrypted content to a server. The server scrambled the information to hide the identity of the sender before forwarding the message to a network of servers that would then decode and deliver it.

In his 1982 dissertation, "Computer Systems Established, Maintained, and Trusted by Mutually Suspicious Groups," Chaum outlined other foundational pieces of blockchain technology, including a consensus node (agreements on data points), the connecting (or chaining) of data blocks, and the verification (digital time stamping) of these transactions.

Chaum's paper "Blind Signatures for Untraceable Payments," a year later, described a new type of digital signature that masked communications so that the verifying individual or groups (signer) wouldn't know the content. The concept was similar to the envelope in which a voter places a completed ballot. The election administrator can verify that someone has participated without knowing the individual's choice.

In 1983, Chaum also introduced eCash, an anonymous, cryptographically protected currency. Software that Chaum developed would store a digital form of money on a user's computer to spend at retailers accepting eCash. The system protected the user's identity via a public key—a sort of passcode—and digital signatures created from the private key. Seven years later he launched a company, DigiCash, as the vehicle for introducing his system to a wider audience. The timing seemed right for this cash and credit card alternative.

By the early 1990s, Chaum's blind signature technology had inspired a group of libertarian-leaning computer scientists who were deeply concerned about the intrusiveness of government and distrusted massive financial services organizations who provided the world's financial services framework.

The Cypherpunks, so anointed by one of its members, the hacker Jude Milhon, communicated at first with electronic mailing lists. The group later held regular gatherings at Cygnus Solutions, a San Francisco–based software support company cofounded by John Gilmore, who was also one of the three Cypherpunks cofounders. The Cypherpunks believed that central authorities—government and private enterprise—had become too intrusive, and that improved cryptography and technologies that protected individual privacy offered the best opportunity for societal change. "Privacy is necessary for an open society in the electronic age," opens their 1993 manifesto authored by Eric Hughes, a Cypherpunks cofounder.

Hughes wrote that individuals have the right to choose what financial information they divulge. "Since we desire privacy, we must ensure that each party to a transaction have [sic] knowledge only of that which is directly necessary for that transaction. In most cases personal identity is not salient. When I purchase a magazine at a store and hand cash to the clerk, there is no need to know who I am."

Central authorities that have served as intermediaries for transactions compromise privacy, Hughes, Gilmore, and their members believed. "When my identity is revealed by the underlying mechanism of the transaction, I have no privacy. I cannot . . . selectively reveal myself," he wrote.

The manifesto was meant to spur individuals to action because central intermediaries such as banks and government had a vested interest in maintaining the status quo in which only they have access to information. "We must defend our own privacy if we expect to have any. We must come together and create systems which allow anonymous transactions to take place . . . The technologies of the past did not allow for strong privacy, but electronic technologies do."

Although they filed multiple lawsuits against the US government related to privacy and export of encryption software, the Cypherpunks operated largely out of the limelight. Their quasi movement never grew much beyond a couple thousand members.

DigiCash was a different story, one that started promisingly but ended sadly.

Chaum raised $10 million from multiple investors, including David Marquardt, an early Microsoft investor. He hired Nicholas Negroponte, founder of MIT's influential Media Labs, as chairman, and signed Deutsche Bank and Mercantile Bancorp of St. Louis, a midsized commercial bank, as clients.

Broader signs also pointed upward. A Congressional committee called on Chaum to testify about electronic currency. Two potential rivals, CyberCash and First Virtual, had sprouted.

But about three years after contracting with the two banks, and intriguing other financial service providers, DigiCash folded. Some observers blamed management issues, principally Chaum's supposed missteps, a charge that he disputed over the years. In a 1999 *Forbes* article, Chaum cited users' lack of "sophistication" for DigiCash's demise. "It was hard to get enough merchants to accept it, so that you could get enough consumers to use it, or vice versa," he wrote.

The topic of virtual currencies was still big even a decade later at Yahoo!, where I was working in the early 2000s. My bosses asked me to explore virtual currencies with my team of about 20 computer engineers. Yahoo! saw virtual currencies as an extension of the online communities that were central to its business. But my group's work was limited in scope and didn't move much beyond the theoretical stage. The reality is that it's hard to launch a successful virtual currency system from scratch.

As with most failed business stories, it was probably a little bit of everything, or perhaps simply DigiCash was ahead of its time; it was providing a solution for a problem that in most people's minds didn't exist because they hadn't seen a compelling enough reason to think beyond paper money and traditional banks. The first mobile payment apps and major hacks were still a decade away.

The world just wasn't ready. DigiCash filed for Chapter 11 bankruptcy protection in 1998 and sold its remaining assets four years later. CyberCash followed a similar path, filing for Chapter 11 protection in 2001 and selling most of its assets to the electronic authentication services provider VeriSign. After nearing bankruptcy, First Virtual Holdings merged with the UK-based company Email Publishing to focus on email communications under the new name MessageMedia. The British smartcard company Mondex ended its digital currency initiative in association with a small number of banks in New York, Canada, and Hong Kong by the late 1990s after generating little interest. The digital currency space is hard, and it's littered with failed companies and broken hearts of entrepreneurs and passionate hobbyists.

Credit cards continued to dominate the payments industry, offering consumers all the convenience they felt they needed. This success was assisted by the invention of loyalty reward programs for credit cards. PayPal, an emerging online company, cofounded by Max Levchin, Peter Thiel, and Elon Musk, provided an alternative to the dwindling number of merchants who didn't accept credit cards. In 1999, I was an early PayPal customer, using my Palm V personal digital assistant device to make mobile payments using just an email address. Around this time, banks began expanding their retail payment services, prompting some digital currency observers to suggest that these banks had early concerns about electronic currency's potential to undermine their businesses.

Chaum sold his patents and moved on to other privacy- and currency-related projects. The Cypherpunks' work continued largely in the shadows. But by the early 2000s, a seismic shift in the retail financial services terrain was occurring, generated by technological advances such as faster internet speeds; smaller, lighter personal computing devices; and increasingly feature-rich websites. It was a strange, transitional period filled with possibility and interesting ideas, a few years after the dot-com bubble. On January 9, 2007, Apple introduced its iPhone, ushering in a movement of app development and society's rapid migration—some might call it an addiction—to mobile devices.

A larger, more acute change occurred a little over a year later when investment banking giants Lehman Brothers and Bear Stearns collapsed. Their demise came from their overexposure to the subprime lending market, a new risky type of investment that had fueled massive, rapid, but unsustainable growth in the real estate market. By the end of 2008, the subprime crisis threatened the viability of every major bank in the United States and reverberated throughout the global economy.

It was against this economic and technological backdrop that a mysterious figure named Satoshi Nakamoto was working on his Bitcoin paper. Few if any know Satoshi's identity, and I certainly don't know for sure either. His identity has generated much speculation, some of it scandalous. For example, a friend of Pablo Escobar, the late Colombian drug kingpin, told the industry publication *Cointelegraph* that Satoshi Nakamoto was actually Yasutaka Nakamoto, a former drug runner for the Escobar cartel. Yasutaka Nakamoto, who may be deceased, had the technical skills to create the Bitcoin protocol, the article suggests, while leaving certain key questions unanswered. More famously, the Australian computer scientist Craig Wright has steadfastly said that he is Bitcoin's creator, although skeptics have raised multiple issues with his explanations. The late Dave Kleiman is a popular candidate for being Bitcoin's creator, or at least being a member of a small team that is behind the Satoshi Nakamoto moniker. Another possible person is Phil Wilson, also from Australia. Phil, who is known as "Scronty" online, wrote the "Bitcoin Origins" story, in which he claims to be a member of the three-person team behind Satoshi, along with Craig Wright and Dave Kleiman.[9] The trio is my top pick.

Satoshi's identity is not a key issue for me. What I can say is that he, she, or they were clearly gifted in computer science and passionate about the same ideas that Chaum and the Cypherpunks examined. More importantly, they possessed the unique gift of visionaries to link ideas together where others saw no pattern.

You would be hard-pressed to find an invention that did not draw together threads from different sources, from the waterwheel through the technological inventions of recent years, including Google, Amazon, Facebook, and Apple. Exhibit A: A number of companies were creating computers in the 1990s, but only Steve Jobs understood that machines combining form and function would resonate on a mass scale. "Originality often consists in linking up ideas whose connection was not previously suspected," wrote the Australian pathologist W. I. B. Beveridge in his 1957 book, *The Art of Scientific Investigation.*

I wish that I had taken the time to understand how operations such as hashing, distributed ledger, and proof-of-work might link together toward a higher purpose. My Yahoo! project treated virtual currencies as akin to loyalty points in an airline rewards program, with Yahoo! as the central authority controlling their distribution and use. This was not blockchain or a currency.

I didn't read "Bitcoin: A Peer-to-Peer Electronic Cash System" until 2013, almost two years after I'd begun mining bitcoin. By that time, I had already recognized Bitcoin's potential to change the financial services world as it presented a true working model of an alternative to our aging monetary system. The white paper is remarkable for how much Satoshi packed into so little space—3,675 words including abstract and a bibliography that lists works from early electronic currency pioneers Wei Dai, Adam Back, and Ralph Merkle. Dai, a former Microsoft computer engineer, is best known as the creator of the Bitcoin predecessor called B-money. Back invented another predecessor technology called Hashcash, which is a proof-of-work system.

GENIUS

It's difficult to know how much the economic downturn—or at least the potential of a crisis—played into Satoshi's thinking. Most likely he was already well along to releasing his new idea.

(I will use the singular masculine from here on simply because the inventor's pseudonym is masculine.) What's clear, either intentionally or unintentionally, is that Bitcoin addressed many of the issues that the economic crisis revealed. The banking system rested on public trust that big organizations would protect their customers' interests with clockwork efficiency. Yet, these institutions don't always have their clients' best interests at heart and are subject to human misjudgments and other failings. As Satoshi noted in his introduction, these institutions' influence has only increased with time, even as services moved online.

Internet commerce relies "almost exclusively on financial institutions serving as trusted third parties to process electronic payments," Satoshi wrote. He added quickly that although the system was fine for "most transactions," existing internet commerce had "inherent weaknesses." Rather than facilitating financial interactions, those flaws had become intrusive.

Unimpeachable, or what he termed "non-reversible transactions," were not possible before Bitcoin. Traditionally, payment transactions always had the ability to be reversed or canceled, necessitating the involvement of these big banks to mediate "disputes" of all shapes and sizes. Entrenched in people's lives and emboldened by their size and power, these banks could tack on fees with the cost add-ons "limiting transaction size and cutting off the possibility for small casual transactions."

But Satoshi zeroed in on some more corrosive features of internet commerce: namely that the current banking systems created an atmosphere of distrust and dishonesty. "Merchants must be wary of their customers, hassling them for more information than they would otherwise need," he wrote. "A certain percentage of fraud is accepted as unavoidable."

Physical currency worked fine in some circumstances, but nothing existed that would allow for dealings over the digital internet without an intermediary. "What is needed is an electronic payment system based on cryptographic proof instead of trust, allowing any two willing parties to transact directly with each other without the need for a trusted third party," he wrote. Computer cryptography had been around for more than half a century, yet it had never been used fully in the realm of payments and money. This was all about to change.

Satoshi then outlined the bones of a system almost flawless in its logic, controlled by consumers and focused on their best interests. Banks and other central authorities would have no role. Bitcoin would create a network, borderless and open to anyone interested in participating and connected to the internet. The participants could buy and sell goods and services, or simply serve as witnesses to every transaction. The ultimate fail-safe mechanism to making this new currency valuable: Satoshi would release no more than 21 million bitcoins. Their value would rise over time as the system caught on. No one prior to Satoshi had the foresight to limit the amount of money in a currency system—though in hindsight, we all know that monetary supply is a key component of every centralized economy.

In addition, the distribution of bitcoins would be equitable, available to anyone, not just to a wealthy elite. An individual's background was irrelevant. If people had the computing power to connect to the internet, then they could participate and get rewarded by mining bitcoin.

It is worth pausing over some of the terminology at this point because it has confused and intimidated casual observers of the cryptocurrency movement. The terms will also be repeated throughout this book.

Digital coins—bitcoin—are a series of numerical codes, also called signatures (which are themselves made from private keys). They allow the receiver of the bitcoins to determine with absolute confidence that the transaction history of that bitcoin is unaltered and comes from a genuine, trusted source. Think of it as an electronic fingerprint unique to the individual creating the payment transaction.

In Satoshi's system, the owner of a digital bitcoin can transfer it to someone else's account, called a Bitcoin wallet. Another number, called a transaction hash, records the transaction as part of an ongoing list or ledger, not unlike what accountants once recorded with pen and paper, and more recently, via online programs. Or consider the transaction hash system like *Reader's Digest*, which assembles abstracts of articles into monthly tomes, or the check recorder of your checkbook.

"The only way to confirm the absence of a transaction is to be aware of all transactions," Satoshi writes. "To accomplish this without a trusted party, transactions must be publicly announced, and we need a system for participants to agree on a single history of the order in which they were received."

A web of servers, each equal to the other, participate in this verification process. When the miners in this peer-to-peer network reach a consensus, the transaction is recorded. The whole process is known as proof-of-work.

Ignore the tech speak. What Satoshi built is a system that creates trust by eliminating the need for trust. You don't need a central organization or intermediary person to verify that a payment transaction took place. This is because the math in cryptography establishes the system's foundation, authenticating and arranging every transaction in a logical sequence. Every transaction is provable by anyone in the Bitcoin community. It is universal public visibility that gives Bitcoin integrity.

The system keeps itself honest.

And because it functions without the need of traditional intermediaries, it eliminates costs and restrictions that have steadily eroded trust in banks, delayed our transactions, and charged fees for the most basic services. Think of the $15 to $30 penalties that are common at larger banks when someone else's check does not clear, or fees for moving money electronically, a service that barely takes any time or effort.

Satoshi introduced the concept of mining as an incentive for people to participate. Solve the algorithmic equation confirming each transaction and earn bitcoin. While the size of bitcoin rewards would decline every four years, eventually declining into fractions, the price per bitcoin would most likely increase as its usefulness became increasingly apparent and global.

The system would ensure privacy by eliminating all personal information from each transaction. Bitcoin network participants would see via a public address—the equivalent of a checking account number—that someone had received or sent bitcoins. But that was as far as the identification would go. Here again, Satoshi designed his system with an almost perfect reasoning, relying on numbers that would be difficult to trace to the real person behind the transaction.

BEGINNINGS

If no one buys a product, how does anyone know if it's any good? Enterprises fail because they can't generate a following. Satoshi created his own action, mining what he termed the genesis block of Bitcoin and selecting people who might participate in early transactions.

Satoshi shared the white paper on a cryptography email list, an audience he smartly figured would be receptive to his ideas. The email list included people with a computer science background who would appreciate what he had built, and those with a record of thinking differently about online privacy and social issues. To be sure, their initial response was decidedly muted. Many of the recipients of the Bitcoin white paper had other work priorities, were unimpressed, or were skeptical about the future of an electronic currency, since many earlier innovators had failed.

This reticence may also have underscored the powerful grip that traditional financial institutions have on our allegiances. Bitcoin faced an uphill struggle to convince people to consider alternatives to paper money and coins, and the checking and savings accounts that they use. Money, bank accounts, ATMs, and debit cards have worked in society for the most part. Even if

Bitcoin functioned as the paper's argument indicated it would, what reassurance existed that it could ignite enough popular support to make it take off and succeed?

Bitcoin was a bold step into the dark.

It took about two months for Satoshi to earn his first convert. Others followed in the ensuing months, although hardly enough to raise much awareness outside the small Cypherpunk community. There were no exchanges, no competing cryptocurrencies, no wallet firms, and no debates on government regulations. Someone pitching a Bitcoin ETF or even discussing the possibility of purchasing any real-life goods and services with Bitcoin might as well have been speaking Navajo. There were no crypto conferences or dedicated mining hardware, and certainly no one was searching for geographic regions with low-cost electricity for mining.

For the first 18 months, bitcoin's price hovered in fractions of a penny, with a small group of Bitcoin users setting the price through their infrequent transactions. If you were tuned into this fledgling movement and had a little extra time and the right computer with the Bitcoin software, you could have acquired thousands of bitcoins just by pressing a few mouse clicks on the Bitcoin software's simple user interface. Back then, they were as useless as the prize in a Cracker Jack box, but they would be worth millions of dollars today. In those early months, no one was accepting bitcoin. On May 22, 2010, on a lark, the Florida-based computer programmer Laszlo Hanyecz paid 10,000 bitcoins for two pizzas worth $41, a rate of about USD 0.004 per bitcoin that day. This famous transaction is now immortalized as the first ever commercial transaction paid by bitcoin. Those 10,000 bitcoins would be worth over $500 million today.

But there were also some promising developments. Three months before Laszlo's pizza purchase, Bitcoin Market, the first Bitcoin exchange, had appeared. Another exchange, Mt. Gox, launched a couple months later. In a few months, Bitcoin's value rose into the pennies. The network was growing.

In 2011 when I started mining, bitcoin was selling for about $20 and the industry had a total market value of under $150 million. It could be 5,000 times that—or more—by the end of 2021, if bitcoin's price reaches $100,000 as some Bitcoin observers have projected. In late 2019, Citibank Managing Director Tom Fitzpatrick, a banking veteran of four decades even predicted that bitcoin would reach $318,000 by December 2021.

Why do I mention all this?

It's to reassure readers. Understanding and projecting the value of Bitcoin or any other cryptocurrency can seem daunting, especially when you compare it to other better-known assets. But while the path is never a straight line, Bitcoin continues to grow in interest and appreciate in value. This is an argument I'll make repeatedly in this book.

What you'll be facing a dozen or so years into Bitcoin's (crypto's) evolution won't be much different in some basic ways than what I encountered about three years into its history. It's still an unknown for much of the world. It's still working out its kinks, albeit more sophisticated kinks than earlier in its history. Government regulation and concerns about security will determine its short-term path. The activities of the major financial houses that once scorned Bitcoin but are now paying attention will determine Bitcoin's growth.

There's more at stake now.

Consider that a blessing. The industry that you're observing has a toehold on the Mount Everest of financial services—more like a few toes.

The issues in question are less about making consumers feel comfortable and more about the organizations that feel threatened by cryptocurrency—central banks and financial service giants. They hope to control Bitcoin's growth through delays and restrictions that cast doubts and limit the opportunities of individuals to acquire crypto. Secretly, I think that governments and corporations want first access to acquiring Bitcoin, but they're all too afraid to admit to this strategy. But note that a number of these entities have already launched their own crypto initiatives, including custodial services, research groups, and even their own cryptocurrencies. With just a blink and a hand wave, these doubters seem to have become believers.

I liken Bitcoin's current status to the early days of commercial aviation, just a couple of decades after the Wright Brothers took off at Kitty Hawk in 1903. The first pilots and passengers took the big chances. Their followers who traveled the first routes a little over a decade later followed with trepidation, but also a sense that flight technology was safer and ready for something bigger. There were also naysayers, people who thought flight was only safe for birds, and that rail was good enough. Their numbers probably included some of the rail barons who felt their livelihoods threatened.

This is almost always the way that innovation and inventions proceed, with some people accepting and others rejecting what's new. There's lots of jaw-clenching and handwringing, lots of doubt, and plenty of debate. A new industry may even take a few steps backward before advancing.

One of the guiding principles of this book is, apologies to Winston Churchill, to simply keep calm and carry on. That is, ignore the hype—good and bad—and consider Bitcoin analytically. Does the argument for Bitcoin add up? Does it work for you as an investor?

In history, things that are good and worthwhile have a way of proving themselves. Everything else is just noise.

THE THREE HORSEMEN: MINING, WALLETS, AND EXCHANGES

Let's move to the fundamentals: mining, safeguarding, and trading of cryptocurrency, or what I call the Three Horsemen of Cryptocurrency.

My metaphor may sound ominous, particularly for fiat currency's defenders who see crypto as a mass-scale, disruptive threat.

But do not confuse my Horsemen with the New Testament's Four Horsemen of the Apocalypse—war, conquest, disease, and death—whose arrival on red, white, black, and pale horses in Revelations foreshadows a near end of times.

My Three Horsemen are an enabling force for good. The world's banking systems haven't been working as well as most people have always assumed. They do not protect our privacy or deliver high-quality service, and they bleed us in small fees.

Ironically, given the criticism of cryptocurrency, bank scandals, such as Wells Fargo creating fictitious customer accounts to generate fees, have been increasing as more banking occurs via electronic devices.

But for people to change over to Bitcoin, they'll need to understand the mechanisms to acquire, trade, and make purchases with it the same way they understand checking and savings accounts and other services with which they've grown up. Cryptocurrency usage doesn't take place without the Three Horsemen.

Not to worry: There's nothing fancy about how the Three Horsemen work. Mining, wallets, and exchanges as they relate to cryptocurrency may sound technical, but that's only because cryptocurrency is so new. The lingo hasn't infiltrated our daily conversations.

We fear what we don't say daily. Some of my friends who know I'm American and educated in American schools marvel at how I can seamlessly switch to Chinese when I'm taking an overseas phone call. They don't realize how easy the transition is because I spoke Chinese so frequently during my childhood. Likewise, younger generations today who grow up with Bitcoin will know the vernacular of cryptocurrency and will have no fear of using it as they get older.

In guides explaining Bitcoin, you may see terms like:

- *Nonce*, a 32-digit number that is arbitrarily formed with the creation of each block. Think of it as an initial identification number.

- *Hash* (also called a cryptographic hash), a 256-bit "signature" number that is generated for every transaction and for every block. Consider it the security lynchpin of the blockchain system that differentiates one transaction from another, and one block from another.

- *Nodes* can represent any electronic devices but are almost inevitably computers that create a record of transactions and keep the blockchain going.

I like *nonce* and *node*, which sound like something from a Lewis Carroll poem. But you don't have to know any of these terms to invest in Bitcoin.

HORSEMAN ONE: MINING

Mining is a clever way to describe an online activity that at its root is the same as the physical process of unearthing precious metals and gems. Bitcoin or gold? In both cases, you're trying to attain a valuable commodity. And in both cases, the degree of difficulty has increased as the unclaimed amount has declined along with the payoff (gold hasn't had much of a run-up compared to major stocks over the past few decades). While the supply of bitcoins is limited, be assured that there will always be an opportunity to acquire bitcoin, as a miner or through other means.

The difference between gold and bitcoin mining is that instead of digging in the dirt to hit a payload, you're using math algorithms and a computer to acquire a virtual object. Mining in Satoshi Nakamoto's vision rewards individuals who solve an equation, which proves beyond reproach that a transaction has occurred. The verified transaction then joins others in a virtual ledger. Think of it as the online equivalent of what accountants in the not-so-olden days maintained on paper, except in this case everyone involved is theoretically an accountant able to flag attempts to spend the same bitcoin twice or manipulate transactional data that form the blocks in blockchain.

Some Bitcoin observers compare the Bitcoin system to Google Docs or another program in which everyone who has access can view the same document. But it differs in that Google Docs allows people with editor status to make ongoing changes, while with Bitcoin, only a winning miner can append the ledger (blockchain) by adding to it. That's the rule of the Bitcoin ecosystem, and it is enforced through group consensus.

The process requires miners operating high-powered computers built specifically for mining to solve a complicated math problem that verifies the payment of goods and services in bitcoin. Mining initially involved individuals, but it has become so complex and competitive, involving nodes worldwide, that it is now impractical for anyone except groups—called mining pools (which I will cover shortly) to mine bitcoin. Mining is now an ongoing, global competition between teams of nerds generating verified transactions that become part of a block that is added—chained—to earlier blocks of data reflecting other transactions.

For example, if you were to use bitcoin to purchase a Samsung washer and dryer on the Best Buy website (this is currently not possible, although you could buy a gift card with bitcoin via Gyft or eGifter and use it at Best Buy), miners would ensure that you had enough bitcoins in your virtual wallet, and that you were not trying to use the same bitcoins that you had already spent. Solving the double-spending issue had been an Achilles' heel of earlier digital currency systems. Once the transaction is executed, it becomes part of the ledger and might follow someone else's bitcoin purchase for a new couch, car, or other merchandise.

A miner (or mining group) solving the mathematical algorithm for a block would earn—as this book went to press—6.25 bitcoins, plus some additional transaction fees. Note that mining algorithms themselves ensure random distribution; it's much like a global lottery that awards the 6.25 bitcoin prize roughly every 10 minutes to the first miner who has worked out a winning solution—the equivalent of holding a winning lottery ticket. I compare the process to a lottery because of its sheer arbitrariness. Anyone with the smallest computing power to run a one-hash calculation can take home the full prize, although not necessarily cost effectively. However, the more hash power you have—equivalent to holding a larger number of lottery tickets—the greater your chances of winning. And it bears highlighting that the process does not favor a particular group or geographic region. The first one to solve the equation is the winner. This global free-for-all has been ongoing for over 12 years. That's not as old as the Staatsloterij, the Dutch national lottery, which is the world's oldest ongoing lottery, dating back to the early eighteenth century—but Bitcoin has a wider reach and brighter future.

The combined output of Bitcoin mining is a public, distributed ledger, which is available for viewing to anyone participating in the Bitcoin network. If you had nothing better to do, you could check any block of transactions in the blockchain, dating to its origin in January 2009.

Mining addressed an issue that earlier digital currencies could not solve: namely, motivating enough people to participate, with bitcoin rewards serving as the incentive. It was key to building a community. Mining also ensured that Bitcoin would have the refereeing to give people confidence—an element of objectivity and fairness that was missing from traditional banking and payment systems. In other words, no one in the world can control the transactions flowing through the Bitcoin system because no single entity can control global bitcoin mining, as it is truly permissionless, and open to everyone.

In the first four years of its existence, a mining node (again, these are computers that participate in the Bitcoin network) earned 50 bitcoins about every 10 minutes for solving the hash equation (algorithm). That average 10-minute cadence continues—sometimes the reward comes after 11 minutes or more, and other times fewer than 9 minutes. But the reward amount has decreased by half three times from its initial 50 bitcoins in 2009, to 25 in late 2012, to 12.5 in mid-2016, and then to the current 6.25 bitcoins in mid-2020. Such so-called block "halvings" will continue to happen at similar four-year intervals through the year 2140, when the last of the supply of 21 million bitcoins are distributed publicly to miners.

Mining equipment has become increasingly sophisticated and expensive. When I started mining in Shanghai in 2011, I used PC gaming graphics cards plugged into a custom PC computer. I optimized every piece of computer equipment needed for the process, including the power supply unit. The software that I downloaded, an improved version of the original version 0.1 Bitcoin program, was no harder or time consuming to run than the SETI@Home software I used to run a decade earlier to search and analyze potential extraterrestrial signals from outer space. This was another hobby of mine. Since I was a boy, I've been interested in space and the possibility of finding extraterrestrial intelligent life.

By 2011, Satoshi had already departed the Bitcoin project—or at least issued his final communication to the BitcoinTalk forum he had created, saying he was "venturing into more complex ideas." Gavin Andresen, a Princeton-trained computer scientist whom Satoshi had placed in a leadership position, and a group of smart technologists committed to Bitcoin's development, continued to eliminate bugs and improve performance—a task enabled by the open source nature of the program.

That summer, I spent a few hundred dollars to gear up and then let the software quietly hum in the background to collect bitcoins. Their value by the end of the year would not even have covered a single round-trip airline ticket between Shanghai and San Francisco, where my brother was also busy mining bitcoins. The competition for rewards was minimal, perhaps a few thousand people globally operating on computers you could buy at a Circuit City or an online retailer. I considered Bitcoin then an amusing hobby that didn't absorb a lot of my time and might lead to a little extra cash. A jump in bitcoin pricing that autumn caught my attention, but so did a fallback to under $5 by year's end. The biggest downsides to my foray into Bitcoin was the extra $1,000 I paid for electricity and a toasty apartment in a city known for its hot, humid summers. But Bitcoin had triggered my neurons. I forged on.

My experiences are quaint by today's standards, the equivalent of comparing an old shopkeeper to Amazon. CPU mining quickly gave way to graphics processing units (GPUs), circuitry developed at the end of the twentieth century for rendering digital images but whose specialized processing power could accommodate Bitcoin's higher needs. In 2013, miners began using computers tailored to Bitcoin problem solving, called application-specific integrated circuits (ASIC). ASIC-based miners, which have grown increasingly powerful, can cost upward of $10,000, not including the electricity to run them over long periods of time. Meanwhile, the chances of earning a block reward with one computation have dropped to about 1 in 21 trillion (as of March 2021). That's about 32 million times harder than the odds of drawing a royal flush in poker (about 650,000 to 1).

The skyrocketing costs and increased difficulty have turned bitcoin mining into an industrial activity, far beyond the reach of the solo hobbyist. It has led to the establishment of mining pools, in which miners combine their processing power to solve equations together, and then divvy up the rewards based on their individual contributions. This is similar to a lottery pool, where everyone in your office might pool together all the purchased lottery tickets, and then if any individual ticket wins, the group would share the prize money. Mining pools are not for the semi-committed or the faint of Bitcoin heart.

Although China has been cracking down on cryptocurrency trading since 2017 as it strives to exert more control over the industry, it still has the most bitcoin mining participants in the world. These large mining groups control more than 60 percent of the world's mining power, also called the hash rate.[1] Over a one-year period from early October 2019, the country's four largest mining pools, F2Pool, AntPool, BTC.com, and Poolin, commanded almost 60 percent of the hash power. Of the 10 next largest mining pools, which controlled roughly 30 percent of hash power, most were China-based. The largest non-Chinese mining pool, Bitcoin.com, has less than 0.5 percent of the world's hashing power.

China's mining dominance reflects not only its deeper interest in cryptocurrency but an abundance of cheap electricity. In 2011, when I first became interested in Bitcoin, electricity in China cost $0.08 per kilowatt hour for consumers.[2] By comparison, electricity cost $0.12 per kilowatt hour in the United States,

$0.26 per kilowatt hour in Japan (which would become one of the most crypto-friendly countries), and $0.30 per kilowatt or more in several European countries. This difference in cost between China and these other major industrialized countries has remained roughly the same over the years. The cost of electricity in China remains about $0.08 per kilowatt, slightly more than half of the cost in the United States. The cost of electricity is now $0.29 per kilowatt in Japan and over $0.30 per kilowatt in Germany, Belgium, and Denmark.[3]

To be sure, this low cost stems partly from China's lax environmental regulations and poor electricity transmission infrastructure, including an outdated network of power lines. The country generates about three-quarters of its electricity from coal even as other countries have reduced their use to improve air quality.

Most bitcoin mining in China relies on another cheap source of power: hydropower electricity, which is generated by dams that harness the country's many streams and rivers. China is awash in unused hydropower because its feeble transmission infrastructure can't move it to other regions. The country has been trying to improve this infrastructure, but the initiative will take a long time to complete. So, expect China's miners to continue their vigorous pace in tapping these pockets of underutilized electricity generation. Many of them have moved to areas with these cheap sources of power.

Note one last similarity to gold in bitcoin's evolution from individual prospectors to organized groups. Gold mining is now the domain of huge companies (sometimes state-owned) using energy-intensive and industrial-strength equipment to mine increasingly hard-to-reach, limited supplies of the precious metal.

Do not consider my descriptions above as an endorsement of bitcoin mining. From a practical perspective, if you're going to acquire bitcoin, you'd be better off not investing big bucks in mining gear, or your time. Instead, make the much easier commitment of buying bitcoin directly, by allocating some percentage of your investment portfolio for bitcoin, acquire a wallet, and register for an account on an exchange.

HORSEMAN TWO: WALLETS

What does it mean to have bitcoin? For starters, it is very different than having fiat currency.

If I was trying to pay you $300 for groceries or some other household necessity, I might just grab the dollar bills from my leather wallet. Or I could engage my bank, credit card company, or electronic payment service to pay the amount. We would both have a tangible sense of what those types of payment methods look and feel like. We'd accept them as payment—as would the outside financial services organization—as commonly accepted units of value.

Bitcoin hasn't reached this point yet. There's no physical manifestation of bitcoin, even if the Bitcoin symbol of a ₿ on a gold-colored coin is increasingly well known. You can't just grab a bitcoin. Distilled to their essence, bitcoins are a series of digital numbers, with each bitcoin account having its own unique sequence (the private key and the corresponding bitcoin address). And these digital sequences are not yet commonly accepted. Although Fidelity and a few other financial services institutions have established custody services for bitcoin investors—they provide a place to hold your bitcoin and track performance—the vast majority of financial institutions do not. I predict this will change in the coming years.

Of course, custodial services run counter to Bitcoin's ethos because they involve outside authority. Bitcoin's beauty is that you can have full control of your digital bitcoins, with no intermediaries or custodians needed.

If you wish to possess bitcoin, you'll need a Bitcoin account, in the form of a wallet—digital or otherwise—that allows you to store your bitcoin. Technically you'll be storing the number sequences (private keys) representing individual bitcoin accounts (addresses) used for purchases or trading. You'll access the wallet via a master private key, a randomly generated 64-digit number that only you will be able to locate.

There is one caveat: while you can keep your bitcoin on a custodial wallet, offered by many exchanges, this option requires you to entrust the security of your bitcoin to the exchange. You will be relying on the exchange, just as you rely on your traditional bank to safeguard your bank deposits.

The digital wallet may conjure images of a traditional wallet or a super safe bank account, and I'm fine if this conceptualization helps someone understand how a wallet functions. But there's really no equivalent product or service among current, consumer-facing banking systems. Bitcoin wallets are unique in how they combine security and control. The closest product I can think of is a chip-based debit card, which has an account number on the front for someone or some entity to send you money, and a pin code of four or more digits that gives you access to your assets. But these debit cards, even with the most carefully scripted security measures, lack a Bitcoin wallet's cryptographic security.

There are five types of wallets in two categories: hot and cold storage. Desktop, mobile, and web-based—also called online—wallets are considered hot storage wallets because they are always connected to the internet, and thus always active and "hot." Hardware and paper wallets are cold storage wallets that are not connected to the internet and thus more secure; they are considered offline and "cold." Each category and wallet possesses advantages and disadvantages in security and user-friendliness. One overriding piece of advice: research wallets as you would any financial service product to ensure that it is reputable and addresses your needs.

Most importantly, you should only choose a wallet that is easy enough for you to use. This final piece of advice may seem obvious, but many people miss it. I've found that often with personal finance technology people opt for the more complicated solutions, believing that they are superior in quality or safety because of their complexity, when they would be better off choosing a more user-friendly product. If you don't feel comfortable about a product because it is difficult to use, you'll be less inclined to use it no matter how good its reviews. A system that is intuitive, safe, and suits your temperament is the better choice.

Desktop Wallets

Desktop wallets downloaded to a personal computer allow users to establish a bitcoin address for acquiring and sending bitcoins. These wallets present a particularly good option if you tackle most of your personal finance decisions at one workstation—such as your desk or the kitchen or dining room table.

Advantages: Desktop wallets do not store private keys on third-party servers, reducing your vulnerability to hacking. You'll never have to keep track of separate external hardware devices.

Disadvantages: You won't be completely impervious to a security breach. You can only access your cryptoassets from one machine. That's going to be increasingly inconvenient as more transactions take place with cryptocurrency, and at unpredictable times and places. Desktop wallets might not be the best option if you plan on making purchases with bitcoin or trading, or if you're planning to be active and may want to execute bitcoin transactions while on the move.

Mobile Wallets

Mobile wallets, such as Jaxx Liberty, Bitpay, and BreadWallet, are apps that you download to your mobile device. They offer the same features but greater flexibility than a desktop wallet; that is, you can receive and spend bitcoins anywhere you can bring your smartphone. That includes buying items at retailers, a number of whom already accept bitcoin via a Quick Response (QR) code.

Advantages: These wallets, which operate on iOS or Android devices, are more convenient than other options, and their usefulness is likely only to increase as the world moves more of its financial affairs to mobile platforms.

Disadvantages: Mobile wallets carry a higher risk of cyber-attack than desktop or cold storage options. Their vulnerability comes amid a rise in malware attacks on mobile devices. One 2019 study by the software and hardware provider Check Point found a 50 percent increase in malware strikes over the first six months of the year compared to the same period a year earlier. An increasing number of these attacks have targeted cryptocurrency wallets as bitcoin's price has risen.[4] You may also lose all your cryptocurrency if your phone is lost, stolen, or badly damaged.

But these types of incidents are rare and share one common thread. They require the wallet holder to make a mistake or let down their guard. Treat mobile wallets as you would any sensitive personal technology and your bitcoin will be secure.

Web-Based Wallets

Web-based custodial wallets, including those offered by exchanges Coinbase, Gemini, Kraken, Bitstamp, and Binance, store your bitcoins and cryptocurrency transactions on a third-party server, run by the exchanges.

Advantages: They offer wide accessibility—from potentially any computer or mobile device with online connectivity. They tend to be the easiest to set up, are often faster than other types of wallets, and allow for trading in multiple cryptocurrencies.

Disadvantages: Because they involve a third party, you're relinquishing control of your assets and your privacy. Online crypto wallets are also more susceptible to hacking, identity theft, and online scams. Among their weaknesses, custodial exchanges can themselves be hacked and have funds stolen. One high-profile attack on Bitfinex resulted in the theft of more than $65 million in bitcoins. A number of exchange wallets have suffered from software vulnerabilities. Banks must meet certain standards for ensuring their technological security, but cryptocurrency operates outside this framework—for now. Exchange employees—the individuals ensuring that technology is safe and user-friendly—have in a number of cases been the weak link and have been exploited by hackers. But these issues have grown increasingly rare as these types of wallet providers improve their technology.

Hardware Wallets

Hardware wallets, as the name suggests, store cryptocurrency on a hardware device, which look like a traditional USB thumb drive. Popular hardware wallets such as Trezor and Ledger store cryptocurrency offline, although an internet connection is necessary for completing transactions.

Advantages: They offer a high level of security and are excellent for storing large amounts of cryptocurrency.

Disadvantages: They are typically the most expensive among wallets and can be very difficult to set up, especially for someone who isn't adept with technology. The latest Trezor or Ledger device can cost well over $100. There are also potential hardware or software vulnerabilities, which require software and firmware updates in the future. The seed backups for these devices can also get lost, damaged, or compromised.

Paper Wallets

Paper wallets store private keys on a piece of paper and provide arguably the highest level of security of any wallet, provided that you generated them securely and have a safe place to store them.

Advantages: You have total control over a paper wallet's setup, usage, and security. They are invulnerable to online hacking.

Disadvantages: You have to find a safe place to store this wallet. You might consider making a backup, although this option carries its own pitfalls. Paper and ink are also fragile materials that can tear, fade, run, or be destroyed by moisture or fire.

Crypto investors with significant holdings mix and match their wallets, diversify their storage, and don't put all their eggs in one basket. One smart idea is to use a hardware cold wallet for large amounts of cryptocurrency that you might keep over time and use a mobile hot wallet for smaller sums that you're allocating for regular use. Or you might also keep a portion of your assets in paper wallets as a diversification strategy.

One last note. In the interest of full disclosure, I've listed the major weak points of these wallets. As a conscientious shopper, you would probably ask about these failings the way you would about any other product. My purpose, however, was not to alarm you. The latest wallets are fundamentally safe. Take your time to understand each product and service, including which provider makes you most confident and which ones raise concerns.

While wallets promote the notion of security, be aware that security always comes with technology hurdles, meaning that the higher the security features, the higher the required technological sophistication. In other words, there is a genuine downside to using the latest high-tech security, as the core technology could overwhelm the consumer, causing accidental misuse and loss of funds through user error. This is the notion of achievable security, where effective security is only what the user can technically achieve.

HORSEMAN THREE: EXCHANGES

Okay, you have a place to store your cryptocurrency. Now you're ready to start acquiring some. Let's assume that you're not going to be one of the few new investors with the time, money, and interest to mine bitcoin. You could acquire cryptocurrency from someone you meet in person, or even someone online. But that would require you to do the grunt work of reaching out to someone in the Bitcoin network and setting up the transaction in person or otherwise.

More likely you'll be working through a cryptocurrency exchange.

At this point, you might ask if exchanges are those same organizations that facilitate traditional financial transactions, exactly what Bitcoin is supposed to eliminate? Technically you'd be right. They even charge fees for purchasing and selling bitcoin, transferring money into a wallet, and for currency conversion. These fees can run high and take a bite from your investments.

While it's understandable to be skeptical, cryptocurrency exchanges bear little similarity to financial services organizations that impose too many regulations that limit how much and when you can buy or sell. As central organizations go, cryptocurrency exchanges have a light touch and are more akin to a bazaar or marketplace that brings shoppers and sellers together than a modern bank. And there are such things as decentralized exchanges (DEXs) that allow for direct trading between buyers and sellers without any funds in central custody. I'll cover DEXs later in this chapter.

Exchanges make it easier for buyers and sellers of cryptocurrency to meet and execute their transactions. In the first few years of Bitcoin's history, there were few exchanges, even as Bitcoin became global and its following grew.

I recognized the need for this type of platform when I launched the BTCChina exchange in 2013. It was China's first bitcoin exchange, and its resources were rudimentary. I had a vision of what it could be by following solid business practices that I had learned while building divisions in my earlier corporate jobs. I raised money and hired experienced software engineers.

The Bitcoin landscape was different then. There was little competition. The security threats that snagged Mt. Gox and other exchanges had not yet emerged because bitcoin wasn't valuable enough (although that was going to change soon). For the first couple of years, we operated strictly as a website—no mobile apps. As we grew, we learned about what made for the best and safest user experience. We had grown from just a few thousand users to more than a million by the time I exited in 2018.

I would be remiss at this point in not addressing the giant bitcoin in the room: security.

Breaches of crypto exchanges have been industry low points, tainting its reputation with parts of the wider public.

No breach was more damaging than the Mt. Gox hack discovered in 2014. Launched in 2010, the Japanese exchange grew rapidly, and by 2013, it was handling about 70 percent of all bitcoin trading worldwide. But in early 2014, the company reported that hackers had stolen about 850,000 bitcoins. Mt. Gox later revised this estimate down to 650,000 bitcoins, or about $450 million, and declared bankruptcy. Most of the coins disappeared from a Mt. Gox hot wallet over an extended amount of time.

Mt. Gox subsequently suspended withdrawals of bitcoin and later filed for bankruptcy, saying that it had almost double the amount of liabilities as assets. In the aftermath, the company's CEO, Mark Karpelès, who had been harshly criticized for his poor people and management skills (a *Wired* magazine story reported that he had failed to include commonly used version control software to ensure that coders didn't overwrite each other's work as they were updating the platform[5])—and was found guilty by a Japanese court of trying to mask Mt. Gox's financial problems. Karpelès received a 2.5-year suspended sentence that was reaffirmed by Japan's highest court in 2020.[6] He has steadfastly maintained his innocence of any wrongdoing.

In October 2014, I met Mark Karpelès in Tokyo. I didn't know him personally, but as we were both running major exchanges (Mt. Gox was the most famous) and served on the Bitcoin Foundation board, I was interested in comparing notes, so I emailed and contacted him during a brief weekend trip to Tokyo. He kindly agreed to the meeting and suggested that we meet at his office in a low-rise building with a tiny elevator in downtown Tokyo. We met in a plain conference room with gray walls.

Investigations into Mt. Gox had already begun, but Karpelès, who was dressed in jeans and a T-shirt, couldn't have been more gracious. He was happy to share his experiences running an exchange and a little nerdy like so many technology professionals. He told me a little about the problems that Mt. Gox was having, and I believed him when he said that they were the result of unintentional mismanagement. I knew from running a fast-growing Bitcoin exchange successfully that it wasn't enough to know something about technology; management experience was critical, something I'd gathered in big doses at several companies. I had a sense that Mark didn't have the needed management background or skills and had gotten overwhelmed.

But my biggest takeaway from meeting Mark was a renewed sense of responsibility in running a Bitcoin exchange. That was the year when we assumed the ceremonial title from Mt. Gox as the world's largest exchange by trading volume. After Mt. Gox shut down, we became the world's longest-running Bitcoin exchange, but in hindsight, that was not significant. Most importantly, I realized that I needed to be truly responsible to my users in protecting their bitcoin deposits from hacking or otherwise.

The theft of Mt. Gox fed crypto skeptics' contention that bitcoin, which dipped 36 percent as the Mt. Gox hack became public news, was unsound. Mt. Gox, which had experienced at least two other smaller hacks, became synonymous with crypto's riskiness.

Exchange woes weren't limited to Mt. Gox. Hackers stole roughly $1 billion in bitcoins in 2018 alone, including a $60 million heist of the Japanese exchange Zaif. In 2016, hackers removed over $70 million from Bitfinex. A 2019 incident cost well-respected Binance about $40 million in bitcoins.

Nothing in technology or anything else is impregnable, which is why we have locks and security systems on our homes. No question, hackers will keep trying to steal bitcoin, which is why users should always be wary about storing their cryptocurrency on custodial exchanges. Even if they're regulated, it doesn't mean they're risk-free. I simply would not advise my family or friends to store bitcoins on an exchange.

A 2020 report by the research group Chainalysis noted that as exchanges served as the middle point for an increasing number of transactions, they became more targeted by hackers. However, the report also found that the incidence of hacking had declined since peaking in 2018.

Don't be afraid of using exchanges, as they are a needed service in this industry, and they play a central role for anyone who wants to buy or sell cryptocurrency. If you wish to reduce the possibility of theft, don't use the custodial wallet services that exchanges offer. There are safer options for storing your bitcoin, as I've already noted.

There are dozens of reputable exchanges that have worked hard not only on security but also in providing user-friendly interfaces. I won't recommend any one exchange over another or provide an exhaustive list here.

Think of exchanges as local movie theaters that are showing the same films. Just like local movie theaters, each country or region has its own local crypto exchanges. They are fundamentally a regional business since exchanges need to interface with their country's banking and payments system; no two countries are alike. They offer the same basic service everywhere, although they may offer certain amenities that cater to customer preferences based on the region. Once you purchase a ticket, it's up to you how you want to use it. You decide whether to buy a lot of bitcoin, a little, or none at all, just as you could choose to sit with your back to a movie screen. Do your research, choose one—or a couple if you're planning to acquire a lot of bitcoin—and use the exchange as it fits your needs.

The website coinmarketcap.com lists more than 300 exchanges, and I predict there will be many more in the coming years. About one-third of them have 30-day trading volumes of well under $1 million. A number of these sites cater to niche populations. But the 30 or so most active exchanges that dominate the industry, including Coinbase, Binance, and BitStamp, each generate trading volumes well into the billions of dollars. However, don't always trust the trading volume numbers from exchanges. Trading volume numbers are self-reported by the exchanges, and there are tremendous incentives to exaggerate. Many exchanges have reported fake trading volumes, especially those that aren't regulated.

Opening an account on an exchange is a multistep process, similar to what a bank or other financial services organizations might require for opening an account, though often with even higher security and identification requirements. You'll need to provide proof of identity, usually by submitting copies of your passport or ID, in addition to a photo of yourself. Some exchanges might even run a test deposit into your bank account. Regardless, you may have to wait a day or two before you can start making deposits and begin to trade.

You purchase a cryptocurrency, let's say bitcoin, using your credit or debit card, or by depositing fiat currency from a bank account. With a credit or debit card payment, you'll receive your bitcoin right away, but you'll pay a higher transaction fee. Transferring money from a bank account will cost less, but you won't have access to your bitcoin for several days. You also have the option to transfer money via a payment platform or bank wire, although those options tend to be more complicated.

As is the case with stock brokerage accounts, you can purchase cryptocurrency using market or limit orders. With a market order you'll buy coins at the best possible price, as demanded by the seller. With a limit order, you'll set a maximum price for making the purchase. The latter option gives you more control over your trading by enabling you to set an acquisition price with which you're comfortable. Some exchanges now allow for margin trading, which means you can borrow money to purchase cryptocurrency, but this is inherently more risky.

Decentralized exchanges (DEX), such as Uniswap, offer another possibility. These platforms function without a central authority to custody user deposits. DEXs do not store currency but create a sort of forum for cryptocurrency buyers and sellers to interact freely. They are fast, and many are open source, so at least theoretically, they should be able to incorporate changes quickly based on user trends. One natural limitation is that DEXs only allow for crypto-to-crypto exchanges, and cannot support trading with fiat currencies.

Some cryptocurrency users believe that these peer-to-peer exchanges are more in tune with the decentralized nature of cryptocurrency's systems. They say that decentralized exchanges are less susceptible to illegal trading, price tampering, and hacks. That's largely because banks and other intermediary organizations, each potentially with vulnerabilities, are not part of the trading process. These exchanges also do not collect as much identity information about users as centralized platforms. A few do not even require a formal registration process.

But their decentralized nature also means there are fewer safeguards for users than on centralized platforms in the unlikely event there is a dispute or someone feels cheated. Not all of these exchanges are used widely, which may also limit someone's trading options. They also do not allow margin trading, lending, or stop-loss trading where you can pinpoint the price you want to sell or buy bitcoin. If you're entering the cryptocurrency market cautiously, this latter inability alone may be a reason to start with a centralized exchange.

So, these are my Three Horsemen—hardly apocalyptic. They're nothing more than building blocks that will enable you to invest in bitcoin and participate in the cryptocurrency economy. Remember that smart investors, regardless of the asset, take their time to make decisions based on research and common sense. So it is with the horsemen. Choose the solutions that make the most sense for you.

Regarding wallets and exchanges, there are a lot of great options. That wide selection has been among the most encouraging developments in Bitcoin, the fruit of many smart, inspired people possessing the same excitement about cryptocurrency that I developed not long after I first encountered it. Consumers couldn't ask for more than an expanding market with a variety of great tools to use.

DARK UNDERBELLY OF THE FIAT BEAST

Most people know what's fair and unfair in life.

It's fair when you make an investment and it grows into a larger investment based on performance criteria. It's even fair—albeit undesirable—when you make an investment and the investment shrinks or generates smaller-than-hoped-for increases, as long as you understand beforehand that the investment may decrease.

But it's unfair when an investment shrinks without good cause or prior notification. This may occur because of investment advisor or custodial incompetence. It may stem from a scam in which someone makes empty promises to purposely lure a consumer into using a service.

Or it may happen because of what I call systematic benign neglect, in which a financial services model limits or reduces an asset's value. That is, the system's design, although not malicious or inherently unfair, nevertheless reduces the value of the investment over time. This decline in earning power occurs through no fault of the asset owner.

Systematic benign neglect describes our current banking system.

Banks that claim to want to help customers instead chip away at their ability to access and spend their money. This inherent negligence is what I mean by fiat's dark underbelly. Yet we don't fight this system because it is so deeply ingrained. We know only the monetary systems that our parents used and that have provided us with the infrastructure for personal financial management.

In my presentations at cryptocurrency conferences, I sometimes pluck an old $100 bill that I keep in my wallet to make a point about the value of money. It is a 1979 note with a small quarter-view portrait of Benjamin Franklin wearing a fur collar haloed in the center and the words "Federal Reserve Note" and "The United States of America" bannered across the top in the familiar Banknote Roman font. In design and texture, it feels like a relic. When I first received the old Franklin, as I tell my audiences, I could have bought two pairs of top-line Nike running shoes, my favorite brand. Now the note won't cover one pair of a similar model. This same $100 bill is worth a lot less now.

The same fate awaits the current Benjamin Franklin note, with a blue ribbon bisecting the roughly 6.14-by-2.66-inch rectangle slightly right of center, and a larger portrait of Franklin to the center left. This crisper, more colorful Franklin, which I also show audiences, probably won't buy much more than a pair of Nike shower slippers in 10 years. Currency's purchasing power decreases rapidly over time.

It may seem sacrilegious to question a monetary system with roots hundreds of years old, which has as its whole purpose the service of our needs—and does so without too many kerfuffles. Over the centuries, our monetary systems have helped the world discover new lands, develop its most valuable resources and greatest inventions, and spawn history's most significant manufacturing, technological, and agricultural movements. Some of our most influential thinkers, people with a view of the future and deep belief in humankind's potential, have shaped these systems, as well as wider philosophies about the role of government and the private sector in generating economic growth. We could argue back and forth about the merits of each, but they are largely rooted in the idea of a central guiding authority, including:

- The early, nameless creators of *metallism*, in which monetary value derives from silver, gold, and other commodities
- Scottish Enlightenment thinker Adam Smith's *invisible hand of commerce*, arguably history's most influential economic theory, which argues that markets should find their way effectively without government or other interventions but operates under the assumption that banks are part of a financial ecosystem
- Early twentieth-century economist Georg Friedrich Knapp's *chartalism*, which theorized that currency resulted from state authority
- Mid-twentieth-century economist John Maynard Keynes's *Keynesian economics*, which argues that states should stimulate growth
- And *supply side economics*, a Reagan-era philosophy that argues for less government involvement, but within current economic frameworks

But monetary systems, and by default the institutions that serve as their bulwarks, have failed on multiple levels. We just haven't noticed because they've been a part of our lives for so long that we accept them without question. Investing, spending, savings, business transactions, and personal purchases all involve long-established, centralized frameworks that most people have placed beyond reproach.

Our love affair with the institutions themselves has fogged our judgment and committed us to an irrational devotion. We trust them, not because we've taken the time to analyze whether the services they're providing are high quality, but rather because they've been around for decades or more as stewards of personal and professional finance.

We do not question how they do business. We do not question why the money we deposit in banks is worth less every year. We do not question governments that claim they are working to ensure low inflation.

I won't debate here the necessity of a little inflation. Most economists would agree that a little inflation boosts economic growth by ensuring consumers purchase goods before they become more costly in following years, and that the wage growth that accompanies it keeps workers happy and productive. Without inflation, firms would not feel compelled to increase salaries. Inflation also increases tax revenues that pay off debt.

"The most important thing to remember is that inflation is not an act of God; inflation is not a catastrophe of the elements or a disease that comes like the plague. Inflation is a *policy* . . ." wrote the twentieth-century economist and philosopher Ludwig von Mises, in his tome *Economic Policy: Thoughts for Today and Tomorrow*.[1]

Von Mises also argued that governments could eliminate inflationary policies. "A policy can be changed. Therefore, there is no reason to give in to inflation," he wrote. "If one regards inflation as an evil, then one has to stop inflating. One has to balance the budget of the government. Of course, public opinion must support this; the intellectuals must help the people to understand. Given the support of public opinion, it is certainly possible for the people's elected representatives to abandon the policy of inflation." I cannot agree more!

What is difficult to argue from banks' perspectives are the costs they impose on their customers—costs that are outsized relative to how much time and effort they require to impose, including:

- Thirty-dollar fees or more on wire transfers, even sometimes from one account to another within the same bank
- ATM charges for out-of-network machines
- Two-day delays before we can use money for checks deposited into a bank account
- Platform updates preventing online access to our accounts

This is all not to mention our receptiveness to data harvesting that banks employ, sometimes paying brokers to analyze our online behavior and to suggest what will likely motivate spending decisions.[2] Some banks even gather information on our social media activities and movements throughout the day. How intrusive!

We are equally accepting of the email and messaging that has as its only objective to get us to respond. Banks conduct these daily under the guise of concern, but they really are trying to develop keener insight into what might tempt us to purchase additional banking products and services—which of course will increase their revenue. Do the annoying tailored messages we frequently receive when we log into our accounts online bother you as much as they do me? I've never liked the Orwellian sensation that any institution, financial or otherwise, was tracking my activities.

But this monitoring is something we accept because we respect and trust banks. Even in an age where bank scandals regularly make headlines, many people still think of them as benevolent guardians of our assets, icons of respectability. This masquerade is part of fiat's dark underbelly.

I have fond memories of my earliest childhood trips to the bank with my parents, and later, when I opened my first bank account at BayBank, a small local bank next to The Lawrenceville School in New Jersey, where I started high school as a boarding student in 1989.

The branch, where my father parked $1,000 for my spending during the school year, had comfortable furniture and calm efficiency in processing the paperwork we needed. They asked a few questions; they were clearly used to Lawrenceville families making similar requests over the years. Over the next few years, the suited bankers there treated me with the same respect they did older customers every time I walked in for bank teller service.

I have a number of friends in executive positions at some of the world's most famous financial services firms. My professional dealings over the years have also been overwhelmingly positive. I've been able to attain mortgage loans to buy homes, and I've never worried that the money and valuables I've deposited with these institutions was vulnerable.

Our main problem has been in failing to ask questions about our monetary systems and the institutions—not to mention the people behind them. Is the way they do things really so efficient and customer friendly? Couldn't there be a better way? Are they even needed anymore in a world with digital cryptocurrency, where everyone can be their own bank?

MONEY'S TRUE VALUE

Learning about Bitcoin prompted me to ask questions about our institutions and how they operate. Increasingly, I came to dislike our current monetary system. It wasn't just that bank services always came at a cost; rather, the whole system seemed geared against us, designed to lessen our holdings in one way or another. This anticonsumer streak is our monetary system's dark underbelly.

Consider money's value. It's worth depends on the decisions of the individuals responsible for its issuing, not on the materials—the paper and metals—from which it is created. There are no mathematical formulas to support its value, no foolproof methods to ensure that its value is exactly what it should be at any particular time. Even airline loyalty point systems or coupons for mooncakes—the Chinese sweets filled with sweet bean or lotus seed paste that people give as presents during the country's Autumn festivals—have a more stable value.

Contrast that to the cost of a McDonald's hamburger, 15 cents in 1955, not long after Ray Kroc franchised the business. The burgers are the same size and have roughly the same protein-to-fat content today, but now cost $2.50—clearly, some things are forever and some things are not. Our money loses value with time. You don't see this decline daily, but over a period of years and decades, it's abundantly clear.

Why this happens doesn't make sense, except that it's been the modus operandi.

We take on faith that something's price has been well considered and is fair to us. And we're willing to pay more for some things over time when we believe they've been improved. But why prices increase as much as they do on an ongoing basis doesn't make sense when you think about it, particularly when the ingredients and processes are the same. They reflect the human frailties of central bankers who set policies determining money's value.

These bankers face enormous political pressure from the people who appointed them not only to stimulate a struggling economy but to maintain economic growth rates when conditions seem likely to change. Witness President Donald Trump's rage following the Federal Reserve's decision in 2018 to raise the interest rate that the central bank charges other banks to borrow money. As is his habit, Trump relentlessly attacked, at one point calling the Fed the biggest single threat to the US economy and suggesting he would fire Board Chairman Jerome Powell. Within a year, despite saying that he would never bow to political pressure, Powell had cut the rate three times.

To be sure, growth was slowing, but GDP was hovering at over 3 percent and the job market was near an all-time best. Fed critics questioned the cuts and Powell's motivation. Why outside of political pressure would the well-respected Powell opt to stimulate the economy, the usual reason for a rate cut, when it showed few signs of bogging down? The timing was at least worrying.

Was it the right move long-term? The coronavirus made the point moot by early 2020, ushering in an economic collapse so severe that the Fed had no choice politically or otherwise but to keep interest rates at all-time lows.

But central banks have a history of gumming up conditions. Usually the problem is overreach, although they are often guilty of profound insensitivity and an inability to understand how their decisions affect people.

Consider the Republic of Cypress. In 2012–2013, the eastern Mediterranean island nation and mythological birthplace of Aphrodite suffered a severe economic crisis, the aftermath of a prolonged recession and overspeculation in commercial property. Nonperforming loans rose over 6 percent, a stunning figure for a small economy that depends on tourism. This sent shock waves through Cypress's banking sector, which held $22 billion debt, an amount that outstripped the country's gross domestic product.

In 2013, the Cypriot government froze all withdrawals and instituted severe austerity measures to secure a roughly 23 billion euro emergency bailout package. As part of these measures, the government seized nearly 50 percent of account holders' savings in excess of the insured limit of 100,000 euros at Cypress's two largest banks, the Bank of Cypress and Laiki (Laiki was later merged into the Bank of Cypress). The account holders received a pale consolation prize, shares in the Bank of Cypress. The Cypriot government said that the capital raised from what it called a tax on account holders would stabilize the country's teetering banking sector and economy.

"This constitutes an important step in the stabilization of both the bank, and the Cypriot economy," said a government spokesperson.

But as is the case with many institutional decisions, there was a darker subplot to the story. An *Atlantic* magazine article pointed out that Cypriot bank assets were eight times the country's GDP, with much of the money coming from what the author called "tax-dodging" Russians, including "oligarchs and mobsters."[3] The article noted that Cypress had become "dependent on central banking financing to stay afloat."

But I believe part of the government's justification was an assumption that if people had more than 100,000 euros in their accounts, they were probably rich enough to absorb this loss. I also agree with the *Atlantic* point that some of the money was part of a scheme among some wealthy Russians to avoid their tax obligations, or to launder ill-gotten gains.

The policy rippled downstream, sending even those account holders with smaller balances rushing to withdraw their cash, creating long lines at ATMs. Everyone was fearful there would be a bigger bank run. Cyprians swarmed the streets, demanding, among other actions, that the government nationalize the banks, freeze the army budget, and institute a federal tax. Two weeks before Christmas in 2012, groups stormed the country's parliament and threw rocks and eggs at legislators. I understood their anger. Here was our banking system's greatest weakness on display.

By decree, and with little warning, a financial institution wiped out millions of euros in deposits. It is as if the assets never existed. And there was nothing technically illegal about Cypress's actions. That is extremely disturbing. To be sure, Cypress recovered, and had several solid years of GDP growth prior to the onset of COVID-19. But the question remains. Should banks have the right to take away your deposits, your hard-earned money, in the event of an economic crisis? Should they wield such enormous power over your life?

Casual observers might write off Cypress's problems as unique to a small country of minor global importance. But it has executive, legislative, and judicial branches, not unlike the US model, and its problems are the same that many larger countries have experienced at some point in their history. Unfortunately, we are likely to see this happen again in another country.

Recall the iconic US Depression-era photos less than a century ago of crowds lined up outside banks and at teller windows, panicked by rumors that banks did not have the cash to cover their accounts and desperate to get their money in hand. From the crash of 1929 until the end of the 1930s, some 9,000 banks failed—4,000 in 1933 alone. Bankers' colossal misjudgments cost depositors more than $140 billion and, in many cases, destroyed livelihoods and businesses as the depression steepened. Frank Capra portrayed the feeling of helplessness in his film *It's a Wonderful Life* in a scene where customers storm the Bailey Brothers Building & Loan, an institutional pillar of the fictional Bedford Falls community.

Eighty years later, in 2008, circumstances were different, but US bankers erred in a similarly spectacular fashion, ignoring the downside of their commitment to a new asset, securities that were created by packaging so-called subprime mortgages, which enabled people with woeful credit to purchase homes. For a short period, the companies investing in these securities and facilitating their sale reaped huge windfalls. In *The Big Short*, Michael Lewis wrote of one investment banker who earned roughly $40 million buying and selling subprime securities.

But when the Federal Reserve raised interest rates, many homeowners defaulted on their loans and the value of subprime mortgage–backed securities cratered. The list of failures and near failures represented a near who's who of commercial and investment banking giants. They included Lehman Brothers and Bear Stearns, which both collapsed, and Washington Mutual, the country's largest savings and loan whose assets were acquired by JPMorgan Chase. Wachovia, the fourth largest bank in the United States, was folded into Citibank, and Merrill Lynch, another esteemed securities broker, was acquired by Bank of America.

Consumers bore the damaging effects of the banks' colossal misjudgments and carelessness on multiple fronts. Many lost their homes, fueling the collapse of the housing market. Others lost investments they had entrusted to their respected institutions. Account holders from Washington Mutual and Wachovia had no alternative but to become Chase and Citibank customers.

Sometimes a one-off incident or rumor is all that's necessary to put a bank on the defensive and customers in a bind. In Sweden in 2011, a rumor that two banks, Swedbank and SEB, were having difficulties spurred long lines at ATMs and teller windows as nervous account holders waited to see if the institutions could cover their deposits.

But banks are like any company under stress. Leadership makes decisions with their own but not their customers' well-being in mind. They can move accounts, limit access to capital, rein in credit, and delay services—often with only the most opaque explanations and little warning. The lack of transparency is perhaps the most galling facet of retail banking for me.

Banks determine the value of money through their control of supply. They can flood markets with new notes, remove currency, or even eliminate a currency altogether. The reasons for these decisions reflect faulty thinking. Witness post–World War I Weimar Germany, which experienced the worst hyperinflation of any industrialized country in history as it struggled to pay off massive war debts stipulated by the Treaty of Versailles's harsh terms. From 1919 to 1922, with the German economy reeling, the mark fell in value by over 99.999 percent and Germans used some of their worthless currency for cooking and heating fuel. The debacle directly led to the rise of Hitler's National Socialist German Workers' Party. This tragic episode in history shows that there can be severe global political consequences when societies are pushed to extremes through monetary injustices.

But there are recent, less politically dramatic but nevertheless disturbing examples of devaluation. In the 1990s, Zimbabwe's economy crumpled after the newly elected government initiated reforms to distribute lands more fairly between white landowners who had ruled the country for decades and black subsistence farmers. The poorly conceived initiative—the black farmers lacked training in managing larger farms—ruined the country's agriculture industry, which accounted for a third of its foreign exchange earnings.

Zimbabwe's banks collapsed amid severe declines in food production, corruption, and sanctions imposed by European countries and the United States against the dictatorial regime. To prop up the economy, Zimbabwe began printing Zimbabwe dollars in sums more fitting for a board game, including 100 billion- and trillion-dollar Zimbabwe banknotes. Inflation continued, and the government kept printing larger and larger banknotes, with the highest value banknote reaching 100 trillion Zimbabwe dollars. In the end, Monopoly play money was probably more valuable than Zimbabwe dollars! The currency did not possess any foundation to give it value. The country's people, foreign investors, and entrepreneurs that might have done business there lost all faith in the government.

Countries can even replace or eliminate currency—or parts of it. In 2016, with no notice, Indian Prime Minister Narendra Modi made a bombshell announcement on television that the government would immediately withdraw the 500- and 1,000-rupee notes from circulation. Modi said that the move would check the use of counterfeit bills for illegal activities and terrorism. After a long delay, the government issued new 500- and 2,000-rupee notes as replacements, but limited how much money bank customers could exchange, and subsequently how much they could withdraw. For several months, the Indian economy lingered at a near standstill.

Cash shortages led to violence, and there were reports of deaths among customers waiting too long in bank lines looking to exchange notes and make withdrawals.[4] GDP dropped a whopping half-point amid sudden sharp declines in agriculture and manufacturing, and a paralysis of the trucking sector, which couldn't pay for fuel. India's stock indices hit six-month lows. Indian economists, some of whom had supported the initiative, quickly revised their thinking.

Holders of the old currency had few options, and in some cases lost years of hard-earned savings, because of their inability to convert to new bills in a timely manner. The episode was yet another stark demonstration of how institutions hold all the power in the bank–customer relationship.

India's decision resembled a 1969 decision by President Nixon to yank $500 and $1,000 bills featuring, respectively, the portraits of William McKinley and Grover Cleveland, from circulation. Nixon's reasoning: the bills were easier for international crime syndicates to move. As I was writing this book, the European Central Bank was considering withdrawing the 500-euro banknote from circulation. So, if cash can be used by criminals anonymously, should law-abiding citizens be prohibited from using cash anymore? Governments would love nothing more than to force society to use a form of money that can be fully tracked and controlled. I vehemently disagree.

Even more recently, we've watched the Venezuelan economy take a historic tumble and its currency, the bolivar, turn to dust. Venezuela had arguably been South America's wealthiest country, awash in oil and free of the political upheavals that have afflicted other countries in the region. But with the arrival of Hugo Chávez and his corrupt successor, Nicolás Maduro, the country has made one wrong turn after another. That includes antagonizing the United States, which imposed sanctions against the Maduro regime, forcing it to deplete its oil reserves.

Inflation hit around 1 million percent, while the bolivar lost 95 percent of its value against the US dollar. According to a 2018 BBC report, it cost more than 14 million bolivars for a five-pound chicken and more than 10 million for two pounds of meat.[5] A 2019 *New York Times* article reported that more than a tenth of the population had left the country.[6] Many of those who couldn't or wouldn't leave dined on unrefrigerated organ meat and scrambled to find clean water and basic services amid regular power blackouts. A Harvard economist quoted in the *Times* story, Kenneth Rogoff, called it the biggest "human tragedy of this scale outside civil war in nearly a half century."

SERVICE FAILINGS

Early in my Bitcoin experience, as I scrutinized fiat currency systems, I recognized how often they had failed me and my family. Consider the scenario I encountered in 2018 when I tried to enter the World Series of Poker (WSOP) tournament in Las Vegas, the world's most prestigious poker tournament with prize money in the millions. From the time I learned the game after college, I had always enjoyed playing small stakes poker. After selling BTCC, I had time to improve my skills by playing more poker tournaments. I won enough against good players to believe I could do well at the annual WSOP tournament. For the opportunity to test myself against poker legends and rising stars, I had to pay the $10,000 entry fee. This was one of the world's largest tournament entry fees, and it was supposed to prevent less skilled players from entering on a lark.

I had banked at Wells Fargo for over 25 years and had more than enough money in my main checking account for this withdrawal. I planned to withdraw $20,000 in cash, $10,000 for the WSOP tournament entry fee and another $10,000 as extra cash as I planned to play in poker cash games or other table games at the casino. But when I stopped into a bank in a suburb about five miles from the famed Las Vegas Strip, accessing what was supposed to be my own money required my enduring an awkward, nearly half-hour-long series of conversations with suspicious bank tellers and an even more skeptical branch manager.

They asked questions that were framed to seem innocuous but were meant to determine if I was going to do something illicit—or at least marginal—with my withdrawal. Due to the large cash withdrawal amount, the bank teller had to get a bank manager to complete the task.

"Mr. Lee, this is a large cash withdrawal. Would you instead prefer a cashier's check?" asked the bank manager. I declined the offer and asked for cash.

"What do you need this cash for?" was her reply.

I was perplexed, and immediately responded, "I mean, this is Las Vegas! I'm going to go gambling at the casinos."

"What games do you play?" the banker asked.

I told them I played craps and poker, and I needed the cash for the WSOP poker tournament entry fee.

The bank manager again suggested that I could take a cashier's check and use that to pay the tournament entry fee at the casino. What she did not mention was that banks charge a fee for issuing a cashier's check, whereas they couldn't charge me any fees for withdrawing cash—for essentially taking back my own money.

So, for a final time I responded, "No thanks. I'll take it in cash please."

As a long-term customer with a large bank balance, I initially thought of letting Wells Fargo know about my displeasure. But I decided to answer the questions sincerely while not sharing too much information. I felt that this approach would deflect any additional suspicions. I let the bankers know that I needed the amount for the tournament and provided a few details about the competition. But really, was it their business to inquire about what I wanted to do with my own money? This wasn't like it was a bank loan, where I had to ask them for permission to borrow the bank's money, and they had a responsibility to judge the worthiness of awarding the loan. This was my own cash! My own money!

There were additional delays as the bank counted out hundred-dollar bills. The bankers had to count the amount twice: once in the machine in the bank, and once more in front of me, one $100 bill at a time. The bills formed 10 neat stacks that

I quickly assembled, tucked into an envelope, and then placed in the black Tumi backpack that I had brought with me. I saw irony in a bank asking questions about a cash withdrawal in a town where big sums change hands regularly. And yes, sometimes big sums change hands illegally. But the more I pondered the situation, the more it concerned me. Do we have freedom over our own money? Or should banks have such a large say, as if we're still children needing permission from adults for our daily life choices and activities?

The bankers' queries were a direct invasion of my privacy. If I hadn't answered truthfully, they most likely could have denied my request for the cash withdrawal, and probably cited antifraud and anti–money laundering rules and regulations. They probably would have claimed that denying the cash withdrawal would be for account security and for my own protection. And worse yet, they could have even red-flagged my account, or filed a suspicious activity report to the banking regulators. What would have been the consequences of that? I don't know.

It was not their business if I spent the money on a poker tournament entry fee, to buy 300 Hawaiian shirts at a local Walmart, or to buy a pound of weed at a local marijuana dispensary. (Yes, recreational marijuana smoking is now legal in Las Vegas, Nevada.) Moreover, anything they needed to know about my accounts was readily available on one of their computer screens. But banks frequently ask these needless questions in the alleged interest of account security. That raises an additional irony because banks and other financial services organizations regularly fall short in protecting our personal data.

Exhibit one was the 2019 Capital One breach that compromised personal information of more than 100 million customers. A software engineer was able to hack into the company's platforms to steal the information. Or consider my longtime bank, Wells Fargo, which is still trying to fix its reputation after its upper management—experienced banking executives all—sanctioned a program charging unsuspecting customers fees associated with fraudulent debit and credit cards and lines of credit. The bank paid $185 million in penalties for the con, and its CEO, John Stumpf, agreed to a lifetime ban from the banking industry. The company's marketing campaigns have continued to focus on issues of trust.

Over the years, I've experienced ongoing problems with WeChat Pay, the Chinese payment platform I used to send money to my friends and family. WeChat Pay has a roughly $30,000 yearly limit on how much people can transact. So, I've had to parcel my transactions carefully throughout the year.

Separately, one of the banks I use in China recently instituted a fee for its SMS message alerts, where they notify me of any account activity. I don't use that account much, so the irony is that every month, I get a single SMS message from that bank, notifying me that they've deducted that special SMS service fee from my bank balance. So literally, I pay them every month to notify me that I've paid them. I often wonder whether I should just request to turn off the SMS notification feature and save the monthly fee. This scenario and my experiences with WeChat Pay and Wells Fargo Bank underscore my lack of control over my assets.

I'll repeat again that I have nothing against traditional currencies. I come from a family that thrived using fiat monetary systems (and gold, which gave them their initial start on a new life in Hong Kong). They used cash to build their businesses, particularly in Abidjan, the Ivory Coast's business hub where my parents settled in the 1970s and used cash as the lingua franca of daily commerce—and sometimes US dollars, often stacked in large bundles and tied with rubber bands. My family withdrew it from old-fashioned bank tellers where they held longstanding accounts.

These dollars, originating in the world's leading economic power, were a sign of reliability. Few if any people argued that dollars would hold up over time.

In word and action, my parents taught my siblings and me how to use the fiat monetary system. They taught us how to budget, save, and bank; the difference between savings, checking, and brokerage accounts; and how, if you planned wisely, you could put money to work in ways that would ensure a high standard of living. We heard many times how they had moved to the Ivory Coast when it was ripe for enterprise and saw the fruits of their labor—a factory that shipped products domestically and abroad, a home with enough rooms for everyone to have a bedroom in a country where some families squeezed into one- and two-room shanties, and trips and school abroad. And their success allowed us to acquire the latest personal computers, which started my lifelong passion in technology.

My ability to earn and curate fiat money as a successful businessman and investor has allowed me to venture widely and cultivate interests in French food, wine, and poker. I have homes in the United States and China, and one day my children will likely follow my path to attend university in the United States. I agree with Henry David Thoreau, the American essayist who touted the virtues of a simpler existence but also said that "wealth" was "the ability to fully experience life."

Until businesses latch onto Bitcoin more widely, I will largely pay for most things the way that I always have with fiat money, using credit cards, cash, payment systems, and other tools of personal finance. I have accounts with dollars and renminbi. I even admire many of the fintech tools developed to serve customers; they've turned our smartphones into mini banks.

I say all this to make the point that my attacks on fiat currency are nothing personal. I'm not some antiestablishment renegade looking to bring down our current ways of doing business.

The United States, as we know it, might not exist without central European banks in the late eighteenth century loaning money to the patriot cause, and a new national banking system buttressing the Union side in the Civil War. Throughout history, banks have fueled exploration, entrepreneurship, and property ownership.

Without bank loans, Sam Walton, the namesake of my old firm, would not have been able to turn his general store into a retailing empire. Bank loans continue to help small business owners who fall under venture capital's radar. In 2019, Wells Fargo, following its well-publicized travails I chronicled just a few paragraphs earlier, originated nearly $85 billion in mortgages, and Bank of America, another $55 billion.

Traditional monetary systems have a place in the world for now. They have given us a good foundation in how to value objects and services and for executing financial transactions fairly. On a personal level, I remember fondly the cushioned chairs in which my father and I sat in the BayBank branch in Lawrenceville, New Jersey, at the start of my freshman high school year when we opened my first checking account.

That said, I can also look at monetary systems and the institutions that are central to them with a clear head. This age-old system has grown out of control. Our money is worth less every year, and its value depends on the judgment of bureaucrats who aren't looking out for us. In contrast, bitcoins steadily gain value due to their deflationary nature, which was purposely designed into Bitcoin.

But banks also have too much say over what we can do with our money, require too much personal information for us to use their services, charge too much, and don't provide the level of security or service that should make us want to continue using them. Because they function within the larger monetary framework, they also don't feel obligated to change their focus. They feel largely impervious to criticism that they operate at the expense of consumers. As is the case with all longstanding systems, their primary goal is to protect themselves. Again, in contrast, Bitcoin serves its community and only its community.

WHY REGULATORS ARE SLOWING ADOPTION BUT SHOULDN'T

How much regulation do people need to live peacefully and productively? When do rules and restrictions overstep their bounds, interfering instead of enabling people?

These are two parts of one big question, debated through the ages by some of history's greatest philosophers. They assume that most people are good—a reasonable premise in my mind, but in need of some correction, a rulebook or codification to rein in our lesser impulses and give us clarity. And this applies to all endeavors, including monetary systems, even Bitcoin.

We may not like rules, but we need a few of them.

"If men were angels, no government would be necessary," James Madison famously penned in Federalist Paper 51, one of 82 he authored or coauthored with Alexander Hamilton, adding, "In framing a government which is to be administered by men over men, the great difficulty lies in this: you must first enable the government to control the governed; and in the next place oblige it to control itself."

Madison understood the organizational challenge that political leaders have always faced. It is an issue that I started pondering more deeply as I immersed myself in Bitcoin and thought of the myriad ways my financial institutions were failing to serve me. It also had me thinking of more situations where government and other organizations complicated instead of eased my life.

Civilizations have answered these questions differently, depending on their cultures, the social and economic challenges they faced, and leadership. Regulation has a long history.

From 2,500 to 1,700 BC, the area between the Tigris and Euphrates rivers, one of the four cradles of Western civilization, spawned the earliest recorded codes of law. The most famous of them, the Code of Hammurabi—named for the powerful Babylonian ruler—was etched into a massive black diorite pillar, part of which now stands in the Louvre Museum.

Hammurabi, a great military leader, appreciated the need for governing his rapidly expanding empire, which stretched 30,000 square miles over parts of modern-day Iraq, Turkey, Iran, and Syria. His collection of 282 laws sought to shape appropriate social and commercial behavior, based on what were probably the most frequent areas of interpersonal conflict.

Some of these statutes were remarkably brutal, but others seemed genuinely concerned about treating people fairly. To ensure sound record keeping, the code required customers of grain, wool, and oil merchants "to write down the value" of the goods they purchase and take a receipt with the amount they paid. "If the agent is careless and does not take a receipt . . . the money not receipted for shall not be placed to his account," according to law 105 in the code.

The code also delineated a payment system. A field laborer received eight gur of grain annually; a herdsman, six gur (I question the fairness; herding seems more a management role); and "a man who hires an ox, 20 sila of grain is his daily hire." Doctors who saved a life received anywhere from 2 to 10 shekels depending on the class of patient—freeman, plebeian, slave.

The Egyptians, Greek, and Roman Empires over the ensuing millennia established their own rules and regulations, many of them financial, as a way to maintain order in their vast geographies. Underlying their actions was a concern that people could not treat each other fairly without rules to govern them. Their systems included built-in mechanisms for ensuring individuals obeyed the law. The idea of a financial network or legal platform in which the participants did not have to entrust a third party to verify the correctness of a transaction had yet to take root.

While written artifacts are scarce, perhaps the closest to this blockchain fundamental was the Egyptian notion of Ma'at, which although not easily translatable, described a sort of natural balance based on the rule of law. Ma'at applied to all aspects of culture, including the just completion of business and personal interactions. It ensured that everyone from the near divine Pharaoh to the poorest peasant would behave virtuously.

The system covered a range of civil issues. The Palermo Stone, so named after its nineteenth-century purchase by a Palermo businessman and probably the oldest historical narrative of Ancient Egypt, suggests that Egyptians believed in a census, and by extension, the recording of personal property and land that could be transferred. A legal papyrus from the reign of Kahun II describes a man's attempt to collect a debt on behalf of his father.[1] Other documents addressed land contracts and labor and bartering agreements, the latter often involving the exchange of work for commodities.

Aristotle saw city-states as the perfect organizational extension of man's political nature and need for order. The city-state ensured that men would live ethically, safely, and productively. Rules were important. "Just as, when perfected, a human is the best of animals, so also when separated from law and justice, he is the worst of all," he wrote in his *Politics*.

Politics cast a wide sweep over financial issues. It provides an account of Thales, the mathematician and astronomer who is sometimes considered the first great philosopher, engaging in an early form of futures trading and a peer-to-peer interaction. According to Aristotle, Thales earned a handsome windfall after paying the owners of olive presses for their use the following year. He based his investment on the expectation of a strong harvest. Aristotle makes no mention of a regulatory body. Thales dealt directly with his counterparts in the transaction. Was Thales the father of peer-to-peer financial systems?

Yet Aristotle also offers one of the earliest formal definitions of money, describing it as a commodity or unit of value that provides the means of exchange and accounting. He touts the advantages of monetary systems over more unwieldy, inefficient bartering, which had been the norm, provided the unit of exchange is easy to carry, store, and use in calculations. In addition, it should be durable and have value itself. Yet he also expresses some cynicism toward money.

"Money is a guarantee that we may have what we want in the future," he wrote in the *Nichomachean Ethics*. "It ensures the possibility of satisfying a new desire when it arises." I like that definition.

What could be a bigger endorsement for Bitcoin, which increases in value over time?

A little more than a half-century before the birth of Christ, the orator Cicero addressed what he saw as the breakdown of the rule of law in the Roman Republic. As a rising political leader and later one of the Republic's two consuls—sort of co-emperors—Cicero had watched the government's elaborate system of checks and balances deteriorate as the upper classes and provincial governors who controlled political life made bribery and extortion common practice. Cicero feared this decline would result in the unraveling of human rights and the formation of dictatorship

Here was central authority overreaching. Sound familiar?

Later in his career, over two volumes, *The Republic* and *The Laws*, and in his famed speeches, Cicero urged the Roman Republic to return to a more honorable time consistent with natural law, which he saw as a guide to individual behavior. "Law is the highest reason, implanted in Nature, which commands what ought to be done and forbids the opposite," Cicero wrote in *The Laws*.

The law must treat everyone equally, Cicero believed, both to ensure a just society and to guarantee individual liberty. Respect for law leads to good government, encourages the right behaviors, and discourages the wrong ones. Isn't that what current legislators aim to do?

Underlying these philosophical contemplations was a question of how to achieve balance and fairness in society via individual and institutional action. One theme held firm: namely, that the state (and I use the term to encompass all their forms of government), for good or bad, had to set limitations.

CENTRAL VERSUS NONCENTRALIZED AUTHORITY

More than a millennium later, the Magna Carta was drafted. It marked a significant step away from purely autocratic rule by ensuring that England's king was subject to the law and by limiting his powers, including the levying of taxes without parliament's consent. It also guaranteed free men the right to trial, setting the base for the 5th Amendment in the US Constitution. The push and pull of rule by a central entity versus a more dispersed system that gives states, cities, and individuals additional autonomy would grow more intense and thought-provoking over time.

The eighteenth- and nineteenth-century political philosopher Thomas Hobbes wrote of compromises and exchanges that man makes to ensure his survival. His overlapping Enlightenment contemporary John Locke saw government as a way of protecting natural rights of "life, liberty, and property." Locke's principles strongly influenced Thomas Jefferson as he crafted the US Declaration of Independence and James Madison and the other authors of the American Constitution. Jefferson favored states' rights and less power to a single centralized authority.

Over the years, the pendulum has swung back and forth between more centralized or diffused power, and between more or less individual freedom. I will not divulge my own political beliefs in these pages, but merely as an observation, I think we've been inclined to less restriction of late, particularly in financial affairs. This trend reflects distrust of the people in charge. Look at how many voters, whether in city, state, or national elections, say they don't like any of the candidates and complain about government. They feel the same way about most big companies, a result of the scandals that have plagued many of these institutions and perhaps bad individual experiences.

The coronavirus pandemic only exacerbated these concerns. Should the government have the right to require us to wear a mask and maintain six feet of distance between us? Should it be allowed to close the economy in the interest of public safety? Or are these actions heavy-handed, infringing on an individual right of each of us to determine what is in our best health interest? And what of government's right to change the terms of our economy by pouring more—freshly printed—cash into the public domain in the interest of stimulating a sagging economy? Should our lauded financial institutions change their hours, suspend online operations, and restrict our ability to execute transactions or access cash?

The pandemic, particularly in its early days, reminded individuals of the lack of control they have over their assets, as some banks closed branches, reduced banking hours, and delayed a variety of services and customers encountered issues as they tried to pay for expenses and move money. The lines of panicked consumers that formed outside grocery and drug stores with dwindling supplies of staple goods were distant echoes of the Depression-era soup lines. Would cash reserves at local banks follow the model of flour, bread, toilet paper, and eggs? As the pandemic raged, I thought occasionally of the famed scene from *It's a Wonderful Life* where Jimmy Stewart's character, George

Bailey, parcels out all but his savings and loan's last two dollars to a frightened, angry crowd and rescues his bank.

I was not completely confident in my banks' abilities to protect my money as the pandemic evolved, and the experience prompted me to consider the experiences of families in the early days of the Great Depression. Are the systems that have grown painstakingly over decades or more weatherproof? Are the people running the esteemed organizations behind them making sound decisions? Andrew Ross Sorkin answered these questions with a definitive *no* in his book *Too Big to Fail*.

The lasting impact of recent events will, if anything, increase our receptiveness to alternative systems free from the intrusiveness of central authorities. Bitcoin, as I've already stated, will no longer seem so exotic, and a growing number of people will be drawn to its infallible logic, efficiency, and cost savings. And given the more libertarian tenor of the times, it will give people a sense of control and freedom that many are craving. People will understand and appreciate the meaning of a publicly available system that is absent the interference inherent in traditional monetary systems with central banking. They will relish a pure financial independence—no banks, cards, or other central authorizing organizations.

BITCOIN WON'T NEED A LOT OF REGULATING

Here we arrive again at a unique aspect of human nature: the need to be as free as possible but also to have agreed-upon rules of engagement. Bitcoin won't require a lot of help, which is among its biggest advantages. But to satisfy the human craving for some order, it will require a few directives. How should Bitcoin stack up against other types of assets such as ETFs, mutual funds, and stocks? Who should ensure that entrepreneurs with honest intentions and the right resources are entering the industry? And in those few instances where there is malfeasance, who can consumers turn to, and what remedies will be available for them? How should Bitcoin (and other cryptocurrencies) be taxed when someone takes profits, or if the individual receives bitcoin compensation?

"A clear regulatory environment that fosters innovation while protecting investors is an important step in digital currency's evolution as a technology," said a March 13, 2018, post on Coinbase's blog.[2] "Regulatory clarity will encourage and accelerate entrepreneurial activity in digital currency, ultimately resulting in new products and services that benefit consumers and businesses." I completely agree.

Historical legislation, passed decades before digital currency was technologically possible, offers some guidance, but understandably could not anticipate many of the issues that cryptocurrencies raise today. The Securities Act of 1933 and the Securities Exchange Act a year later, by-products of the Great Depression, were designed to protect stock investors from fraud by requiring firms to provide clear, accurate information about their business, leadership, financial performance, the nature of the securities being offered, and to ensure a fair environment. The Securities Exchange Act created the Securities and Exchange Commission (SEC), one of the most fearsome regulators in the United States today.

In 1946, the Supreme Court's decision in *SEC v. W.J. Howey Co.* clarified the definition of an investment. In a six-to-one ruling (the chief justice position was vacant, and one justice, Robert Jackson, did not participate in the case), the justices determined that an investment based on the framework of the Securities Act of 1933 was any "contract, transaction or scheme whereby a person invests his money in a common enterprise and is led to expect profits solely from the efforts of the promoter or a third party."

Some current lawmakers and others considering cryptocurrency issues have invoked the "Howey Test" to determine if cryptocurrencies are securities. They view bitcoin investment as a speculative activity and should incur the same capital gains taxes that investors pay on stock sales. But regulators have yet to fully accept this argument. In a mid-2019 decision, the SEC rejected the assertion by the Cipher Technologies Bitcoin Fund, a so-called closed-end investment fund, that bitcoin should be considered a security. "We do not believe that current purchasers of bitcoin are relying on the essential managerial and entrepreneurial efforts of others to produce a profit," the SEC held.

I thought that this determination made sense. Bitcoin itself isn't a for-profit enterprise. It is a decentralized network that has created an alternative to our current monetary system. Its goal, as much as you can say the Bitcoin platform has any goal, is to win converts, not profitability. Bitcoin is better considered as a digital commodity, as an asset, just like any other asset or property that people can own.

In July 2020, a federal judge weighing an altogether different set of facts in *United States v. Harmon*, concluded similarly: Bitcoin was a type of money.[3] Money "commonly means a medium of exchange, method of payment, or store of value," wrote Chief United States District Judge Beryl A. Hall, adding "Bitcoin is these things." The ruling allowed prosecutors to proceed with money laundering charges against Larry Dean Harmon, the operator of an unlicensed Bitcoin exchange, under the Washington, DC, Money Transmitters Act. The ruling covered a small jurisdiction but dovetailed with federal and state agencies' approach to Bitcoin regarding money laundering.

While limited in scope, these are meaningful decisions that bode well for Bitcoin. They affirm Bitcoin's status (and usefulness) as a currency. They also offer hope that the obstacles to passing effective, wider ranging regulation are surmountable. If the SEC and a court can respond on a limited scale to regulatory questions that companies pose, then government agencies have the ability to issue wider edicts. Of course, broader decisions can only occur when these agencies have a firm understanding of how Bitcoin works and why they shouldn't try to regulate it as if it were like any other sort of asset.

And they should be careful not to try to pretend that they can severely limit its use or worse. Such a draconian perspective at this point would be akin to trying to return a tiger to its cage with your bare hands.

I believe regulators have already taken too long to settle most regulatory issues involving cryptocurrency, but as an evangelist, I'm eager to move to next steps.

I do understand that there are a few nettlesome issues involving taxation and security that will need settling. There's also a psychological component that becomes apparent at US conferences, where people often ask me about the future legality of ETFs and consumer protections in the cryptocurrency space. I often sense that they are looking for the added assurance that government brings via legislation or code of guidelines. They are showcasing an aspect of human nature present in even the most libertarian individuals: we are hardwired to look for the approval of a higher authority.

A SLOW START

Government by nature moves slowly as lawmakers gauge the potential impact of their actions on their political futures. By calling into question traditional ways of conducting business, they also raise doubts about the need for the institutions behind them. In the case of cryptocurrency, those institutions are commercial banks and the mighty central bank. Commercial banks compose the largest part of the vast financial services industry. It is a major constituency that also has a big influence over policy. While I appreciate that political leaders often need to take their time as they weigh important decisions, in cryptocurrency's case, I think they've been dragging their feet to avoid offending banks.

Note that the US Congress and state legislators have been latecomers to the regulatory party, holding their first hearings years after China and other countries passed their first laws targeting Bitcoin. For example, the People's Bank of China (PBOC), the Chinese central bank controlled by the government, declared in 2013 that Bitcoin was not a currency, and barred its banks and businesses from accepting bitcoin. Wrong decision in my opinion, but at least they were taking notice.

Some of the regulatory discussions in these other countries centered on a minor issue: what they should call cryptocurrency. The names included:

- *Digital currency* in Argentina, Thailand, and Australia
- *Virtual commodity* in Canada, Taiwan, and China
- *Crypto-token* in Germany
- *Payment token* in Switzerland
- *Cyber currency* in Italy and Lebanon
- *Electronic currency* in Colombia and Lebanon
- *Virtual asset* in Honduras and Mexico

They're all different! For me, *cryptocurrency* works just fine. And I don't think we need to reconsider Bitcoin as a name, even if it sounds like a virtual gaming currency. "That which we call a rose by any other name would smell as sweet," wrote Shakespeare. But I think such discussions do reflect the uncertainty that surrounds all new movements.

In this book, I've used *cryptocurrency* to refer to the digital currency movement, *Bitcoin* to refer to the platform, and *bitcoin* to refer to the currency. They are three distinct entities. Note that many legislators and investors mistakenly interchange Bitcoin and cryptocurrency. Bitcoin's creation led to the current cryptocurrency movement. You could even say that without Bitcoin, cryptocurrency would not exist today.

Note that some legislative bills also reference blockchain, which is Bitcoin's underlying technology, with proponents dreaming of wider, potentially groundbreaking applications in business, entertainment, government, and other sectors. Rather than separate blockchain-focused bills from the passages below, I will cover them as another sign of Bitcoin's impact and the importance of its underlying technology: decentralized public blockchain.

Witness the remarks of then LabCFTC (the Commodity Futures Trading Commission financial research unit) director Daniel Gorfine during a July 2018 hearing on cryptocurrency before the US House Committee on Agriculture.[4] A lawyer by training, Gorfine spoke optimistically of a "fast-evolving" financial world driven by "technology-driven innovation."

"This has changed the way market participants interact, trades are formulated and processed, risk is assessed and hedged, and business operations are executed," Gorfine said. "No longer do market participants rely on face-to-face interactions and telephones. Instead, markets have become increasingly electronic, digital, and interconnected. This new world, in turn, creates new market and regulatory opportunities, challenges, and risks," including cryptocurrency.

Gorfine spoke of a bigger, "shared goal to bring clarity and certainty to the market" to ensure cryptocurrency would achieve its larger goals. But he also advocated for a "thoughtful" approach that would "not steer or impede the development of this area of innovation.

"While some may seek the immediate establishment of bright lines, the reality is that hasty regulatory pronouncements are likely to miss the mark, have unintended consequences, or fail to capture important nuance regarding the structure of new products or models."

Gorfine added that it was "important that we're not hasty in figuring out . . . the contours of applying securities law and . . . the commodities framework."

Former CFTC chair turned MIT Media Lab senior advisor Gary Gensler, who spoke after Gorfine to the same committee, struck a similarly upbeat but measured tone. He likened blockchain technology and crypto finance to "new technologies in the past, from railroads in the 19th century to the internet in the late 20th century," which also spurred serious regulatory debate.

"Operating within policy frameworks, though, has helped foster traditional capital markets for decades and are just as important for crypto finance, even if the details for achieving the goals may be adapted to accommodate new technologies," Gensler said. He offered a short list of public benefits from these frameworks, including better tax compliance, guarding against money laundering or terrorism financing, promoting financial stability, fostering economic inclusion and growth, and protecting investors and consumers.

Gensler added: "Achieving these broad public policy goals fosters economic growth and is consistent with promoting innovation. Such core principles of investor protection and market integrity are embodied in U.S. securities and commodities laws regardless of the form of investment. Such common-sense rules bolster confidence in markets and enhance our economy."

But the speakers to the Congressional committee, who also included Amber Baldet, then JPMorgan's blockchain lead and now the cofounding director of blockchain startup Clovyr, and Scott Kupor, managing partner of the powerhouse venture capital firm Andreessen Horowitz, received a mixed response, with one legislator, Minnesota Democrat Collin Peterson, likening crypto to "a Ponzi scheme." "What's behind it?" Peterson asked. What Peterson didn't understand was that for something to be valuable, it doesn't have to be backed by something else. This is a common misconception.

But this was not partisan skepticism. Witness Minnesota Republican Rick Allen's expressing doubts about creating "another money supply . . . I just don't know how that works," Allen said. "Our dollar sets the mark for the world." This kind of comment shows a lack of understanding about the difference between fiat currency (where the value is declared by fiat) and a valuable commodity, where it has inherent value due to its usefulness and scarcity. Gold, as an example, has inherent value because it can be used for industrial and other business purposes (including as jewelry), has unique chemical properties (dense, inert, and stable), and is scarce (relative to other metals and natural elements).

There are even harsher critics among American back benchers, none more intense than California Democrat Brad Sherman, who called cryptocurrencies "a crock" in a March 2018 hearing of the US House Subcommittee on Capital Markets, Securities, and Investment. He connected them to a range of illicit activities. "They help terrorists and criminals move money around the world. They help start-up companies commit fraud, take the money, and one percent of the time they actually create a useful business, but then again I daresay that some tiny percent of all larceny and crime helps finance something that turns out to be useful."

A year later, Sherman called for a complete cryptocurrency ban, saying it would protect the US dollar's power and influence in global markets. "An awful lot of our international power comes from the fact that the dollar is the standard unit of international finance and transactions," Sherman said, adding that "it is the announced purpose of the supporters of cryptocurrencies to take that power away from us. . . . The advantage it has over sovereign currency is solely to aid in the disempowerment of the United States and rule of law."

About the same time, at a hearing to consider Facebook's ballyhooed Libra cryptocurrency, Sherman's outspoken fellow Democrat Maxine Waters raised concerns about "privacy, trading, national security and monetary policy concerns"[5]—all issues for other types of assets.

Yet I believe Sherman, Waters, and others with similarly negative views and concerns are a declining minority. Most legislators who have studied cryptocurrency understand its potential, or at least recognize that Bitcoin is too firmly entrenched to outlaw or restrict via regulation. And I expect some of the naysayers will become converts. As an early and frequent cryptocurrency supporter, Minnesota Republican Tom Emmer, said in a 2018 hearing of the House Financial Services Subcommittee on Capital Markets, Securities, and Investment: "People tend to fear what they don't know." He added: "If people sailing the oceans at the time of Columbus had believed the world is flat, we wouldn't have had the great discoveries of the New World."[6] Very well said. The reason you are reading this book is that just like Columbus, you refuse to believe that the world has to be flat. You're making the effort to learn about Bitcoin, just like how Columbus took the risk to sail west, beyond the end of the world. And he didn't fall off the edge of the world, but rather made possible a new beginning. The same is true for Bitcoin.

Yet Congressman Emmer, who had expressed concerns in another Capital Markets Subcommittee hearing that lawmakers' overzealousness would quash cryptocurrency's "entrepreneurial spirit," also acknowledged a need for some regulation. He introduced three separate cryptocurrency and blockchain bills in late September 2018: Resolution Supporting Digital Currencies and Blockchain Technology, Blockchain Regulatory Certainty, and Safe Harbor for Taxpayers with Forked Assets Acts.

The Resolution proclaimed Congress's "support" for the "development of" cryptocurrency in the United States and recommended "the federal government . . . provide a light touch, consistent, and simple legal environment." The two other Acts addressed protections for miners and other "blockchain entities" and consumers holding a cryptocurrency that has forked—in other words, splintered from another digital currency.

"The United States should prioritize accelerating the development of blockchain technology and create an environment that enables the American private sector to lead on innovation and further growth," Emmer said in announcing the bills.

"Legislators should be embracing emerging technologies and providing a clear regulatory system that allows them to flourish in the United States."

A year later, Emmer joined 20 other congressmen in asking IRS Commissioner Charles Rettig to clarify how taxpayers should report cryptocurrency, particularly how they should calculate and track the asset's cost basis—its original price plus other factors. The request for guidance was Emmer's second in less than a year. "Guidance is long overdue and essential to proper reporting of these emerging assets," Emmer wrote. "The bipartisan support this letter has received should send a clear message to the IRS that clear guidelines for reporting virtual currency are necessary." I agree with Emmer and I like all of his points, except for how he refers to Bitcoin and cryptocurrency as *virtual currency*. Though this term has stuck in government and legislation, I think it's a wildly inaccurate way to describe Bitcoin. There's nothing "virtual" about Bitcoin, any more so than emails and websites are virtual. Bitcoin is as real an asset and currency as any other.

Emmer concluded: "My colleagues and I are optimistic that the IRS will issue the guidance needed for taxpayers struggling with these reporting requirements."[7]

The following month, Rettig promised to provide guidance "very soon," but the agency has yet to follow through fully, although in July 2019, the IRS started sending letters to over 10,000 cryptocurrency investors, advising them to pay back taxes on their crypto transactions. "The IRS is expanding our efforts involving virtual currency, including increased use of data analytics," Rettig said in an IRS statement.[8] "We are focused on enforcing the law and helping taxpayers fully understand and meet their obligations." The letters came a year after the IRS launched a Virtual Currency Compliance campaign.[9]

In July 2019 remarks, during the House Financial Services Committee to discuss Facebook's Libra cryptocurrency, North Carolina Republican Patrick Timothy McHenry described "the world that Satoshi Nakamoto envisioned—and others are building" as "an unstoppable force." McHenry raised concerns similar to Emmer about legislators overplaying their cards. "We should not attempt to deter this innovation, and governments cannot stop this innovation," he said. "And those that have tried have already failed."[10]

In remarks that month at two hearings of the Senate Banking, Housing and Urban Affairs Committee to consider Libra, Idaho Republican Senator and Committee Chair Mike Crapo raised concerns about privacy, but also came down decidedly on the side of cryptocurrency. "It seems to me that digital technology innovations are inevitable, could be beneficial, and I believe that the U.S. should lead in developing these innovations and what the rules of the road should be," Crapo said. "The digital currency and blockchain ecosystem is diverse, and care must be taken in determining what gaps may be present in the existing framework and developing a more comprehensive approach."[11]

As this book went to press, Congress had introduced at least 30 cryptocurrency-related bills designed to clarify the regulatory landscape. More than a third of the bills attempted to provide a standardized regulatory foundation for cryptocurrencies and blockchain. Roughly the same number targeted crypto's use for money laundering, human trafficking, and terrorism. The remaining bills addressed the US government's potential use of blockchain technology and a digital dollar.

At least two of the bills addressed concerns about Facebook's entry into the crypto space and potentially other large tech companies with the resources and followings to introduce a new currency. I note here again that neither Libra nor other cryptocurrencies share Bitcoin's unique characteristics or promise as a universal store of value and a globally accepted means of exchange. But both bills anticipate important issues that will only enhance the public's estimation of Bitcoin.

The Protecting Consumers from Market Manipulation Act, introduced by Jesús García (D-IL) and Rashida Tlaib (D-MN), is supposed to help ensure that tech companies developing successful cryptocurrencies face the same regulatory oversight as financial services firms. The Financial Stability Oversight Council, a US Treasury agency that the Dodd-Frank bill created to protect consumers from a repeat of the 2007 banking implosion, views cryptocurrency as a financial market utility, fancy speak for a payment system. "Big tech companies like Facebook and Google are moving to the financial services sector where they currently evade existing banking regulations," García said in introducing the bill. "Congress has a responsibility to protect working families and keep banking and commerce separate."[12]

Let me be clear here again that while I am a Bitcoin evangelist and confident of the broader future for cryptocurrencies, I understand the need for regulation. I am also realistic that Bitcoin (and the wider crypto universe) are early in their evolution and still working out basic issues—and a few smaller bothersome ones—that one day soon will be second nature. Regulation is part of what I call the clarifying work common to new business innovations. On a smaller scale, the West African countries where my grandparents settled faced similar phenomena as they reckoned with foreign enterprises. The governments had to determine what they would allow. As time went on, their decisions became easier as they saw these businesses fuel their economies.

REGULATION DEBATE OVERSEAS

Cryptocurrency regulatory debate is hardly unique to the United States. Some countries are farther along in settling their approach to cryptocurrency. Some have made misguided efforts to regulate it, usually overstepping—witness China's supposed crypto ban and similar efforts by other authoritarian governments. Others are at the beginning stages, with some countries unsure what to do amid soaring interest within their borders.

One thread common to many of these countries' attitudes toward cryptocurrency has been concern for consumers. In a 2018 survey-based report on cryptocurrency regulation in 130 countries and other geographic areas that have offered some legal guidance on the topic, the Law Library of Congress, Global Legal Research Center found that many "jurisdictions" issued notices about potential pitfalls of crypto markets.[13] The warnings, which have generally come from central banks, were largely centered on explaining the differences between state-issued, fiat currencies and cryptocurrencies. But the warnings also addressed risk and volatility, "and . . . that many of the organizations that facilitate such transactions are unregulated."

The report also found that many governments warn consumers that they may not have legal means to recoup losses due to errors or misdeeds, and they have highlighted cryptocurrency's potential for illegal use, particularly money laundering and terrorism. As I've mentioned, although Mt. Gox and other hacks have been severe, I believe that critics have overstated Bitcoin and other cryptocurrencies' vulnerabilities to hacks and misuse, conveniently overlooking the ongoing security weaknesses among traditional financial service institutions.

Nevertheless, the report found that many countries amended their money laundering and organized crime financial laws to address cryptocurrency transactions. They are now requiring higher levels of scrutiny among banks and other financial service companies.

The countries and jurisdictions with the most stringent regulations or that have issued full or partial bans have tended to be the most authoritarian. As this book went to press, Algeria, Morocco, Bolivia, and Pakistan had banned all cryptocurrency activities. Maybe no surprise, these countries are operating either under a form of dictatorship, constitutional monarchy, or single-party rule. Qatar and Bahrain, which have traditionally placed severe limits on their citizens' actions, allow consumers to participate in cryptocurrency only outside their national boundaries. At least a half-dozen other countries, including most significantly China and Iran, have prevented financial services organizations inside their borders from facilitating trading or any transactions related to the sale or purchase of goods with cryptocurrency. This mini trend is logical. Authoritarian regimes and those under severe social and economic stress (Iran, Bolivia) are naturally wary of relinquishing control of any aspect of their economy, particularly the means of exchange.

But they are on the wrong side of this issue. Here I will make another observation about the nature of society and make a confession. I didn't realize that there were as many mixes of political systems within countries as there are until I became an adult. That is, some alleged democracies and socialist systems can have authoritarian threads, while more authoritarian governments can adopt certain democratic reforms.

Witness China's transition to a freer market economy over the past two decades, which has led to huge annual surges in GDP, a historic accumulation of wealth and consumption of luxury goods, and a mushrooming middle class that has more freedoms than it did in the 1990s or before. My own ability as someone with an American passport to work unimpeded for years in Shanghai and subsequently to launch a business in the country are testimony to the new freedoms after decades of harsh authoritarian rule. The country has retrenched in some areas, as the Hong Kong demonstrations attest. I am aware that in China, I have to watch what I say more carefully, and I do not enjoy the same freedoms as I do in the United States. This complex environment, welcoming at certain times and less so at others, only intensifies my belief in Bitcoin.

Bitcoin transcends limitations, regulatory or otherwise, because in the end, Bitcoin is just information (wallet private keys). Most of the time, it's just electronic digital information, so you can't see or touch it. It's practically invisible, yet it is so powerful, both as an idea and in daily usage. Its functioning depends on the wallet private keys that afford you full exclusive control of your funds and allow you to participate safely and pseudonymously in the Bitcoin network. As long as you have these private keys at your command, you can acquire or sell bitcoin, or use it for purchasing goods and services. Most importantly, with Bitcoin, you never have to depend on any intermediary third party. You are always in full control, and that is its beauty.

And with Bitcoin, it doesn't matter if you're transacting in hundreds, thousands, or tens of thousands of dollars; or where or when you want to execute a transaction. Bitcoin will never face restrictions on any of these issues or require extra approvals and permissions. Its processes won't change even if the style of government evolves to become more authoritarian and restrictive. Bitcoin is immune to censorship and crackdown. It was designed and built to be like that. Once alive, it can never die. And remember, despite efforts to curtail it, Bitcoin is alive and well, and has been for the last 12 years.

I'm encouraged that even countries that do not recognize cryptocurrency or are at the early stages of reckoning with its future see potential in the future of digital currency and the technology behind it. They seem sincere in their efforts to create a friendly cryptocurrency regulatory environment. Among others, Spain belongs to this group. I am also encouraged, perhaps strangely, by other countries' interest in developing their own cryptocurrencies. While these initiatives have little to do with Bitcoin, they are yet further proof of Bitcoin's influence. It is the tossed stone that keeps creating ripples in the pond. But don't be confused. Bitcoin is the one, and every other cryptocurrency is just a copycat.

ICO TOKENS ARE NOT BITCOIN

A quick word about initial coin offerings (ICOs), which fell under regulatory scrutiny following a series of mega offerings, including two crossing the $1 billion mark in 2017 and 2018. In an ICO, an entrepreneur or project team issues tokens to raise funds from the public to fund their blockchain project. Investors often have the option of using fiat currency, bitcoin, or another leading cryptocurrency to purchase the tokens, and they may receive a healthy return on their investment if the project has a successful launch. Aside from falling under the general dome of cryptocurrency, these ICO tokens are unrelated to Bitcoin. You might as well compare cryptocurrency to subway tokens or arcade game credits. They operate on different premises and do not hold the same investment potential. I am not disparaging these interesting, possibly transformative projects. Some of these projects are forging new applications for blockchain technology, but again, blockchain by itself is not Bitcoin, and ICOs did not enable Bitcoin.

I mention ICOs here only because they remain a concern among regulators and the wider public, both of whom have been simultaneously awed and concerned by the great sums of money they raised. Did they reflect greed, similar to other money-raising enterprises in history that were eager to take advantage of a thriving new trend? Were they scams? In some cases, the ICOs connected to projects that were still eons away from producing a final product. Investors seemed to be paying for an idea or the notion of an idea, perhaps worthy but maybe not. They were buying into hype, and hoping to sell it to the greater fool, with an even larger appetite for hype.

For a while in 2017 and 2018, it seemed like every young blockchain and crypto entrepreneur I met had a token offering in the works. Many of them were deeply committed to blockchain applications, but I sometimes felt the ideas were half-baked at best, more the result of fear of missing out on the next big trend than anything else. As gambles go, I was more inclined to purchase promising tech shares in the stock market than to buy the token promissory notes for many of the blockchain projects being pitched.

While I won't pan any single project, consider the following projects that raised huge amounts of money—and controversy:

- Block.one (aka EOS), a creator of open-sourced software targeting blockchain technology, which raised $4.1 billion even before the company had a formal project to offer the world.
- The encrypted messaging app Telegram, which allows people to send messages, photos, and audio files, raised $1.7 billion.
- Distributed file storage provider, Filecoin, which raised $258 million.
- Tezos, a provider of distributed database technology and famously featured in a *New York Times Magazine* story, which raised $232 million.

But ICOs also created problems, with some projects failing and others promising more than they seemingly could ever deliver. A number of these projects still have not taken root. Telegram delayed the launch of its platform and proposed new terms for refunding investors, after being fined $18.5 million by the SEC for its unregistered securities offering. Tezos suffered through C-suite disagreements about the company's strategic direction and financial management. It also endured a series of legal disputes.

To be sure, ICOs tailed off as crypto prices cooled. But some countries saw an opportunity to protect consumers from what they worried would be future rogue ICOs. As this book went to press, China, Macau, and Pakistan ban ICOs entirely. New Zealand and the Netherlands engage the appropriate regulatory agency to regulate ICOs depending on whether they classify a particular ICO as a security or other type of asset. And in the United States, an ICO offering has to comply with SEC rules, making one difficult to launch.

A TAXING PROBLEM

Similar to the United States, taxation in many countries remains a vexing issue that should clarify itself over time as legislators, regulators, and business leaders acclimate to cryptocurrency's wider usage. Although most countries do not tax mining profits, the current global landscape offers a patchwork of approaches. They reflect not only different taxation systems but also the different stages of acceptance. To varying degrees, they address the root problem of how to categorize cryptocurrency as an asset, including the gains from mining and selling bitcoins or other cryptocurrencies. Should profits be considered capital gains, income, or something else? Should they treat businesses and consumers differently? Among the solutions now:

- Israel, which has emerged as a center for technology innovation, taxes cryptocurrency as a financial asset.
- Switzerland, whose Zug region is among the world's crypto and blockchain hubs, treats cryptocurrency as a foreign currency. Zug and Ticino, which are near the country's traditional banking centers, already accept bitcoins as a means of payment, as do Mexico and the Isle of Man (the list will soon grow).
- Great Britain requires corporations to pay a business tax on cryptocurrency gains; unincorporated companies, an income tax; and individuals, a capital gains tax.

Some observers of Bitcoin and other cryptocurrencies are discouraged by the disjointed nature of regulation and the uncertain future. Do I wish we had a list of rules already in place? Yes, of course. Do I think this should have already occurred and that we are unnecessarily complicating matters? Yes again.

But I'm buoyed by where we are. I think about how far the industry has come in a dozen or so years. Tom Emmer was still a state legislator in Minnesota when Satoshi Nakamoto published his white paper, and although I've never met Emmer, my guess is that cryptocurrency wasn't part of his vernacular much before he won his House seat in 2014. Nor were most other lawmakers familiar with it.

Now, Congress has a Blockchain caucus, and multiple committees and subcommittees are regularly interviewing experts and having hours-long debates about the potential role of Bitcoin in America's financial system. And to be sure, the conversations—representatives Brad Sherman, Maxine Waters, and other skeptics notwithstanding—are more about when and how than *if* Bitcoin becomes a daily reality.

I was particularly appreciative of Senator Mike Crapo's optimistic remarks in the Banking Committee. Crapo is no millennial or Gen-something who grew up with technology. He's a 70-year-old, Harvard-educated lawyer with a receding hairline from one of the country's reddest states. It's not a place you quickly associate with anything that sounds even remotely newfangled. Idaho's most famous industry is potatoes, and although its tech and science sectors now account for a quarter of the state's business, it is still better known for agriculture, manufacturing, and service industries.

But Crapo, in his sensible blue suit, speaking in one of the Capitol Building's paneled rooms, clearly understood cryptocurrency's—and by extension, Bitcoin's—value. And when you think about this, it makes sense. Idaho has a low tax rate compared to most other states, the fewest regulations of all states,[14] and a business-friendly environment. When I think about so-called red states that favor more libertarian values, I am optimistic that lawmakers and regulators will pass laws favorable to Bitcoin and other cryptocurrencies.

I'm also confident that new laws will preserve Bitcoin's unique properties. Most lawmakers favor business-friendly products and services, and there are none more business-friendly than cryptocurrency. In allowing peers to interact directly, cryptocurrencies strip away almost every process that could interfere with a transaction.

A CRYPTO CZAR?

That said, now I'll make two recommendations that given my arguments for decentralization may seem counterintuitive. I favor the creation of a crypto czar and agency at the federal level focused on regulation and all other issues related to cryptocurrency.

Yes, you've read correctly. I'm suggesting the formation of a command-and-control organization to oversee an industry largely built on the premise that centralization weighs us down. But I see no contradiction or irony in this proposal.

Government czars, given the right mandate and clear instruction, have served the United States capably throughout recent history, sometimes with short-term goals but on other occasions with longer-term objectives. Franklin Delano Roosevelt made ample use of czars in World War II to win the battle of propaganda and coordinate food production and supply chains. Barack Obama named czars to shepherd the recovery of the banking and financial services industries following the 2008 recession. AIDS czars helped find solutions to that health crisis. And while the Department of Homeland Security has deservedly received criticism for its politicization over the past five years, it has largely succeeded in making airports safer.

I'm not sure whether the czar and agency would be a permanent fixture or a short-term solution. That issue will resolve itself, depending on how quickly cryptocurrency achieves wider acceptance. But I'm certain that a czar or agency will not need to involve itself directly in crypto lawmaking; rather, they would serve as a guiding force, untangling the knotty issues that have hamstrung lawmakers, business leaders, and consumers. Instead of multiple agencies fumbling around, often covering the same ground, a single point of expertise could establish clear lines of discussion. This clarifying action would, in turn, help legitimize cryptocurrency and spread awareness. A czar and agency would be a fostering, not limiting, force.

The czar should come from within the industry: an investor, entrepreneur, technologist, or some combination of the three, possessing deep, wide-ranging knowledge. He or she should comprehend the major concerns of the various stakeholders in cryptocurrency, understand consumers' worries, and display an openness to change. In addition, the person should have good relationships with lawmakers and financial service industry leaders. And he or she should possess diplomatic skills, advocating where advocacy is necessary, and ratcheting down tensions on other occasions to steer policy in the right direction. This individual should also be able to demystify and clearly explain cryptocurrency to the general public, to the broader business community, and to policymakers and elected representatives.

As for my second recommendation, I believe the czar and the agency devoted to cryptocurrencies should create a Cryptocurrency Bill of Rights that outlines in clear, concise language what people can do with cryptocurrency and limits the ability of government or any authority to discourage its use. The bill would offer an easy reference point for consumers, businesses, and the legal community, guaranteeing cryptocurrency's permanent place in the financial services universe as an investment and store of value and a means of conducting transactions. It should clearly delineate that governments and any other authorities cannot capriciously limit cryptocurrency's usage. Not unlike the US Constitution's Bill of Rights, the bill will protect a fundamental right: in this case, allowing an individual or business to conduct transactions in a legal currency of their choosing. I might include the following:

- Consumers will have the right to buy or sell cryptocurrency directly, with no limits.
- Consumers will have the right to use cryptocurrency for legitimate transactions, without any third-party involvement or authorization.

- Consumers will have the right to invest in funds that hold cryptocurrency, such as mutual funds and ETFs.
- Consumers will have the right to hold their cryptocurrency directly, by managing their own private keys on unhosted wallets, without divulging any information to the government.
- Government will guarantee the right of operation for legitimate exchanges and other service providers that help people acquire and trade cryptocurrencies.
- Government will ensure that cryptocurrency can operate on equal terms with fiat currencies and other types of assets.
- Government cannot confiscate cryptocurrency holdings arbitrarily.
- Government cannot tax cryptocurrency beyond how it treats other types of assets.

Will this solve everything? Hardly. And my expectation is that this Bill of Rights will see additions as the Bitcoin and cryptocurrency industry evolves—just as the US Bill of Rights has grown. And we are also likely to see changes in whatever agency might one day oversee cryptocurrency activity. This is all to be expected. Bitcoin is in a sorting-out stage with the normal regulatory uncertainties. But more importantly, the industry's fundamentals are strong and the basic perception of Bitcoin is improving.

What encourages me even more is that Bitcoin has never been classified as illegal in any free country. That's a telltale sign that even doubters don't feel strongly enough to throw up the most formidable of all roadblocks. This makes sense because once you boil it down, Bitcoin is just digital information in the form of private keys of the wallets and the open-source software that runs the nodes on the Bitcoin network. The only countries where Bitcoin has been ruled as illicit have been authoritarian, and they're more inclined to outlaw anything that seems threatening. Is it surprising that Vladimir Putin or Xi Jinping dislike Bitcoin, which is completely beyond their control? And despite this, Bitcoin activity in Russia and China flourishes, as even these countries can't stop it.

North Korea? Iran? They have bigger problems.

Perhaps you should ask yourself how any entity could even stop or extinguish Bitcoin, which is just essentially a long string of letters and numbers. Could they force someone to share their private keys under torture or duress? Again, I'd say that that type of society would have bigger issues than the perceived threat of a new monetary system.

Bitcoin is like a child in a big meadow that other children once had to themselves. As more children play in the meadow, a municipality has to start making a few rules to ensure everyone stays safe.

But it's still a big meadow filled with potential.

LET'S GET PHILOSOPHICAL: MONEY IS A NATURAL RIGHT

It may seem odd to consider money as a natural right. Natural rights are a concept meant to define the core entitlements of human existence. The nineteenth-century English philosopher John Locke and his disciples believed that men possessed inalienable rights, undeniable by any institution or individual. "Man . . . being all equal and independent, no one ought to harm another in his life, health, liberty or possessions," Locke wrote in his Second Treatise of Government.

Nearly a century later, the English statesman Edmund Burke, who veered away from Lockean theories about human nature and governance, called "the natural rights of mankind . . . sacred things."

Some misers—and nervous consumers in a recession—may consider money sacred, but not in the way that Burke meant. I have to admit that for most of my life, I never thought of money as a natural right before. For me, money was a tangible object, coins and bills that you used almost daily, and in that regard no different than a toothbrush or coffee mug.

But when I became interested in Bitcoin, I started to think of money in more abstract terms, as a store of value that just happened to have a physical presence. The currencies that various civilizations created were the practical solutions to representing these stores of value. What else could they do? The Babylonian creators of the first coins, the Tang rulers in early China who printed history's first paper notes, the Medici, and various iterations of central banks worldwide through the twentieth century didn't have the technology to produce an alternative method of representing value, like Bitcoin.

Bitcoin allowed me to think of money differently. I determined that money was more profound than the physical objects that people for centuries accepted as the means for exchange—dollars, francs, marks, pesos, yen, euros, and otherwise. These fiat currencies are relics from societies that were part of a different world. They don't address the fresh challenges that have arisen amid rapid technological, economic, and political change. They restrict consumers and businesses that have a strong desire to unshackle themselves from traditional commercial systems.

The more I pondered the essence of money, the more I realized that money represents the fruits of our labor—the results of our past work. And any money that we don't spend immediately, we can save for future use. Money is proof of someone's work, a way to store value for future use.

Against this backdrop, I began to see money as a natural right. By that I mean that it should provide a pure, unvarnished freedom to do whatever someone wants to do with it at the time and place of their choosing. No institution should interfere with this freedom. Having control of our system for valuing things should be as natural as being free and physically safe in the world. In fact, I saw money and life, liberty, and property as interconnected.

I know that many people will not understand or accept what I'm proposing. They grew up believing that fiat monetary systems took good care of them. Their upbringings inoculated them to the weaknesses inherent in fiat systems. Most of all, they mistakenly believe that they have total freedom in what they do with their money. How do you dissuade someone of a belief when they don't know better?

I created a freedom-of-money test. My belief is that when confronted with the truth, people recognize that they don't possess perfect freedom of money, or anything close to it. In turn, they recognize that Bitcoin does provide that type of freedom, and that money should be a natural right.

Judge for yourself. Take the test. There are seven questions requiring yes or no answers. There are no wrong answers. Your answers depend entirely on your experience.

1. When you deposit a check, do you have access to the full amount immediately?

2. Do you have immediate physical control of money that you keep in a checking, savings, or money market account? That is, except for the cash you keep in your wallet, can you use the money whenever and wherever you want?

3. If you want to send someone money, can you complete the transaction immediately without the intervention of a bank or other financial services organization?

4. Can you withdraw or transfer any amount of money at all times?

5. Can you complete the transfer, payment, or withdrawal without having to pay an exorbitant banking fee?

6. Does your money, including any interest accrued, have the same purchasing power today as when you first deposited it into the bank?

7. Disregarding the cash in your wallet, can you do anything with your money without the presence of a third party?

If you answered no to any of the questions, then you do not have true freedom of money. In truth, I have the same problem, in spite of my acquisitions of bitcoins over the years. I don't have perfect freedom of money because I continue to hold fiat currency and work with traditional financial services organizations. That's because only some businesses accept bitcoins. That's the reality for now, although I'm optimistic this scenario will change in the coming decades. The case for money as a natural right is too strong, and Bitcoin with its ability to guarantee perfect freedom of money is the only path forward.

These seven questions illustrate almost perfectly the lack of control we have over our money whenever an outside third party is involved. In the cold, hard light, we have little if any say in the pace at which massive financial institutions complete our transactions. We have little if any say in the fees they charge or the rules they set that restrict our personal and business finance activities. In poker terms, they always hold a royal straight flush no matter what hand we have. In chess terms, they always control the board. I, for one, don't like that feeling. I like to think that I have decent odds to accomplish what I want to.

I felt a sense of helplessness when a Wells Fargo branch kept me waiting when I tried to withdraw $20,000 of my own money to pay my 2018 World Series of Poker main event tournament entry fee and to gamble in the casino. I had a similar feeling when the same bank—a different branch in Santa Monica, California—two years later made me wait over an hour before I could transfer $100,000 to a friend's account in Hong Kong, using an international SWIFT wire transfer.

Never mind the banks' sophisticated technology, or the fact that I was a customer of 28 years and I was appearing in person with suitable government-issued identification. Perhaps the size of the transfer, particularly as it was headed overseas, made the branch uncomfortable. The bank manager said that their decision to reject the transfer was for my own protection. They seemed concerned that I might commit or be the victim of fraud.

Never mind that I was physically standing inside the bank branch, as opposed to conducting my banking by phone, or via the bank's website. I could have understood a bank raising concerns about a transaction of that size if they couldn't see the individual behind it. But there I was, in flesh in blood, the person who owned the account and who should have had ultimate authority over the money in the account.

Once they had my money, I had to play by their rules. And the lack of transparency throughout the process was galling. Apparently, the $100,000 wire transfer amount was too big, particularly as it was headed to Hong Kong, China. The branch bankers kept me waiting while they cleared the transfer with their fraud department. I resented the delay, which in the end took over an hour, and the lack of transparency about what the fraud detection professionals were weighing in their deliberations or who finally okayed the transaction. The situation was absurd. Did they really think a longstanding account holder would show up in person to complete a transaction of questionable legality? And who were they to judge how I should use my money? This was my money. I wasn't borrowing money from Wells Fargo and then sending it to Hong Kong. Should a bank really have a right to deny a wire transfer to someone I designate? And then, Wells Fargo, a bank with nearly $2 trillion in assets under management and an eagerness to rehabilitate its reputation from a fraud scandal just a couple of years earlier, added to this injury by being noncooperative and obtuse. To this day, I don't know who made the decisions to delay my transaction, and then subsequently, to okay it. I tweeted my displeasure that same late winter day. To Wells Fargo's credit, a customer management executive called back a few days later to hear out my complaint.

Wells Fargo was also no different than my Chinese bank, which had a policy to limit international deposits and transfers to $50,000 total per year, as per the capital control rules in China. This bank was just obeying rules set by the central bank, rules that came down from the central government, which wanted to control the flow of money into and out of the country and to stimulate economic growth. Why can't you have free capital markets *and* economic growth?

BEGGING FOR YOUR MONEY

The relationship between bank and customer reminds me of a parent and child relationship, in terms of the child having to ask the parent for permission to buy anything. The bank sets the rules, and it doesn't matter how big your account is or how long you've been a client. Everyone has to obey them. But this is an unavoidable part of being a bank customer. Few people protest the counterproductive delays and bank rules.

Such delays are costly, counterproductive, and more importantly, sow distrust.

As I've dived more deeply into Bitcoin, I've found people's lack of protest sometimes puzzling. It's almost like people turn into zombies after they hand their money to the banks.

It is a strange oversight, particularly in the United States, a country that originated from a rebellion against the denial of basic freedoms. It is yet stranger in light of the current political climate, which is consumed with the same issue. If you're on the right, you're worried about your ability to use religious principles to govern your nonreligious actions, to conduct your business affairs without interference, to own a gun, and even to wear a mask. If you're on the left, you're concerned about freedom of reproduction rights, freedom to express yourself and assemble peaceably, and now even to vote. I offer here no bias as to where I stand on any of these issues, except to observe that both groups believe society encroaches on their freedoms.

Most Americans, I believe, have at least a passing knowledge of the first line of the US Declaration of Independence, which states that "all men are endowed . . . with certain unalienable Rights, that among these are Life, Liberty and the pursuit of

Happiness." There has been some debate historically over what the Declaration's author, Thomas Jefferson, meant by happiness, although it seems drawn from Locke's *Two Treatises on Government*, in which he theorizes that government exists to protect an individual's "life, liberty and estate."

In Locke's time, property equated to land, the primary source of wealth in England dating to the Dark Ages. The acquisition and use of such land went largely unchecked until William the Conqueror created the first English property law in his Domesday Book. William, a French noble whose victory over King Harry in the Battle of Hastings in 1066 is commemorated by the Bayeux Tapestry (I've always been amused that the English had a French king and spoke an early version of French for official business), created a code that included rules for land ownership and taxation. Credit to William's foresight, the Domesday code served as the foundation not only for subsequent English law, but also for the legal systems in countries that England colonized. It offered certain protections and limitations against seizure, and these strictures were strengthened and improved over the centuries.

To be sure, homeowners know well the frustrations of rising property taxes and lengthy permitting approvals for construction projects. Fall behind in certain payments and homeowners will also know the pain of a tax lien. But if they follow reasonable financial management, they do not have to worry about the government confiscating property arbitrarily, or more seriously, artificially reducing its value—at least not in a free society.

English property law made no mention of currency. The central Bank of England, a seventeenth-century creation chartered largely to fuel the country's endless wars for European hegemony, set English monetary policy for centuries. It loaned money, established rules for transactions, and, of course, printed legal tender. It was an ingenious way to raise cash at a time when the government's credit standing was poor. The bank remained privately held—technically controlled by shareholders—until it was nationalized in the mid-twentieth century. The bank's governance model, which included establishing the terms for transactions and printing of legal tender at its discretion, gave it an all-encompassing role in business affairs and the economy.

As I've already noted, this centralized system was also flaw-ridden, overcontrolling, and subject to the often poor judgment of the bankers who set policy. I do not say this harshly. The creators of central banks, including the US Federal Reserve, an early twentieth-century innovation that was started in response to a geopolitical crisis, did the best they could with the resources and knowledge they had at their disposal. There just was no better solution technologically.

And as I've also written, these institutions, including powerful central banks in France, Germany, Japan, and now China, have worked well enough. They funded war efforts; nurtured postwar recoveries and supported industrial, medical, and technological revolutions; and helped build burgeoning middle classes that propelled economic growth through billions in annual spending. They provided the resources for entrepreneurship, and you could even credit them for helping to spawn the rise of developing markets and the globalization of the world economy. China's and India's growth are at least part testimony to the influence of central banks.

But their inherent weaknesses have become more glaring as the world has changed.

The leaders of these institutions are stuck in their ways. They are slow to react and unable to serve or protect a truly free environment in which businesses and individuals can do what they want, when and where they choose. They operate a well-entrenched system that, however well-meaning, is the antithesis to the idea of freedom of money. Whereas freedom of money wasn't all that important years ago, it is important now, especially because we finally have the technology to give everyone true freedom of money, in the form of decentralized digital cryptocurrencies, built on public blockchains.

A DIRECT APPROACH

But practically speaking, can money be a natural right? Is true freedom of money possible? Is there an appetite for change? And if so, what should it look like? If you've already accepted the potential of a peer-to-peer system of money as Satoshi Nakamoto outlined, as millions already have, then you have your answer: a resounding yes to the first three questions. The number of bitcoin transactions has grown from just a handful a decade ago to over a million. Hash rates, the processing power of the Bitcoin network, have continued climbing, year after year, with no end in sight. Bitcoin, with its more direct transactional model, has made conducting business easier by making global payments frictionless. What smart businessperson wouldn't want to get behind that proposition?

As a senior-level executive and entrepreneur, I've always looked to raise efficiency. Most of the executives and entrepreneurs I know feel much the same. They are get-things-done types, advocates of a principle famously named for the Medieval English philosopher William of Occam. Occam's razor, or the law of parsimony, states: "Plurality should not be posited without necessity" (*Pluralitas non est ponenda sine necessitate*).

In other words, the simplest or most direct solution to a problem is best.

They have built important parts of their organizations on the idea that complicated answers are rarely clear and often counterproductive. Would that the culprits responsible for the subprime mortgage crisis and other recent manmade financial debacles had heeded this wisdom instead of looking for ways to game the system.

What principle captures the spirit of Bitcoin better than Occam's razor? What monetary system offers purer efficiency or comes closer to perfect freedom of money? And at a time when society has become more distrustful of big organizations and more receptive—at least in the United States—to libertarian philosophy, what system is more in tune with public sentiment? In recent decades, our society has created a cottage industry of efficiency experts and pundits eager to apply the Occam's razor principle in the interest of higher productivity and profitability. And now we have a new monetary system that embodies these principles. We might have had it sooner had the technologies that have created it existed and if someone with a sense of how to assemble them had emerged.

It is as if Bitcoin's anonymous creator had Occam's razor in mind as he crafted his system based on direct contact and a public ledger that records each transaction with unparalleled immediacy. Was Satoshi one of the first Cypherpunks, or a next generation descendent deeply worried about institutional—government and financial services—intrusiveness? He, she, or they were certainly intent on creating a new, more efficient means for commerce.

It is also safe to say that Satoshi's work was part of a natural maturation of society. Society isn't ready for something until events combine with the right order and timing—that includes perhaps most importantly the political and social climate.

Bitcoin can take hold now whereas it couldn't have 20 or 30 years ago because people are now looking for a greater ability to do what they like without interference. Recent authoritarian movements in the United States, Europe, and other parts of the world notwithstanding, this trend is likely to continue. And in this environment, people will look even more harshly at the hidden costs and controls of our monetary system. They will be more inclined to fight back. Bitcoin gives them a new alternative path. Concurrently, companies that have fought freedom of money have sensed this turn in public sentiment.

True freedom of money is simply the latest freedom for society to embrace more fully, alongside life, liberty, and property, guaranteed by law and unimpeachable—no different than the freedom to speak out or worship as you like. It is the guarantee that our institutions cannot arbitrarily take any part of our money, or freeze or devalue it, and that they cannot stop or delay a transaction, or ask questions to determine how someone might use their money, including using cash in a licensed casino. They cannot set new rules to address crises that are usually of their own making.

It should be a natural state of being, to be guaranteed by the US Constitution and other governments, and a higher level of existence, not unlike Edward Bellamy's utopian vision in *Looking Backward* or other fictional realms that promised higher efficiency. But similar to the original rights that are central to democracies, these new rights will require a fight—not physical, let's hope—in swaying public opinion. Thomas Jefferson would have been a strong Bitcoin advocate. I'm less sure about John Adams and Alexander Hamilton, particularly the latter, who tangled with Jefferson about the need for a central banking system, although my guess is that as believers in free enterprise, they would have come around and embraced Bitcoin.

Bitcoin embodies freedom of money, not only because it leads to an almost complete unshackling from banking and governmental restrictions, but also because it offers an unprecedented choice.

Use it. Invest in it. Sell it. Do all three.

Digital and traditional money are parallel worlds that can coexist peacefully and productively, although I wouldn't be surprised, in the unlikely event that I was reincarnated a century or so into the future, to find Bitcoin and other digital currencies the norm. This will be especially true when the teenagers of today, growing up in a Bitcoin-enabled society, eventually take over the leadership roles at all of the commercial banks and regulatory agencies worldwide, including the Federal Reserve. These same youngsters will be our lawmakers in Congress in no time, and they will chair all of the most important committees with oversight over digital cryptocurrencies. Bitcoin and cryptocurrencies will be natural to them, just as computers, smartphones, and the internet feel natural to us today.

Then as now, Bitcoin will possess the same qualities that make it true freedom of money. What characteristics make Bitcoin truly free? I've narrowed the list to the following five traits:

It Holds or Increases Value

I can see how Milton Friedman and the monetarists think that a little inflation is good for the economy. It prompts people to buy products, which helps fuel the economy. But inflation too often has gotten out of control, and I've been troubled by the approaches of many governments to print money to address self-inflicted crises. Note the troubles that struggling economies have encountered throughout the past century as they printed new banknotes with the misguided notion that it would make people feel more confident. Venezuelans with their 6,500 percent inflation rate (as of January 2020)[1] can tell you why that hasn't worked out so well. And the list of such countries with similar experiences goes on and on.

But even under normal circumstances, money loses its value too readily. And sadly, we've grown accustomed to this trend. Note the example I use in my conference presentations, pulling out the old, single cold $100 bill with the small picture of Ben Franklin. It could buy a lot more when I first acquired it in the 1980s than it can now. Contrast the old Franklin to a bitcoin acquired in 2013 at $100, then considered a breakthrough price. If you used that bitcoin now, you would be able to buy a new Tesla Model 3, or even the upcoming Tesla CyberTruck. Bitcoin may continue to see big increases and drops in price, but its overall arc will be upward—big-time.

It Is Usable Without Interference

My bitcoin is entirely mine. I don't have to pay a fee for access or to hold it as a personal asset. I don't have to answer to some individual representing a third party. If I need $10,000 for a poker tournament, marijuana (I don't smoke), or simply want to give it away to random people, as long as I own and have the bitcoin in my wallet, I can do it.

There's no middle person in the transaction, no legal authority involved, and no one to cast judgments or hold up or decline an activity. And I would add that it offers an immediacy absent from any other payment system. The transaction is broadcast and replicated globally in a mere few seconds, and the money arrives in someone's wallet within minutes. But the moment you depart from Bitcoin, you are relinquishing your freedom. You should have the right to spend as you choose, whether you use that right daily, occasionally, or not at all. Fiat systems don't give you that option.

It Allows Transactions of Any Amount

I've already established that in today's fiat monetary system, outside authorities can delay and censor to whom we give money via payments, transfers, or even gifts. If they don't like someone on one end of a transaction because there's something about the sender or recipient's background that bothers them, or the nature of the transaction, they can insert themselves and block it. They can censor transactions based on the amount being sent. That applies to amounts falling below and above normal thresholds. The latter is more obvious as I've noted in my own struggles to withdraw and transfer tens and hundreds of thousands of dollars. But banks and other financial services organizations restrict smaller, more typical transactions through their fees.

If I decided to transfer money electronically in $1 increments (an admittedly absurd amount), I would likely have to pay the same $15 charge as for other larger amounts. Depending on where people bank and the nature of their accounts, they might pay a fee as well to receive a transfer. Think of the chaos if I were mad at someone with one of these fee-heavy accounts and I just made multiple small-denomination transfers into the person's bank account. Perhaps the better example is people sending remittances to family members living in poorer countries. The fees for simply moving money from one location to another average 7 percent, according to United Nations reporting.[2]

It Enables Transactions at Any Time and from Any Place

You could argue that with mobile apps, we have the freedom to conduct business at any time and place. But those apps are extensions of organizations with their own rules and regulations. True freedom of money offers consumers and businesses the ability to conduct their business entirely on their terms but without the encumbrances built into fiat systems. That includes now quaint-sounding restrictions on when someone or some entity can execute certain transactions. For example, many banks do not complete wire transfers over the weekend. And most business-to-business transactions face limitations in when they can take place and to what countries. Large swathes of the world lack easy access to banks. Bitcoin overcomes those obstacles with ease. Formal banking hours will be a thing of the past.

There Is No Middleman

In true freedom of money, you always have full, exclusive control over your own money. You engage directly with the individual or organization on the other end of a transaction. You execute the transaction and send the money. No other entity is involved, and no one needs to give you permission. Money becomes like air or gravity that you can activate immediately without fear of interference or punishment. It is part of a natural state of being. It only failed to exist in the past because we didn't have the technology, knowledge, and resources to create this freedom. With Bitcoin, now we do, and it is ushering in a new way of doing business.

AN EVOLVING INDUSTRY

When I started to write this book, I assumed that I could safely say that Bitcoin had arrived. What I mean by "arrived" is that it was part of life, not some fringe element or oddity pushed into the spotlight by a devoted band of technology pirates. After all, bitcoin's market cap had already passed $200 billion and, over the long term, it is heading higher. The cryptocurrencies that it had at least partly inspired totaled an additional $60 billion plus in market cap and are clearly heading toward $100 billion. (In February 2021, bitcoin's market cap reached $1 trillion.)

Other key statistics in Bitcoin by the numbers were equally encouraging when I started the book. The 10 leading exchanges were generating daily trading volumes in excess of $15 billion, mostly in bitcoin. (In late January 2021, the trading volumes of these exchanges exceeded $30 billion.) The number of Bitcoin wallets was heading toward 50 million with new products sprouting seemingly every day, each promising a more user friendly, more secure experience than the previous one. All but a little over 3 million of Satoshi Nakamoto's original supply of 21 million bitcoins were in circulation (now less than 2.5 million are uncirculated). The number of verifiable active cryptocurrency traders, meaning they have identifiable, registered accounts with at least one reputable exchange, was already in the tens of millions (it is now closer to 50 million).

If you were around in 2011 when I bought my first graphics cards for mining, or even just a few years ago, this would have seemed like all the proof anyone would need. The market was huge and rapidly growing. The ups and downs that I've told you to ignore notwithstanding, there are few if any success stories to match Bitcoin's narrative.

Among recent investments, Amazon is about the only other asset to achieve similar growth, but its trajectory came only after the company changed its business model to sell everything from automobile tires to xylophones. Remember when Amazon only sold books?

Bitcoin's total value, or market cap as some might call it, now dwarfs IBM, General Electric, Boeing, John Deere, General Motors, and Bank of America—iconic brands in America's business history. And those companies took decades to reach their lofty perches. General Motors, IBM, and the original Bank of America were founded within a decade of one another shortly after the turn of the twentieth century.

Based on its market cap, bitcoin would be somewhere around the twenty-fifth biggest economy, far larger than oil-rich United Arab Emirates, the tech/crypto/blockchain haven of Israel, Norway, Austria, and South Africa. If only 25 million people had registered accounts (some people have more than one), and no one else was interested in Bitcoin (not true), Bitcoin's community would be bigger than the populations of Belgium and Greece combined.

These statistics served as kind of ambient music to my Bitcoin daily dealings and proved that Bitcoin had reached the main stage in the financial services world. Or had it?

One of the great things about writing a book is that it forces you to think more deeply about issues that you think you had settled in the inner round table of your mind. You get to pick apart and re-piece arguments, listen more carefully for the nuance of skeptics, and reconsider information and events with fresh eyes.

So, as I mapped out *The Promise of Bitcoin*, and looked at whether I could safely say it had arrived, I thought about what I might have overlooked. What details and counterarguments had I not fully appreciated? I had successfully established myself as a Bitcoin evangelist. I believed I swayed many hearts and minds to Bitcoin's cause, including a few erstwhile doubters. But my converts came largely in controlled settings—conference speeches, YouTube sessions, and media appearances—and occasionally in more casual discussions.

But if I was really going to live up to my role, I needed to be sharper, and that meant looking critically at even the most basic assumptions, even those grounded in mathematical reasoning.

"Not everything that can be counted counts. Not everything that counts can be counted," wrote the mid-twentieth-century sociologist William Bruce Cameron, a quote often misattributed to Albert Einstein, who understood the inadequacy of some mathematical measurement. Numbers aren't everything.

"Either mathematics is too big for the human mind, or the human mind is more than a machine," wrote Einstein's close friend and fellow genius Kurt Gödel, who also taught at Princeton.

Numerical quantification as a measure of success can be misleading. Brand awareness and the full embrace of new products or services—technological or otherwise—depends on many factors, many of them subjective. Do we need to know how many albums Beyoncé has sold to know that she is a great singer and cultural influencer? Or whether the Yankees' Aaron Judge led the league in home runs to know he's among the most feared sluggers ever to don a baseball uniform? Or how many TikTok users there are to know that it is deeply embedded in society?

Calculating Bitcoin's popularity itself is tricky because of its success in protecting individual identity. We don't know who's behind each wallet address account, and even law enforcement would have to make a Herculean effort to unmask a Bitcoin participant. Privacy coupled with a decentralized distributed ledger technology is what makes Bitcoin special. Cracking a bank vault would be easier.

Bitcoin investors appreciate the control, privacy, and security that Bitcoin gives them. Many with moderate to significant holdings keep multiple wallets to inoculate themselves against breaches. The same person may buy bitcoins at various times using different addresses. I keep wallets on my laptop, mobile phone, and on Ballet wallets, my new startup. If hackers penetrate one of my wallets, they can only steal a small part of my holdings. The rest of my bitcoins are safe in different locations, each with their own private key. Even if someone could link me to an address—almost impossible—they would face an even bigger hurdle using it.

Other prominent investors have used a similar strategy, splitting their bitcoins across mobile devices, laptops, hard drives, and cold wallets. They have created what amount to small bitcoin fortresses.

Then there are Tyler and Cameron Winklevoss, brothers, who shortly after acquiring 1 percent of the world's bitcoin holdings, made four copies of their key, cut each into three parts, and then placed each part in safe deposit boxes at low-key regional banks throughout the central United States.[1] The twins created the private key itself by rolling dice to formulate the key numbers and to reduce the risk of someone figuring out a numerical pattern. But again, how would a hacker even know that the private key they were trying to decode belonged to the Winklevoss brothers or someone else, or for argument's sake, whether the Winklevoss brothers had set up additional wallets over the years to further protect their holdings?

There is no way to know what anyone is doing at any one time in the Bitcoin ecosystem or to know how many people are involved. One wallet holder or registered user of a cryptocurrency exchange does not equal one person. We can only round off broadly how many people hold bitcoin at any one time.

Some Bitcoin observers might point to daily trading volume, which records activity on major exchanges, as indicative of the industry's establishment. And yes, the size and growth in trading into the billions has been impressive. Among other things, it reflects that there is a vibrant, sizable Bitcoin community. But it does not pinpoint how many different people are acquiring and selling bitcoin (or any other cryptocurrency)—with or without wallets, on exchanges or otherwise. The same people could be responsible for multiple transactions. Trading volume does not tell us definitively whether Bitcoin has arrived or if it is a fad that will expire in due course.

All of the above encouraged my thinking that knowing the number of exchanges and people holding bitcoin gave us only part of the answer about whether Bitcoin had truly arrived. These numbers merely confirmed the obvious. Bitcoin has expanded from a few believers, technologists, adventurers, and curiosity seekers in a dozen years to conservatively tens of millions of users. Its growth has not only been among the most remarkable stories in business and technology, but also speaks volumes about its promise.

But the question still exists whether we can say that Bitcoin has arrived. Or is it more correct to say that it's simply heading in that direction?

There's a difference. Arrival means something is definitely here to stay. Heading somewhere isn't bad, but it also suggests its foothold remains tenuous. I would obviously make a stronger case if I could prove the former. Exchange and wallet activity and price increases wouldn't be enough. As I've already said, writing a book tests your thinking in a good way. It causes you to become a keener observer than you were before and to develop a finer appreciation of trends you've been observing.

As I looked deeply into the promise of Bitcoin, I found myself agreeing at least partly with Cameron Winklevoss, and questioning my own understanding of why Bitcoin had arrived. There were other clear signs, well beyond the numbers, that Bitcoin was ingrained in society and had staying power. These were subjective in nature but equally compelling to the analytics that have drawn a disproportionate amount of attention.

I placed these reasons into six categories, which I posed as questions and now share in no particular order. The answers underline my belief that Bitcoin has become a fixture in the global financial world and will only increase in importance.

But I encourage you to think beyond my arguments here and to ask questions. Bitcoin can only grow stronger by parrying reasonable arguments against it.

WHAT COULD REPLACE BITCOIN?

Contrast Bitcoin's growth to other recent technological phenomena that seemed to promise new worlds but gave way to better products—or soon will. No product or service has a future if it can't address demand better than anything else on the market.

No industry reflects this reality more than consumer banking technology. Drive-through bank tellers that popped up in the late 1980s and featured air compression tubes and voice communication systems for depositing and withdrawing money once seemed like the future. As innovative as they were at the time, they quickly lost out to drive-through ATMs with touch screen interfaces that didn't require tellers.

While these machines are still used, and now incorporate artificial intelligence and machine learning to help you with your banking (a creepy sensation), there are fewer of them,[2] as companies conduct more business electronically and people rely increasingly on their mobile apps for banking. If I were betting, I wouldn't lay much money on the future of ATMs because, like it or not, physical cash is a dying species.

Verification technology? Credit or debit card magnetic strips that you slide through a merchant's small, handheld verification device once seemed the height of efficiency and convenience, and a light-years improvement over earlier systems that themselves were improvements over the clunkier equipment required for credit card transactions little more than two decades ago.

Credit cards only date to the 1950s. Remember Diner's Club, the original credit card company? I didn't think so. I certainly don't see this card often. Did you know that before it issued its first credit card, American Express was best known for traveler's checks that you could only get at a cooperating bank or American Express offices? While it could take an hour to get the checks, people were willing to put up with the inconvenience because the checks were more secure than carrying big amounts of cash. They required the bearer of a check to match the signature on the check to use it for a transaction. Now there are contactless cards where you don't need to swipe or insert, but only wave the card at a payment screen. It is a card built for COVID, and if epidemiologists are correct, for pandemics to come—there is no potential for sharing viruses. Apple Pay is a prime example of this contactless card technology, and I use it all the time; I even make payments by waving my Apple Watch.

Look at the sweeping changes in other consumer-facing industries. Gas-saving and hybrid cars with technologies that allow drivers to wring unprecedented mileage per gallon are already yielding to electric cars that do not need any gas. MacBook Airs now weigh as little as two-plus pounds, less than half the earliest models, but with more memory and power than their predecessors; mobile devices are similarly sleeker and more powerful. These personal computers (I use the term loosely to encompass laptops and other smaller devices) now even serve as control centers for internet-of-things households, empowering users to turn appliances on and turn off, adjust temperature controls, and view security systems. The interfaces look like airplane dashboards.

Everything mentioned here had a logical replacement. Now comes Bitcoin as an alternative to traditional monetary systems. It created a more secure, private, and responsive payment system at a time when people were looking for exactly those qualities in financial services. It came as the economy became more global and enabled some of the world's most remote areas to connect financially with no third-party involvement, something that would not have been possible a few years ago. Most of all, it is remarkably well-constructed.

What is likely to replace Bitcoin? What is better at solving the most glaring problems with our current monetary system? What does it lack technically to thrive?

Unless you can think of something that I haven't, your answers were probably "nothing" to all three questions. There is no logical successor to Bitcoin, no project or service that improves upon what it offers. Some advocates of other cryptocurrencies believe that their currencies will supplant Bitcoin. I have nothing against them; moreover, I appreciate the thought and technological prowess behind Ethereum, Litecoin, and others, each of which solves a problem that Bitcoin may not fully address or explores new, related territory. And they reflect a wider curiosity and embrace of cryptocurrency technology.

I am particularly curious to see the influence of Ethereum's smart contracts platform, which potentially could extend beyond monetary systems. The platform may change the nature of interactions in many areas, including the legal profession, loans and mortgages, and public record keeping. But Ethereum is not better suited than Bitcoin to become a globally accepted unit of exchange, or in essence a global reserve currency. Even if the supply were limited (it is not) and trading volume and market cap were larger at this point, the Ethereum project's main concerns do not involve currency and store of value. Parallel systems are likely to sprout but without Bitcoin's popularity or name recognition. Most importantly, none of these new alternative coins can ever overcome the fact that Bitcoin was the first.

As for payment platforms, I have yet to see one that isn't retro in its centralized structure and inferior to Bitcoin. If one comes into existence based on the principle of decentralization, I will welcome it eagerly.

Critics may question the staying power of a system without a central column to anchor it or a company to take charge of its growth strategy, security, and marketing. This gap seems antithetical to how companies have traditionally operated and might seem to provide an opening for something else to replace it. But Bitcoin's very power and potential lie in its ability to address these concerns without having to make any special effort. Security is built in through its use of cryptography, the proof-of-work system, and the distributed ledger that allows everyone to serve as a monitor of accuracy.

And the most encouraging part of Bitcoin's evolution has been its strictly organic growth. Its following has increased into the tens of millions without any one organization spearheading a marketing effort. What that means is that Bitcoin has grown on its own merits with one convert telling another about its benefits, and people coming to understand its usefulness and investment potential through their own devices. This upward trajectory coming without the normal support of the corporate world, and through the various downturns, scandals, and half-scandals, underscores Bitcoin's permanence and the likelihood that nothing will replace it anytime soon. In the same way, I wrote this book to further spread the message of Bitcoin. And you're reading it because you're Bitcoin curious and might soon become a convert.

IS BITCOIN MAKING HEADLINES?

In early 2014, not long after I had turned BTCChina into one of Bitcoin's first major service providers in China, the Chinese business commentator and TV personality Larry Hsien Ping

Lang invited me on his show to debate him about Bitcoin's merits. Lang is a colorful figure, a Jim Cramer–like personality who establishes an easy rapport with his audience by speaking plainly and assuming positions that seem long on Main Street wisdom. I've watched him during my time living in China as he dissected companies and parried with business leaders about events and trends. I also recognized that he was careful to take perspectives that would please Chinese authorities who were sensitive about commentary that seemed even mildly critical of the country's economy.

Bitcoin had already stirred rumblings within the government, which saw its popularity as a threat to monetary policy and control-and-command political philosophy. I knew that Lang would play the role of skeptic, raising Bitcoin's perceived failings. The crowd might even be on his side. I would wear a figurative black hat in defending Bitcoin.

But I appreciated the opportunity to evangelize before a large television audience. Until then, I'd done a few interviews in China, mostly with smaller business print publications. Bitcoin just wasn't interesting enough to merit much attention from mainstream media. It was still considered an oddity, a difficult-to-fathom object with a weird name.

My sense in hindsight is that most news organizations figured the mysterious Satoshi Nakamoto and his oddball group of followers would make good copy, and that China's fascination with the digital currency was noteworthy. But they also probably believed it didn't have much of a future, probably because of its complexity and their false perceptions that it was vulnerable. Anyway, when Lang asked me to debate, I was eager to speak on Bitcoin's behalf.

To this day, I believe I won my 2014 debate with Lang, as certain trends after the event seemed to attest.

BTCChina's clientele and revenues, which had grown, continued soaring, as did mining hashing rates that reflected the country's passion and global interest in Bitcoin. And in one of our more heated exchanges, with a dramatic waving of both hands, Lang flat-out declined a hypothetical free gift of 100 bitcoins. The freeze-frame and video clip of the interchange between us turned into a cryptocurrency internet meme on social media. (To this day, people in China exchange these screenshots and video clips whenever bitcoin prices reach a new high to poke fun at Lang.) I questioned why he would refuse free money, and he snapped back saying it's because bitcoin is worthless. At that time in early 2014, the value of 100 bitcoins was only about USD $50,000. Today, at the time of publication of this book, the value of 100 bitcoins is already well over $5 million, and it will only keep going up! The Bitcoin social media crowd loved my impertinence, and perhaps in some small way I contributed to Bitcoin's momentum. These days, I wonder if people are still teasing Larry Lang about turning down a free gift of 100 bitcoins.

But when I look back, it is the lack of media interest that stands out more than the episode's incidentals. If I had been fielding media requests weekly and receiving invitations to speak at conferences, my debate with Larry Lang would have been one of many. I wouldn't have felt the same exhilaration that I did for my spirited defense.

Contrast my email inbox then to now. These days, I routinely receive media requests for comments or to speak at conferences, and these also come via direct messaging on LinkedIn and Twitter. I've appeared on Bloomberg, CNBC, the BBC, and have been quoted in many of the world's major business and mainstream publications, including the *New York Times*, *Financial Times*, *Wall Street Journal*, and *The Economist*.

A cottage industry of trade publications has also sprouted. CoinDesk, the brainchild of one of the venture capitalists behind the successful music stream app Spotify, had just launched when I debated Lang. Now it has over three million unique monthly visitors[3] and runs a series of conventions worldwide. The 2018 New York Consensus event drew more than 9,000 people, busting beyond the capabilities of the New York Hilton's convention center.

Bitcoin is also now a regular topic on business shows, often accompanied by appearances by leading advocates, many of them investors with records of success. These shows do not address topics until they reach a certain scale. They are aware of their potential influence over viewers. Clearly, for a new asset to break through, it has to reach a certain threshold in public awareness. Bitcoin may not have quite reached the level of FAANG stocks (Facebook, Apple, Amazon, Netflix, and Google), but it's getting there, and it's no less important than some of the small and midsized companies that they discuss. While I do not suggest following their advice, which focuses on short-term positions of interest to these shows' viewers and likely veers from your own investment profile, the growing media attention is the single biggest sign that Bitcoin has arrived.

ARE BITCOIN TOPICS MORE SOPHISTICATED?

This item is the corollary to my point above. You can tell a lot about the maturity of a movement or industry by the nature of the conversations. Are people uninformed about the basics or starting with some knowledge? Are they focused on the big picture—what is it, how does it work, when and where can you use it—or are they sensing patterns and asking about specifics? If they fall into the former, they're likely just starting. If the latter, they are beyond the starting point and are taking the movement or industry as something more permanent. I may be stating the obvious, but remember, most analysis of financial trends or otherwise relies on commonsense observations.

What I noticed as more and more reporters and commentators reached out for my expertise is that their questions and topics had changed. For the three years after I sparred with Lang, even as bitcoin's price broke the magical $1,000 threshold and BTCC (BTCChina was renamed BTCC in 2015 as we extended the business beyond China) grew into a powerhouse with consumers rushing to use the platform to buy bitcoin, my interlocutors wanted to focus on fundamentals and pricing predictions.

Some sent queries in advance. I appreciated the heads-up. I started to be able to predict what they wanted to cover and developed a set of talking points with a few catchphrases that I thought would be succinct and catchy enough for television. I didn't mind the repetition of themes; I felt that I was doing a service not only for my business, but for the Bitcoin industry as a whole. So, I did what I would do in any PowerPoint presentation.

I ensured that I hit certain buzzwords and explained them in user-friendly language: *decentralization*, which was difficult for many people weaned on traditional banking systems to understand; *distributed ledgers*, which were easier to explain if you just painted a picture of lots of accountants working online; *cryptography*, which I described as a sort of super-secret code that let you participate in Bitcoin systems; and *digital currency*, which I likened to gold without the shiny physical object. I repeated my predictions that bitcoin would rise well into five figures and then six and seven figures, although I was a little hazier about when it might hit certain levels, and that the wise investor would see it as a long-term commitment. You may note here that I haven't moved from these positions, so in one respect, I guess that I haven't evolved.

But starting around 2017, when bitcoin's price started to increase again, like the first engine thrust of a rocket ship, and reached $20,000, I noticed that I was hearing different questions. To be sure, people were still fascinated by pricing—and I don't blame them during heady times when everyone envisions making a fortune. But reporters and anchors also wanted to discuss regulation, specific concerns about security, and the potential role of Bitcoin in funds and other financial products. In one appearance on Bloomberg television with Rishaad Salamat, I spent much of my time addressing the potential implications of China's crypto crackdown. In another appearance on a different show, I discussed the obstacles to a bitcoin ETF, and why its approval was inevitable. In a number of interviews, in a sign that I found encouraging, I didn't receive one question about fundamentals or pricing. I could say the same about the queries I received at conferences. The questions were increasingly looking into the weeds instead of generalities.

My experience dovetailed with studies, including a 2018 YouGov survey that found more than 7 of 10 people had heard of Bitcoin[4] and a 2019 Crypto Radar report that more than 6 percent of Americans owned it and another 7.5 percent planned to buy some.[5] While those numbers are not breathtaking on the surface, they represented marked gains for a decade-old industry. The sophistication of my conversations simultaneously reflected a deeper awareness that comes only with subjects that have made mainstream inroads.

HAVE THE PRICING THRESHOLDS STEADILY RISEN?

What I'm about to say may seem counter to my thinking earlier about not reading too much into numbers and pricing. But as I also said, statistics help draw a picture, underlining trends in concrete terms and confirming firsthand observation. In some cases, they may also trumpet the crossing of certain psychological barriers. An industry or movement reaching a certain level of growth attains symbolic value, swaying public opinion.

Some observers believe Bitcoin has hit a number of those milestones. And they would have a good case pointing to bitcoin achieving parity with the US dollar in 2012 and crossing the $10 and $100 marks in quick succession a little over a year later.

Dollar parity prompted some people to think of bitcoin as they would any other currency—the euro was trading only a little higher against the dollar. And $10 and $100 seemed extraordinary in early 2013, as those levels were reached so fast on the heels of bitcoin's penny-stock-like trading days.

But I see greater significance in bitcoin crossing the $1,000 and $10,000 levels. The former grabbed the public's attention because of the speed of its ascent in late November 2013. Bitcoin had spent most of the year trying to stay above $100 and was still floating around that mark in mid-September when it took off around the third week in October.

I was busy hiring more customer service agents and software engineers to meet surging demand for BTCChina services as bitcoin crept above $800 and then $900 and lingered there teasingly for a few days. But I found myself checking the price regularly during this stretch. When I awoke one morning at my usual 7 a.m. and saw the price trading at over $1,000, I knew we had crossed into new territory, and that the Bitcoin world had fundamentally changed.

I would be disingenuous if I said that I wasn't happy to see the fulfillment of my predictions and the value of my holdings soar—I had acquired some bitcoin when it was still trading in single digits. But I didn't have nearly enough to retire on a tropical island. My joy was seeing bitcoin reach an important milestone. Even if $800 or $900 doesn't seem much less than $1,000, I knew that four figures would capture the media's and public's imagination in new ways. At that point, gold wasn't much higher, Amazon hadn't reached $1,000, and Google was less than half that price.

The run-up to $10,000 and beyond was an even bigger affirmation of what I anticipated occurring in bitcoin pricing. Not long after it had passed $1,000 and then retrenched on several occasions to the cackles of skeptics, I told my BTCChina staff and industry newcomers who asked me for advice that bitcoin would see an even bigger bull run within three or four years. I just didn't know how dramatic an increase we would see and how effective it would be in chipping away some individual concerns and moving Bitcoin closer to the mainstream.

Bitcoin had started 2017 at around $1,000 and had quickly tripled to $3,000 when it started rising. Even during that year's bull market for stocks, few equities could match this performance, and none with bitcoin's potential. The frenzy to enter the market resulted naturally from many consumers fearful of missing out, also known as FOMO. (FOMO rallies are when bitcoin prices go crazy high due to the sudden huge demand from a large influx of new investors.)

Regardless of whether bitcoin investors rightfully entered the market at this point because they had developed a more educated appreciation of it, or wrongly were looking for quick gains, the frenzy had the same effect: Bitcoin had taken a major step in becoming less foreign and scary. And those who ignored the sudden hype long enough and looked below the surface could see a rational logic to the price, one that possessed a similar pattern to recent fast-flying tech stocks, including Amazon, Google, and Facebook. They had all risen fast and furiously in their early days before falling precipitously, and then not long after, hitting even higher highs. Concerned about volatility and security? Hadn't tech stock critics flagged and flogged the volatility issue since these companies entered the investment limelight? Weren't tech stocks the high-risk part of a portfolio?

In the ensuing months, even after bitcoin crested above $20,000 briefly in December 2017 and fell to under $7,000 two months later, the mainstream business media swooped in with unprecedented intensity. A few publications assigned cryptocurrency beats. Others commissioned stories, including a *New York Times Magazine* cover story that looked at the rising phenomenon of initial coin offerings. The *Times* piece focused on Tezos, which in 2017 raised a mammoth $232 million. Online traffic to the leading trade publications increased multiple times, and attendance to conferences and other events skyrocketed. And every week, there seemed to be a new publication forming or business blog or forum that was covering Bitcoin.

I was even heartened that these gains came as I was preparing to shutter our domestic China-based exchange following the Chinese government's crackdown on exchanges. Chinese nationals were even then bitcoin's most prolific investors. If Bitcoin could thrive while its biggest market was creating a new, formidable obstacle, it was a good sign. Bitcoin had turned into something that no institution or force could overlook or stop. At $10,000 or a few thousand dollars north or south of that level, economic and political leaders would have to reckon with Bitcoin—and sooner rather than later.

You could argue that Bitcoin is still battling many of the same fears as it has throughout its existence. But the number of people jumping at the slightest kerfuffle has decreased, while Bitcoin's legion of defenders expands. It is now fighting for acceptance from a larger base than it was a year, two, or three years ago. Crossing the $10,000 threshold for the first time had a lot to do with this greater acceptance. It signaled that Bitcoin was here to stay, even if bitcoin prices don't necessarily stay above $10,000.

IS GOVERNMENT MORE INVOLVED?

I'm not a political person. I don't follow the ins and outs of who's winning power struggles in Washington, DC, or China's Central Committee. I lean libertarian because I value liberty and freedom. The less government touches my life—socially, economically, and otherwise—the better, although I appreciate its importance in delivering key services. So, I haven't tracked Congress's Bitcoin deliberations on a micro level. I don't monitor which committees and subcommittees are holding hearings, or who's appearing before them on behalf of cryptocurrency and blockchain.

As I've made clear, blockchain is blockchain, a decentralized technology that is revolutionizing digital money, and Bitcoin is a decentralized digital currency system invented in 2009 that uses blockchain as its undergirding. Bitcoin gave birth to blockchain and raised its profile beyond a small group of tech geeks.

I've never testified at a Congressional hearing of any stripe, although I know several of the people who have. Nor have I lobbied anyone.

But I can identify a number of the most supportive legislators. I know that Congressman Thomas Massie, a Kentucky Republican who proposed legislation to audit the Federal Reserve, quipped at a 2013 convention of libertarians that Bitcoin might replace the Federal Reserve.[6] I noticed Massie because he is the type of individual that Bitcoin needs, an alternative thinker with an MIT engineering degree who built his own solar house. As a libertarian with a STEM background, he could appreciate the creation of a peer-to-peer network that used cryptography and math to ensure the integrity of the currency and its transactions. In hindsight, I am not surprised that Massie was the first congressman to make comments that worked their way into media reports.

I know that Tom Emmer, a conservative Minnesota congressman whom I've already mentioned and a similarly harsh Federal Reserve critic, has been an enthusiastic supporter of cryptocurrency and blockchain, holding the first congressional town hall on cryptocurrency in August 2020 and accepted bitcoin for his 2020 reelection campaign. Emmer supports letting the market determine the fate of cryptocurrency, welcomes Bitcoin's base technology, and is wary of overregulation. But as cochair of the Congressional Blockchain Caucus along with Florida Democrat Darren Soto, he's also driven efforts encouraging the IRS to clearly articulate its guidelines for taxing cryptocurrency and its place in financial services products. I agreed with Emmer's optimism that cryptocurrency would play a larger role post-pandemic. It has to, as there's no going back to a world without cryptocurrency.

"As we come out of the crisis, Bitcoin ain't going away. It's gonna get stronger," the congressman told Morgan Creek Digital's Anthony Pompliano on the venture capitalist's *Pomp Podcast*[7] not long before the town hall—fighting words that I liked along with other evangelists. "You just watch, it has value, when something has value, people are going to take risks and it's going to advance."

Entrepreneur and 2020 presidential candidate Andrew Yang also accepts bitcoin, and Wyoming Senator Cynthia Lummis has expressed her concerns about the dollar losing value. Then there was Jared Polis, Colorado's Democratic governor and founder of two tech firms, who, in a response to Bitcoin critics, penned a sarcastic note in 2014 calling for a ban on US dollar bills as a means of exchange because they were unregulated. As we all know, a lot of crimes get committed using US dollars, including money laundering and terrorist financing, so it seems hypocritical that no one else would ask to ban the US dollar.

I've noted the anti-Bitcoin rants of Donald Trump, who wrote in a series of tweets in June 2019 that it was "not money" and built from "thin air," even as his then chief of staff Mick Mulvaney had supported it. And I read former security chief John Bolton's account in *The Room Where It Happened* of Trump asking Treasury Secretary Steven Mnuchin "to go after bitcoin," although it's still unclear what that means. How would you go after Bitcoin? To be sure, it would have been nice to have a president who supported Bitcoin. But I dismissed Trump as a product of a different time and unwilling or unable to understand Bitcoin. He has plenty of company.

Pro or con, I see the growing interest among political leaders as another big step forward for Bitcoin. When Massie verbalized his pipe dream that Bitcoin was the logical replacement for central monetary systems, my guess is that hardly anyone in the US Capitol, let alone most of the world's other power hubs, had even used the word *Bitcoin*. Why should they have? Few of their constituents probably knew what it was. Politicians go thematically where there are votes. But times are different, and the increased focus of lawmakers on the topic reflects the size of the movement, and their realization that it's getting bigger fast.

WHO'S ADVOCATING FOR BITCOIN?

This is a corollary to the point above. If you want to know that a movement or venture has integrity, consider the company it keeps. Who's interested? Who's involved? Who's running things? If they're reputable folks with a history of sound judgment, there's a good chance that there's something behind it. If the individuals attaching themselves have more questionable backgrounds, the movement probably won't have much staying power. Of course, you'll make this determination after vetting them carefully yourself. News articles, 10-K reports and other financial documents, and in some cases personal references are a good way to evaluate individuals and their commitment to an enterprise.

The same principles hold true for investments. You would be smarter tracking Berkshire Hathaway or working with an experienced wealth manager or a respected wealth management firm than your cousin's friend or an outfit that has contacted you via mail, advertising a free steak dinner if you sign up for their presentation. This has happened to me, and while I like a good steak, I toss those investment scam inquiries in my trash can.

When I'm sizing up investment advice, I weigh the opinion of people who clearly know their products and are not caught up in the euphoria of something that a lot of people are praising. I have always treated the providers of investment advice with care and balance. If someone famous endorses something, I may pay attention. But I'll pay more attention if someone famous can prove why I should pay even greater attention. The rapper Snoop Dogg has made a lot of money entertaining, but he also famously advertises for T-Mobile, Pepsi, Adidas, Chrysler, among other brands. Snoop Dogg also likes to play poker and has spoken favorably about Bitcoin, and I am suitably appreciative. But how committed is he? "You cannot carry water on both shoulders," wrote Charles Porter in his novel-turned-Oscar-winning film *True Grit*.

The best Bitcoin advocates stand up to any scrutiny. They include respected investors, entrepreneurs, and executives from the corporate world. I'll count myself among that group. I spent almost two decades working for a few of the world's best-known tech companies. I'm a product of corporate life and possess all the cautions and business know-how that corporate experiences bring. I've run departments of respected professionals for those firms, and later, started my own company, which I built into one of the biggest service providers of its kind until outside forces conspired against it. You could even say that I smartly navigated those forces by selling BTCC at the right time, before conditions worsened and the business might fail.

And while many people were smart enough to acquire more bitcoin than I, I had enough foresight to mine my own and recognize its potential value to the world. I've adopted the most conservative of investment strategies, based on Warren Buffett's philosophy, which he inherited from Benjamin Graham. Find something you believe in, something that is undervalued by the market, that you know provides an invaluable service, and don't be afraid to hold onto it, even if others are going a different direction. About the most controversial thing I do is play real money poker online, although well within my means. By most measures, I'm well-grounded.

The ranks of my fellow, loudest evangelists and many of Bitcoin's biggest investors include people who have participated in some of recent history's most successful ventures. I know a few of them. They are all widely respected for their business acumen, particularly regarding market demands and a sense of timing. They consider their investments carefully.

A part of Bitcoin's reputation for flightiness stems from a misconception that only people willing to take massive risks or seeking quick gains participate in the platform. Yet the reality is different: the people with the biggest stakes in Bitcoin got to where they are by approaching their work soberly and analytically. They merely used the same approach for Bitcoin. Consider the following people, some of whom are lesser known in the United States.

Argentinian billionaire Wences Casares founded his country's first internet provider, Internet Argentina S.A., and the brokerage Patagon, which he sold to Spain's largest bank Santander. He subsequently started a gaming company, the Brazilian Banco Lemon, and a digital wallet, selling all three for tens of millions, before focusing on Bitcoin. He raised $40 million to launch the popular crypto platform Xapo, which holds more than $10 billion. According to a 2017 story in Quartz,[8] he is responsible for convincing Microsoft founder Bill Gates, LinkedIn cofounder Reid Hoffman, and other tech entrepreneurs into buying bitcoin.

And Wences is not unbridled in his outlook. In a June 2017 post on the Xapo blog, when bitcoin had just climbed over $2,000, he wrote that "there is at least a 20% chance that Bitcoin fails," and that "it may fail very quickly—even without much time to react."[9] He reminded people not to own more bitcoin than you can afford to lose, which for most people is "1% of . . . net worth."

Tyler and Cameron Winklevoss's involvement added glam to the Bitcoin community more than a year before it had broken $1,000. The Winklevoss brothers had participated in the most high-profile feud in tech history with Facebook founder Mark Zuckerberg, chronicled by a bestselling book, *The Accidental Billionaires*, and Oscar-winning film, *The Social Network*, in which the twins emerged as losers and villains despite receiving a $65 million settlement. But the drama overshadowed their capabilities as savvy businessmen who had sensed the potential of online social communities and had a deep interest in technology. Moreover, they were willing to back up their convictions about Bitcoin's future with their bank accounts. "Some people view it as gold 2.0," Cameron said in a 2013 CNBC "DealBook" interview not long after their initial investment became public, and touted its "technological aspect. . . . The idea that payments are increasingly going to use a network like the Bitcoin network to move money around the world."[10]

He added later: "Most people agree that virtual currencies are here to stay."

In the same conversation, Tyler alluded to Bitcoin's advantages for executing financial transactions more securely and privately than traditional monetary systems. "It's based on trust in cryptography and not trust in an individual," he said.

Are they *Bitcoin Billionaires* as Ben Mezrich's entertaining book about their entry into cryptocurrency indicates? I hope so! Regardless, I appreciate their involvement, and they offer optimistic commentary, rooted in common sense, about pricing and other issues. "The small bull case scenario is a $400 billion market cap," Tyler said in the same "DealBook" interview. At the time, bitcoin's market cap was about $4.3 billion.

"It doesn't make sense in a sense" that it isn't 100 times more, he added.

Twitter and Square founder Jack Dorsey has been perhaps the tech world's strongest, most steadfast Bitcoin advocate, regularly touting its benefits and at one point purchasing up to the $10,000 weekly threshold allowed by Square's cash app.[11] By that time, he had already created a Square crypto unit that one day would enable small payments in bitcoin. "For bitcoin to become a widely used global currency—one that can't be stopped, tampered with, or rigged in anyone's favor—improvements to bitcoin's [user experience], security, privacy, and scaling are required," the company wrote in a January 2020 blog post.[12]

In a March 2018 *Times of London* story, even as bitcoin had dropped two-thirds of its value since the year's start, Dorsey predicted that bitcoin would overcome any hurdles.[13] "The world ultimately will have a single currency, the internet will have a single currency," he said. "I personally believe that it will be bitcoin," Dorsey said, adding it would happen "probably over ten years, but it could go faster."

In June 2014, charismatic venture capitalist Tim Draper, whose portfolio of investments reads like a who's who of big tech stocks, including Twitter, Twitch, Baidu, Tesla, and Skype, made headlines by purchasing 30,000 bitcoins at the US Marshals' auction for Silk Road's forfeiture of assets, the platform that had allowed individuals to pay for illegal drugs and other products and services. He invested in Coinbase and has repeatedly predicted—usually wearing one of his trademark Bitcoin ties—that bitcoin would hit at least $250,000 by 2023. In a February 25, 2020, interview with CNBC, Draper said he had moved "a lot" of his portfolio into bitcoin after exiting stocks late the previous year.[14] "I'm just a believer—and I look and I say, 'Hey, this is just better,' " Draper told CNBC. "Long term, people move to things that are better."

Dan Morehead has been arguably the most aggressive cryptocurrency and blockchain investor. In 2013, Morehead's San Francisco–based Pantera Capital launched the first Bitcoin fund, the Pantera Bitcoin Fund, which offered high-net-worth individuals and institutions the opportunity to invest in bitcoin without the bother of storehousing it themselves. The fund was a brave early bet, coming when bitcoin was trading around $60 and still far from impressing financial services firms. Morehead is no gambler. He graduated magna cum laude as a civil engineering major at Princeton and spent about 10 years as a trader and in executive roles at Goldman Sachs, Bankers Trust, and Deutsche Bank before serving as CFO for a hedge fund and founding an electronic foreign exchange platform.

Morehead started Pantera Capital as a global macro hedge fund in 2003 but adjusted the company's focus as he tried to pinpoint the direction of the badly shaken global economy. "We are in the process of trying to figure out if the world is coming to an end (which we still doubt) or if the global sell-off was more a function of $75 billion in futures being liquidated over a U.S.

holiday," Morehead wrote in an early 2008 letter to investors, according to a *New York Times* article.[15]

Pantera targeted Bitcoin after partnering with Fortress Investment Group, Benchmark, and Ribbit Capital, three major investment firms that have been on top of a number of technology and other trends. Benchmark was an early investor in eBay and Uber, and has also taken stakes in Snapchat, Instagram, and Zillow, while Ribbit invested in investment platform Robinhood and insurance company Root (it also became an investor in the exchange Coinbase, which had launched the previous year.)

Pantera Capital assumed the majority position in the Pantera Bitcoin Fund, as is reflected in the name. Its investments have included some of blockchain and crypto's best-known startups, including Coinbase, Polychain, and cryptocurrencies Ripple, Zcash, and BitPesa, the latter of which targets the massive remittance industry in Sub-Saharan Africa. Morehead possesses a pilot's quiet self-assurance. He has weathered bitcoin's various fluctuations and has vastly outperformed equities markets—at one point in late 2017, his funds had returned 25,000 percent over their histories.[16] He raised $13 million for his first Bitcoin fund, nearly doubled that for the second fund, and in 2019, closed on a $175 million fund[17]—marking a further sign of Bitcoin's hook into people's cerebellums. In a lengthy May 2020 newsletter to investors, he predicted that bitcoin would hit $115,000 by August 2021.[18]

"This is a really distressing, massively confusing time," Morehead wrote. "I have no idea what's going to happen in 99% of things right now. However, I strongly believe it's close to inevitable that this will be very positive for cryptocurrency prices."

He added: "One of our principal arguments for bitcoin in a portfolio is that it has had a 209% 9-year compound annual growth rate with essentially zero long-term correlation to stocks, bonds, oil, and other asset classes. From a Portfolio Theory perspective: If you can find something that goes up in the biggest crisis in a century, you should have some of that in your portfolio."

In September 2013, shortly after the Winklevoss brothers and Morehead committed to Bitcoin, former investment banker Barry Silbert created the Bitcoin Investment Trust, the first US-based private investment instrument focused exclusively on Bitcoin. Seven months later, the Trust, part of his company Second Market, had acquired 100,000 bitcoins, worth over $40 million at the time, and Silbert was opening the Trust to retail investors. The latter move was a small milestone in Bitcoin's history, allowing average investors to invest in bitcoin without working through an exchange; the Trust had previously only been available to select investors. In 2015, after selling Second Market to Nasdaq, Silbert launched Digital Currency Group, which has ranked among the most significant venture capital firms targeting early-stage Bitcoin and cryptocurrency companies. An offshoot of Digital Currency Group, digital currency asset manager Grayscale Investments has over $27 billion in assets under management.[19] Silbert has been among the industry's great optimists. As early as 2015, Silbert was already predicting that Wall Street would start trading bitcoin and that banks would provide bitcoin services. Among Digital Currency Group's major investments are the exchanges bitFlyer and Coinbase, and the cryptocurrency payment platform Lightning Network (It invested in my start-up BTCC). The company also owns the cryptocurrency industry's leading publication, CoinDesk.

The same month as the launch of the Bitcoin Investment Trust also saw brothers Bart and Brad Stephens start Blockchain Capital (another BTCC investor). The San Francisco–based venture capital firm has invested in a number of Bitcoin's most important companies, including the payment platform BitPesa, which helps Bitcoin users in developing countries complete their transactions, and the Kraken exchange. The company has also invested in Libra, Facebook's proposed cryptocurrency. Both Stephenses worked in the financial services world for about 15 years before developing their interests in Bitcoin and blockchain technology.

And in February 2021, Tesla founder Elon Musk ignited a bitcoin price surge when his company announced that it had purchased $1.5 billion in bitcoin. The announcement came little over a week after Musk added a #bitcoin to his Twitter profile and later said on the popular Clubhouse social network platform that he regretted not purchasing bitcoin sooner. "I am a supporter of bitcoin," Musk said, adding that he thought bitcoin was "on the verge of getting broad acceptance by conventional finance people."[20]

I could assemble longer lists of other top Bitcoiners with equally respectable and impressive résumés. Coinbase CEO Brian Armstrong spent years as an enterprise risk management consultant at Deloitte. My brother Charlie Lee was a Google software engineer, who later joined Coinbase. ConSensys cofounder Joseph Lublin is ex–Goldman Sachs. Bitcoin payment services provider BitPay CEO Stephen Pair was a software engineer at IBM. Arthur Hayes, founder and CEO of the BitMEX derivatives platform, was an equities derivatives trader at Deutsche Bank.

To be sure, there are others who come from less traditional backgrounds and relish challenging status quo systems. Their outlaw status is consistent with digital currency's Cypherpunk beginnings, which saw mismanagement and even evil in traditional institutions. Why else would they have concerned themselves with a system to bypass existing platforms? But this is what I like about Bitcoin. It allows for people of all beliefs and backgrounds. And yes, that includes the celebrities who have sometimes garnered headlines for their Bitcoin investments and pronouncements.

Let me be clear. I don't attach much value to the Bitcoin endorsements from 50 Cent, Mike Tyson, or Kanye West, although I do find something poetic about William Shatner (the original Captain James T. Kirk of the Starship *Enterprise*) and his Bitcoin embrace and support of an Illinois mining farm. I can't remember currency ever serving as a *Star Trek* plot device, but I can now think of possibilities if they ever reboot the series—alien villain corners the market on intergalactic digital currency?

I see more significance in current leaders of old-fashioned institutions who support Bitcoin or have come to respect it. Fidelity CEO Abigail Johnson comes first to mind. What company in financial services is more bedrock than Fidelity, which cares for almost $2.5 trillion in assets, largely due to its reputation for strong customer service? I appreciate JPMorgan CEO Jamie Dimon's semi-capitulation—enough to have his firm explore developing a cryptocurrency—and SMH Capital CEO (formerly Prudential Securities CEO) George Ball's Bitcoin conversion after strongly opposing it. "I've never said this before, but I've always been a blockchain, cryptocurrency, Bitcoin opponent; but if you look right now, the government can't stimulate the markets forever," Ball said, speaking to the newswire Reuters in an August 2020 video interview.[21]

I've felt encouraged by Reid Hoffman's and even more Bill Gates's mention in connection with Bitcoin, even if they likely don't hold much bitcoin relative to their wealth. "If we were building a financial system from scratch today, we'd do it on a digital platform," Gates said in a video to a cryptocurrency forum.[22] "Digital can lower the cost of a range of transactions by as much as 90%, providing nearly universal access to innovative financial products and services."

And even if it's a stretch to mention Warren Buffett as anything less than a Bitcoin skeptic—at least for now—I would note that he possessed bitcoin for a short time, courtesy of Tron founder and CEO Justin Sun, who paid nearly $4.6 million at a charity auction for dinner with Buffett.[23] During the meal (which my brother Charlie also attended), Sun gifted Buffett a bitcoin on a mobile phone and tried to change his opinion, if only a little, about Bitcoin. Buffett, still not convinced, donated the bitcoin to a lucky charity.

MAY I SUGGEST YOU IGNORE THE TURBULENCE

On July 27, 2020, bitcoin broke $11,000 for the first time in almost a year, increasing $1,400 in less than 12 hours before retreating into the mid $11,000 range. In my Twitter feed that day, I flagged an October 1, 2017, post that I had sent out as the previous bull market was rapidly approaching the same price range, "Why it's #NotTooLate to invest in #Bitcoin today: You're ahead of ~7 billion people, buying into a #gold-like asset class at a 99% discount." Then, I added a new conclusion: "Almost 3 years later, and still true today . . ."

I wasn't trying to be cocky; well, maybe a little. It always feels good when I seem to be right about Bitcoin, particularly given all the skepticism. I see it as an opportunity to convince people to buy, a task that becomes easier, ironically, when the price rises significantly. Two weeks later on August 10, 2020, with bitcoin trading robustly in the $11,000s, I flagged a second 2017 tweet—from February of that year—in which I predicted the price in 2020 "after (the) block halving" would reach between $5,000 to $11,000. (In the 2020 block halving, the amount of the bitcoin reward for miners every 10 minutes went from 12.50 bitcoins to 6.25, which I figured would make bitcoin more valuable.)

"Not a bad price prediction," I wrote in my August 2020 commentary on my 2017 prediction.

In truth, I had been only roughly correct in 2017. I hadn't pinpointed when the surge would occur, and my forecast, while impressive, given bitcoin's $1,165 trading price at the time, now seems almost laughably vague. Other people with some knowledge of technology investment trends could have predicted similarly.

In 2020, I made another bold price prediction when bitcoin was trading at around $10,000, tweeting to Tesla founder Elon Musk on June 2 that I was "looking forward to the #CyberTruck next year! By then, I predict you can buy it with just one #Bitcoin. If $BTC price exceeds $39,900 [the price of the Tesla Cybertruck] by late 2021, I'll GIVE AWAY a FREE @Tesla CyberTruck." By the end of the first week of 2021, bitcoin had surged above $40,000, so I will be giving away a CyberTruck, regardless of where bitcoin's price ends up at the end of the year.

So, I'll give myself a little credit but not too much, and note that my 2017 and 2020 predictions raised a couple of larger truths: (1) Bitcoin is unpredictable, and (2) ignore its unpredictability.

On the first point, all I'll say is that no one has a crystal ball about what bitcoin will do from one short period of time to the next. It could spurt, sink, zig, and zag like a cardiogram.

On the latter point: If you've bought into bitcoin, volatility is part of the package. More importantly, you shouldn't be riding its every ebb and flow on a daily or near daily basis. As I've already written and will write again, if you're a smart bitcoin investor, you're not day trading but instead looking long term.

I've done well with my bitcoin investments. I know more about bitcoin than most people, and I don't get caught up in its micro movements. "Bitcoin's gonna be Bitcoin," I always say, in terms of its moody price behavior.

Accept its qualities the way you might accept your more dramatic friends whom you like as much as your quieter ones. Each character type has its downside, but they all enrich your life. You simply learn to live with all their facets. For the time being, if you want an investment that won't jiggle around, buy bonds or utility stocks, because you're not going to be able to predict with certainty what bitcoin is likely to do over short stretches. Bitcoin defies the usual analyses.

Let's return to the huge gains in July 2020.

The increase seemed to correlate to a unique combination of events—or did it?

On the understandable side, a day earlier, the US Comptroller of the Currency, part of the Treasury Department that regulates national banks among its responsibilities, said that it would allow banks to hold cryptocurrency funds. The announcement represented a small but important victory for Bitcoin. It meant investors would now have the option of storehousing their bitcoin in banks. People know banks but not necessarily digital wallets. Just as importantly, it signaled yet another step in banking and government acceptance of digital currency.

Also on the understandable side, the credit card giant Mastercard announced on the same day that it would partner with crypto service provider Wirex to issue a payment card allowing consumers to exchange cryptocurrency for fiat currency. In addition, in another headline favorable to Bitcoin, Russia declared Bitcoin was a type of property, an announcement that seemed to underline that country's grudging embrace of digital currency, even as it continued to outlaw its use as a means of payment within the country.

During the same period, the COVID epidemic sent shudders through the world economy, there was civil unrest in most major cities throughout the United States, and there were concerns about people's ability to vote in the coming US election. All of this uncertainty had pushed some investors toward the traditional safe haven of gold. Less than a month after breaking its historic high of $1,776 per ounce, gold had climbed over $1,940 per ounce, and by August 6, 2020, it surged past $2,000 for the first time ever. "We've seen gold rally up in 1980 and 2011 after the financial crisis," I told John Riggins in a July 28 *Bitcoin Magazine* podcast. "It's exciting to see gold go up."

But . . .

The backdrop on this Monday didn't differ appreciably from the previous week or other weeks earlier in the month. The coronavirus continued to leave the United States and the rest of the world in various stages of shutdown, with the United States suffering from the highest daily infection and mortality rates. Joblessness in most major Western industrialized countries hovered near or close to double digits amid manufacturing slowdowns. Consumer spending and GDP continued to contract as everyone waited hopefully for news of an effective vaccine.

And equity markets, which had remained stubbornly and somewhat mysteriously high throughout the pandemic, registered another successful day. The Dow Jones Industrial Average gained 100 points, and the S&P 500 and Nasdaq also rose. So-called FAANG stocks—Facebook, Apple, Amazon, Netflix, and Google—which had largely fueled the stock market's success, posted strong gains. If investors were looking for a safe haven as some investment observers maintained, they had options beyond bitcoin. The bottom line that day: major signals were mixed.

Not that bitcoin's performance as an uncorrelated asset should have depended heavily on any of these happenings individually or taken together. Part of Satoshi Nakamoto's premise was to create a currency free from the normal flow of events and human judgment that drags down traditional currencies.

Fast-forward to the opening of the Labor Day weekend 2020. The symbolic if not actual end of summer is usually a quiet time in business as companies ready for the season's last extended holiday. Bitcoin had been keeping its $11,500 orbit with some observers anticipating that it would cross $12,000 again on its way to additional gains in 2021.The Winklevoss brothers were crowing as they touted their new Gemini Exchange on Twitter.

Other prominent Bitcoin personalities were no less optimistic. From my perch in Las Vegas, where I had relocated from China early in the pandemic, I felt optimistic. "This time it feels a little different," I had told Riggins in our interview. Starting in September, bitcoin seemed likely to continue upward.

And then, bitcoin did what it often does, moving in a big way without warning. From September 1 to September 5, it dropped over $2,000, dipping below $10,000, before settling in the $10,000 to $11,000 range for much of the ensuing six weeks. There was no easy way to predict the decline, particularly following so closely after its impressive midsummer performance.

You could practically hear the skeptics renewing their complaints about bitcoin's volatility and the risk it presented to investors.

Yet sitting at my Las Vegas home, I was no more worked up about bitcoin's drop than I had been a month earlier. Bitcoin had merely gone for another one of its up and down rides, but its basic properties hadn't changed. From its summertime performance, it was still a great investment. Those who'd purchased bitcoin in March as the pandemic gathered steam would have gained 200 percent on their holdings. They even would have been up about 5 percent from late July—not great but better than a lot of stocks.

The naysayers were simply making their usual mistake, looking at what happened over the course of a day or a few days—but ignoring the bigger picture. Bitcoin might be volatile, but that's certainly a rate I believe most investors could live with, including Warren Buffett. In contrast to bitcoin, Berkshire Hathaway stock rose only 3 percent over the same midsummer 2020 period.

Note that Berkshire Hathaway returned to its salad days not too long after Buffett fought past his longstanding aversion to what he considered risky technology stocks and became Apple's biggest shareholder. People often forget an asset's weaker moments when it's doing well and that even the greatest investors make mistakes and change their minds. It's also worth noting that any investor, including Buffett, can benefit from an open mind.

The short roller-coaster ride in pricing was a perfect bitcoin microcosm. It could rise quickly, inspiring bouts of euphoria, but also sink so fast that it could raise doubts among even the most forward-thinkers. I also thought that seeing this play out offered great lessons for investors who were paying attention and wanted to learn. Among other things, it demonstrated that volatility is badly misunderstood and not necessarily evil. And indeed, investors who held on through the ride were rewarded when bitcoin approached the $30,000 level in late 2020.

MISUNDERSTANDING VOLATILITY

What is volatility? Perhaps more importantly, what is it not? And also, why shouldn't people be scared of it?

The short definition is that volatility describes the amount that the price of an asset can move up or down. An asset's volatility—sometimes described as *realized volatility*—usually depends on its historical performance. Analysts and publications calculate volatility differently contingent on what they feel is most relevant in pricing cycles. There is also *implied volatility*, which tries to predict future price movement.

To be sure, many investors fear volatility, and it has been one of the biggest obstacles for bitcoin because of its frequent big price fluctuations. A 2020 survey by Fidelity Digital Assets found that volatility was among the main reasons that people chose not to acquire bitcoin.[1]

What is the CBOE Volatility index, which computes the implied volatility of the S&P 500, nicknamed? The Fear Index.

But volatility is not risk.

We've mistakenly mixed up the two because of an internal need to control our environment. Volatility is beyond our control, so it seems inherently risky. With investing, this means that we can't prevent beyond a doubt that our assets won't dwindle in value or even become completely worthless. We fear this possibility and the hardship it would bring. Risk can be scary because of what might happen.

This response is more emotional than rational. Few people risk their well-being when they invest. We find ways to hedge risk, to not put us too close to the edge of something frightening. At the same time, we often forget that losing value on an investment sets up the opportunity for a great comeback.

History is filled with great comeback stories. Henry Ford went bankrupt before his car company succeeded. Walt Disney also declared bankruptcy twice. A last-minute bank loan enabled him to finish *Snow White*, which gave him the start he needed. Even Abraham Lincoln ran a general store into the ground before righting himself. None of these ventures were that risky, by the way. They simply suffered from mismanagement.

Of course, there are assets that embody risk. I won't dwell on this type of investment here because bitcoin is far from risky and its frequently drastic price changes will one day stop.

Suffice to say here that risky investments usually involve startups that have spun off from some larger technological trend or a biotech working on a new therapy. They are the domain of venture capitalists, or occasionally the new phenomenon of crowdfunding, or the investor in penny stocks hoping for a big comeback.

Professional investors and knowledgeable individual investors do not become alarmed if a venture fails. They are able to ride out the waves and irregular growth patterns in risky assets. The leading venture capitalists use mathematical models that enable them to determine where they should invest and their potential success rate. They also possess the resources to withstand a certain amount of loss. Volatility does not figure into their thinking as much as the bigger, long-term picture. In this regard, they are taking calculated risks.

To be sure, VCs and small consumer investors have been taking some of those risks in Bitcoin and blockchain projects. The list of high-powered VCs that have created units focused on these areas or invested in promising projects has grown—and with good reason.

As I've already written, the entrepreneurs behind these projects have been addressing important issues in trying to make the world a better place. But this has nothing to do with pricing volatility. It's merely a calculated risk that some people are willing to take.

Volatility plays by certain rules. We can measure it and sometimes even predict when it will occur. It has a relationship to events, bad and good. Taking it into account and understanding how it works can enable us to make good decisions.

There are assets in which an investor should be willing to accept a fair amount of price fluctuation as they establish themselves because they are fundamentally sound and likely to grow. You just need to be patient and calm—not unlike the captain of an airplane.

"It's amazing what you can get used to," said Chesley "Sully" Sullenberger, the beloved U.S. Airways pilot who landed his Airbus A320 in the middle of the Hudson River in 2009. Sullenberger wasn't offering investment advice, but he might as well have been.

If you're thinking of investing in bitcoin, keep your blinders on about price on any given day, unless you're just curious or there's some signature event that can serve to test a theory about why bitcoin's price increases or decreases. That can be a useful exercise, and you may find some pattern or connection that no one else has seen. If you become an evangelist, you should also check bitcoin's price daily, as I've been doing for years, now with the help of my Apple Watch. As an evangelist, it's important to be current on bitcoin's movement in case someone asks you about it.

I never worry if bitcoin has had a good day or bad, if the pundits are down on it or not, or how other assets are doing.

I determined early on that bitcoin, like any good investment, requires commitment. Investing in bitcoin is a marathon—or better yet, an ultramarathon spanning decades—and not a sprint.

STAYING CALM IN THE FIRST BULL RUN

On November 28, 2013, when bitcoin started the day at $1,003, the first time it had crossed $1,000, I told anyone who would listen to invest, or if they had already bought some, to hold on to it. The term *to HODL* was still three weeks away from appearing on a post on bitcointalk.org forum.[2] The author of the post clearly misspelled the word *hold* as *HODL*, adding all caps for emphasis. The author was admittedly drunk that night. However, the new term *HODL* assumed a life of its own in the online world. It came to describe the idea of holding your bitcoin investments for the long term, possibly forever. Later, HODL became a reverse acronym, and came to stand for "Hold On for Dear Life." Yes, to survive the volatility of bitcoin, you probably do need to hold on for dear life. But I don't see this as negative.

Are you HODLing bitcoin? I am.

Topping $1,000 was undoubtedly a signature moment for bitcoin. Rational or not, it held symbolic value. A thousand sounded more impressive than a number in the hundreds, suggesting more strongly than ever that there was a good case for investing in bitcoin. Investors often seek validation in milestones. And the recent run up to $10,000 is an even bigger milestone. Now that it has crossed $10,000, I think Bitcoin is here to stay.

But the first bitcoin bull run to garner significant attention from the business media—and again I reference breaking the $1,000 threshold—reflected a sea change from an industry insider–driven asset to something that attracted wider interest from the general public. For its first three years, bitcoin's price depended largely on the activities of the small communities that had received bitcoin, in some cases from Satoshi Nakamoto and other early converts, and on mining activity. In those days in 2011, you could probably fit the number of bitcoin investors worldwide into a large ballroom. Exchanges were still a foreign concept with only a few operating—mostly with problems—and others were a year or more away from starting. Among the most successful exchanges today, Coinbase wouldn't launch until mid-2012, a year after my own startup, BTCChina. Binance wouldn't open its doors until 2017.

BitcoinMarket.com and Mt. Gox are widely considered the first exchanges of any note, particularly the latter. They launched a few months apart in 2010. They were visionary in recognizing a market for their services and deserve credit for establishing sizable enough businesses to become part of Bitcoin's history before their ignoble ends. BitcoinMarket.com even saw the inevitable interrelationship between Bitcoin and existing financial systems, signing an agreement with payment service PayPal to enable users to exchange fiat money for bitcoin. But it was never able to improve its ramshackle platform and is more of a footnote in the history of exchanges than a full episode.

Was it surprising then that bitcoin's price languished in double digits until Mt. Gox grew into a juggernaut that made it easier to trade? A product—investment or otherwise—only flourishes when an infrastructure exists to enable wide participation. In the days and weeks before Mt. Gox made some technical improvements and marketed itself more widely under its aggressive new owner, Mark Karpelès, I believe demand for bitcoin was increasing.

A growing number of people, many of them non-technologists, were discovering Bitcoin, and Mt. Gox's platform gave them a relatively easy way to invest. The high trading volumes were validation for other new investors, and the resulting buzz of activity sent prices steadily higher.

A quick word about Mt. Gox: the Tokyo-based company's rags-to-riches-to-rags tale is well known in the industry and unfairly taints it along with the vice-ridden platform Silk Road, conflating human weakness and error with true weakness. Early impressions are tough to shake, particularly when they involve hundreds of millions of dollars and law enforcement actions.

Mt. Gox's story started in 2006, way before the invention of Bitcoin, as a platform to enable players of a fantasy-based game to trade cards online. That card game was called Magic: The Gathering, and its acronym formed the name of this site, MTGOX, with the suffix "OX" to stand for Online Exchange. Its downfall amid the loss of about 650,000 bitcoins is one of Bitcoin's few tragedies, and one that will one day be completely irrelevant. Why will it become irrelevant? Well, as a society, are we still concerned about the big heists of merchant ships in the seventeenth century, with the pirates of the high seas stealing large fortunes of gold, silver, and other valuables? Hardly. I believe that four centuries from now, the big Mt. Gox hack will be no different than the heists of the early days. And, most importantly, it doesn't affect the usefulness nor the value of bitcoin.

I remain firm in my agreement with others who see bitcoin as an entirely or largely uncorrelated asset. But there were other events in late 2012 and early 2013 that enabled bitcoin's first notable price increase. The cryptocurrency payment service BitPay, which had been in existence for about 18 months, reported that by the end of 2012 over 1,000 merchants were accepting bitcoin. BitPay's headquarters was in Atlanta, hardly a tech hotbed, but it underscored Bitcoin's reach beyond Silicon Valley, Boston, and other hubs. Major dating websites such as OKCupid decided to accept bitcoin, which drew notice. An agreement to link bitcoin to M-Pesa, the massive mobile payments service provider in Africa, was an even bigger story.

But none of these events or bitcoin's high that year of near $1,200 on November 30, 2013, mattered. I was no more alarmed when it dropped below $700 less than 10 days later or had sunk to $351 by April 12, 2014, and finally tumbled to $171 by January 2015. The first Bitcoin winter was a long, harsh one. But winters are always hard. George Washington camped in subfreezing temperatures at Valley Forge in 1777 and 1778 before he won the American Revolution.

Are high triple-digit fluctuations, particularly if they are headed in the wrong direction, unsettling? Absolutely. But I would again strongly suggest that they should not be Bitcoin dealbreakers. Here is a Bitcoin aphorism: Bitcoin requires tenacity. HODL. Hold on for dear life.

The next bitcoin bull market offered similar lessons. Bitcoin had started picking up ground in 2016 as more exchanges and other service organizations launched all around the world to serve growing demand. Daily trading volume as listed on CoinMarketCap, which by this time had become a go-to industry source for quick information, had risen from about $30 million to over $200 million. By the start of 2017, bitcoin's price had regained almost all the ground it had lost following the 2013 bull market, topping $1,000 for only the second time ever. A series of small events further stoked the fire. In July 2016, researchers from the United States, the United Kingdom, and Germany found that users were more likely to use bitcoin for "legitimate enterprises" than "sin."[3] According to bitcoin.com, the same years, scholars and others authored nearly 3,500 research papers that mentioned Bitcoin, more than seven times the number four years earlier.[45]

The following January, 2017, a report by media giant NHK found that the number of retailers that accepted bitcoin in Japan, the world's third largest economy, had increased by nearly five times.[6] By April, the Japanese government had legalized bitcoin as a payment method. Each event taken alone didn't make huge waves. But together, they reflected a gathering storm. This was a good storm for Bitcoin.

By early August of 2017, bitcoin had more than tripled in price. At BTCC, I was preoccupied with signs that the Chinese government would be cracking down on domestic Bitcoin exchanges as it looked for ways to control the gathering movement. But I found time to smile. Bitcoin was behaving every bit as well as I had expected. Then it really took off, gaining altitude in big triple-digit chunks. By the middle of October, it had bolted past $5,000. At the end of November, it crossed $10,000. A few days before, flush with confidence about the market, I sold some bitcoin I had acquired in 2013 to take some profit and made an impulse purchase of the new Tesla Model X in China for $130,000. On December 7, bitcoin jumped a whopping $3,700, rising above $17,000, and 10 days later, it soared to its all-time high of $20,089. That was the absolute top, at least until the next bull run.

As happy as I was, I also knew the good times wouldn't last. Some people said the price increase stemmed from the activity of a major bitcoin whale trying to stir interest in bitcoin, and that this investor had pulled back once he accomplished his mission. I've never bought that theory. Bitcoin was already too big for one person to stir the pot that much. I subscribed to a different theory. Bitcoin was merely following a historical pattern of bull markets, where a FOMO (fear of missing out) rally takes hold, common for other tech-based investment categories, and prices soar rapidly. I knew it would retrench quickly and stabilize at a much lower and gut-wrenching price level. I couldn't predict by how much, but when it settled around $6,000 by early spring 2018, I wasn't surprised the least bit.

And again, I wasn't worried by the huge price swings. I was a Bitcoin veteran and I was used to it. In my mind, the sudden breakneck enthusiasm for bitcoin, with tens of thousands of new investors trying to capture the whirlwind, was frothy. The environment for Bitcoin acceptance had changed but not radically enough to merit its meteoric rise. The about-face many new investors and others subsequently executed, as they unloaded some or all of their holdings, was also overdone. Bitcoin hadn't become less promising over the course of a few weeks. By this time, I had sold BTCC to a Hong Kong–based group, so I had more time to gauge public sentiment. Some of the biggest naysayers were ready to sound Bitcoin's death knell, and even some friends and former BTCC employees had doubts. Some of them sold all their bitcoins, to my great surprise and disappointment.

But I was resolute about Bitcoin's future and the best strategy for investing in it: HODL. What they termed turbulence was just a series of adjustments in my mind. The true believers set their investment goals years, even decades into the future. They wouldn't let price movements dissuade them. Without a doubt, I am one of them, a true believer in Bitcoin.

Not then and not now. You just have to be willing to accept the big price fluctuations for what they are, not a mark against Bitcoin, but a reflection of an asset finding itself. Remember, Bitcoin hasn't even reached its thirteenth birthday; so it's technically not even a teenager. It's growing up fast, and it has already achieved so much in just 12 years. When Bitcoin reaches 18 or 21 years, it will truly be a force to be reckoned with. I can't wait for that day.

Want to hear something radical? Bitcoin isn't volatile as much as it is simply letting market forces dictate its path. The eighteenth-century Scottish philosopher Adam Smith had a thing or two to say about market forces. His theory of an invisible hand dictating economic performance has been the bedrock of capitalist society. I'm convinced that Adam Smith would also have been a huge fan of Bitcoin.

BITCOIN IS LESS VULNERABLE THAN YOU THINK

Superman had kryptonite. Achilles had his heel.

The 1927 Yankees led by Babe Ruth and Lou Gehrig, often considered history's greatest baseball team, had trouble beating the sixth-place Cleveland Indians.

Standard Oil got too big for its own good and had to be split up.

Investment banking giants Lehman Brothers and Bear Stearns, which once controlled over $1 trillion in assets and featured some of Wall Street's sharpest minds, succumbed to greed in the subprime mortgage crisis.

The rating agency Equifax, which boasted of its ability to safeguard individuals' financial information that it shares with clients, left a gap in its cyber defenses, allowing hackers to access data for 143 million customers. Hewlett Packard, IBM, Fujitsu, Tata Consultancy Services, NTT Data, Dimension Data, and Computer Sciences Corporation, all companies at the forefront of tech innovation, have been victims of cyber espionage, allegedly from China's Ministry of State Security.

Even gold, a naturally occurring element—AU, number 79 on the periodic table—that no other naturally occurring substance can obliterate, has a weakness if you consider that its price fluctuations stem from macroeconomic events and historical susceptibility to scams. In 1869, war hero Ulysses S. Grant saw his presidency scandalized after his brother-in-law and two acquaintances influenced his decision to stop selling gold, a practice he had used to pay off the country's enormous Civil War debt, so that they could corner the gold market. Grant sniffed out the scheme shortly after it launched, but by that time it had sent gold prices plunging from about $160 an ounce to under $140 in what became known as Black Friday. The drop sent the stock market into a tailspin and led to an investigation in which the revered leader of the Union army was exonerated but at the cost of at least part of his good reputation.

Everyone, everything, and every organization, the biggest and smallest, fictional and nonfictional, in every aspect of life has a weakness. They're all susceptible in some way to attacks or other events that can harm them. This vulnerability is part of the human condition. To be sure, some are more vulnerable than others.

The Grant episode and a few others notwithstanding, gold has largely operated above the fray because of its imperviousness to destructive forces. To be sure, it can be molded into different shapes, but the basic composition that makes it valuable is unchangeable. Gold is a naturally occurring element, as opposed to being a compound, composite, or alloy made of other things. In this regard, gold is uniformly the same everywhere in the world. Superheat gold and it merely melts or turns into another shape. It is extremely dense, and thus heavy, making it hard to counterfeit using lighter substances. In its lengthy history as a store of value, it has been largely resistant to dramatic price swings and misdeeds. It obeys no single authority. Gold is the best physical example of a decentralized asset class. Anyone can find gold, and anyone can own gold.

I suppose Ian Fleming, the creator of James Bond, understood gold's timeless properties best in *Goldfinger*, where the aptly named villain, Auric Goldfinger, doesn't even try to steal the world's largest store of gold, but rather aims to contaminate it with radiation that will last 58 years and boost the value of his own supply. Bond fans remember the dirty bomb stopping seven seconds before it exploded.

This chapter considers whether Bitcoin is vulnerable, and I've indirectly already answered the question. It is vulnerable. But in this regard, it bears another similarity to gold, the asset to which it is most compared.

Coming from a Bitcoin evangelist, this may seem sacrilegious, but part of being a good advocate is offering an honest appraisal. Paint too rosy a picture and people start to doubt. Describe something that has blemishes and it becomes believable.

Bitcoin is not perfectly secure because in life, nothing ever is.

To be sure, Bitcoin, like gold, comes closer than any object of value to being invulnerable. It cannot be demolished, wrecked, or ruined—not because it's a physical element—rather because there is nothing to destroy, unless you count a paper or hard drive wallet, but even then, a savvy bitcoin investor would otherwise know their key or have proper backups. Bitcoin itself doesn't physically exist in a single location. There is no coinage or legal tender. And the system itself does not depend on a single person, company, or institution. Bitcoin is not open to a single point of attack that could compromise its entire existence. Rather, the Bitcoin "system" is spread out across the whole world over the entire internet, encompassing hundreds of thousands of machine nodes, and many millions of users and their computing devices. How would you destroy or turn off something like that?

Its vulnerability, to the extent it exists, comes from individual errors or inaction resulting in loss of funds. If wallet holders share their private key or do not follow certain safety precautions, it could lead to the loss of their bitcoin. It's worth pointing out that even in a scenario of coin loss, the bitcoins themselves have not disappeared, as there will always be a maximum of 21 million bitcoins. Bitcoin is also vulnerable to a foul-up by one of the many service providers that form Bitcoin's growing infrastructure. Such mistakes are often the result of individual misdeed, or more often misjudgment, such as a manager failing to address a gap in a company's defenses or not reacting quickly enough to a new threat. These are all understandable problems.

EVERYTHING IS VULNERABLE

No industry or system can ensure that all its participants are ethical, capable, and intent on following the right practices. If someone robs a bank in Utah, or even if there's a larger cyber event such as the data breach of JPMorgan Chase involving over 70 million customers, do you indict the whole banking industry? Or if there's questionable behavior, such as the Wells Fargo scheme to charge people for services they hadn't requested, or the 2020 lawsuit alleging that Bank of America, Wells Fargo, JPMorgan Chase, and US Bank reshuffled Paycheck Protection Program loans to prioritize those businesses likely to make money—does that mean the whole industry is rotten? The lawsuit, which was still pending at the time of publication, was among the latest blows to the banking industry's reputation. However, I can assure you that the day after the filing of the lawsuit, banks nationwide operated as usual, just as they have following other stressful events. A well-documented 2014 study published in *Nature* magazine found that banking culture fosters dishonesty,[1] and yet banks didn't start shuttering. (To be fair, a 2019 Berlin-based study called the earlier report into question.[2])

Airlines and trains continue to operate even after crashes. The automobile industry survives recalls, not to mention ongoing concerns about its negotiating tactics. The reason is because they are fundamentally sound and continue to provide valuable products and services.

I suggest approaching Bitcoin the same way. The industry has had problems just like any other industry, particularly in its early stages of development. But observers should not misinterpret those issues as a profound problem with Bitcoin itself. The mechanisms that went into the creation of Bitcoin are every bit as solid today as they ever were. And those mechanisms should not be conflated with the wider ecosystem of trading and custodial services offered by a variety of firms. While some of these firms have had issues (and likely there will be more issues in the future), these difficulties should not be used to undermine Bitcoin or other cryptocurrencies, as they themselves are fundamentally sound.

It bears repeating here that the term Bitcoin encompasses two distinct parts of the Bitcoin universe. Bitcoin with a capital "B" describes the overall platform that sends the cryptocurrency into the world at regular intervals and enables investors to hold and trade it. Bitcoin with a lowercase "b" describes the unit of the currency. But this is irrelevant to the issue of vulnerability, unless you consider the companies that service Bitcoin part of the capital B, the Bitcoin system. But this would be an error. Bitcoin is no more responsible for Bithumb's, Binance's, or some other major exchange's security breaches than the Federal Reserve is for the bank robberies or the breaches of Goldman Sachs, Deutsche Bank, or another banking or financial services firm—big or small. Find an industry or any movement that's grown large enough that doesn't have problems, and I'll tip my hat to you. It doesn't exist. In any industry, problems come with scale. As more players whose movements cannot be controlled or monitored establish a foothold, the chances for issues increase.

THE GREATEST PROTECTION

Of course, some people believe that Bitcoin's decentralized nature opens it to multiple points of attack. They postulate that without a central authority, Bitcoin has no sheriff for protection. Theoretically, any participant can strike Bitcoin. In my view, these people are reflecting their own biases toward traditional, centralized systems, conveniently forgetting their vulnerabilities.

Decentralization is the greatest protection of all. It eliminates a single target that can bring down an entire system. Bitcoin has no central computer system managed by an IT department that can be attacked. There are no unscrupulous contractors that might be engaged who could unlock a control tower, giving them access to someone's information or even assets. With Bitcoin, there is safety in the herd, with everyone potentially available to watch for something that doesn't add up.

Think of trying to break into a bank vault with a few hundred thousand people watching you try to crack the combination. Every transaction must add up, with no duplicates allowed, before miners can add it to the public ledger—the blockchain. And miners will continue to participate in increasing numbers because of the bitcoin rewards they can receive. Bitcoin is a self-reinforcing system.

Bitcoin was purposely designed this way, creating a positive self-reinforcing cycle. As it proves itself impervious to serious attacks, Bitcoin becomes more valuable, convincing more people to participate, which widens the circle of potential observers, making it even more secure, and, in turn, more valuable. Or to put things more simply, the greater the global mining hash power, the more secure Bitcoin becomes. To the chagrin of governments and regulators worldwide, Bitcoin has now become a de facto standard as the global digital currency. Ask anyone who understands the industry.

Bitcoin's components, taken together, create an almost impregnable firewall against evil intent. It is nothing short of a scientific breakthrough in its preventative, self-healing qualities and ability to grow stronger as the network expands. To claim that Bitcoin is insecure is to attack scientific logic.

I say "almost" because as I pointed out at the beginning of this chapter, nothing is perfect. The one small opening that Bitcoin leaves is the so-called 51 percent attack, in which malicious miners assume control of over half of a cryptocurrency network's computing power, in order to attack it by slowing down or censoring transactions. This attack was successfully used in 2016 against two lesser-known cryptocurrencies, Krypton and Shift. But the likelihood of a group reaching a similar outcome against Bitcoin's enormous network is less than miniscule. It would take an enormous effort to coordinate such an assault, which is particularly difficult given the number of mining groups and their global spread. I would consider a 51 percent attack a vulnerability in the way that a giant meteor might be a threat to earth. Possible? Yes. Likely? No.

Yet perceptions are hard to shake. The various cyber incidents involving service providers have left the false idea that Bitcoin is more vulnerable than traditional currency. Bitcoin was not the vulnerable piece in those cases. Rather, it was the centralized service providers that got into trouble. We even see people blaming Bitcoin for events beyond its control. For example, in July 2020, Bitcoin critics and casual readers were quick to blame Bitcoin for a Twitter hack, partly because of the distorted headlines of some of the world's most respected media outlets, including the *New York Times*[3] and BBC. The headlines used the term "Bitcoin Scam," although the event exploited weaknesses in Twitter security to access the accounts of Barack Obama, Bill Gates, Kanye West, Elon Musk, and other global figures to trick people into sending more than $120,000 in bitcoins on the false pretense that they could double their money. *The Late Show* host Stephen Colbert, a keen and witty observer of cultural issues, used the term "bitcoin bandits" in his opening monologue a day after Twitter discovered the breach. Even the respected publication *Wired* misrepresented the hack, describing it as a Twitter Bitcoin hack, although Bitcoin itself was not hacked and it was not responsible for the breach.

Police later arrested a 17-year-old hacker for what cybersecurity experts described as a commonplace, amateurish scheme that could have involved nearly any cryptocurrency to defraud Twitter users. Bitcoin just happened to be his choice, an innocent bystander in the caper. (Have you noticed that for online hackers, Bitcoin is always their target of theft, or the payment of choice when they ask for ransom? Why is that? Bitcoin has some truly great features, and even hackers appreciate them.)

But the incident offered yet another reminder of Bitcoin's challenge in overcoming preconceived notions about its vulnerability. After reading the *Times*' typically well-detailed account of the hack and other stories, I wondered if the headline writers were conveniently playing to public biases or were reflecting their own while looking for a catchy turn of phrase. Perhaps both.

Sometimes I call Bitcoin's struggles to overcome misconceptions about it the Mt. Gox syndrome. The massive theft of bitcoins deeply affected those who were following it around that time. (Some of the Mt. Gox account holders who lost their bitcoin life savings gave up on Bitcoin entirely.) But in subtle ways it has affected people who have become interested in Bitcoin years after Mt. Gox. They have heard that Bitcoin is vulnerable with Mt. Gox as the most prominent example.

Yet Bitcoin should no more be defined by Mt. Gox than other strong, vibrant industries should be defined by the stains they've suffered. Looking at this another way, Wells Fargo had about $1.5 trillion in assets under management as the first stories broke about its attempts to defraud customers. It is now closing in on $2 trillion and has more than 70 million customers. The overwhelming majority of its clients never lost faith in the bank, at least not enough for them to choose another bank.

Too many people also conflate weaknesses in the ecosystem with Bitcoin itself. This confusion reflects people's uncertainty about the role of companies serving investors. It may partly stem from the very names of these organizations, which often incorporate all or part of the word *Bitcoin*. If something sounds like Bitcoin, isn't it Bitcoin? Well, no.

And as I've already mentioned, the keepers of fiat systems don't help matters by amplifying unjustifiable concerns at every opportunity and creating obstacles at the regulatory level, or in other ways. They hope to make people fearful by highlighting Bitcoin's alleged weaknesses. Look closely at what they are saying and you'll find a fictional tale. My hope is that Chapter 2 will help clarify what various players in the Bitcoin infrastructure do and how to use them safely.

Deconstructing the misconceptions about vulnerability will undoubtedly take time. It will require an understanding of people's concerns about Bitcoin and patience to explain logically why they are wrong. It will also require clear messaging and ongoing belief in people's desire to learn about something that can benefit them.

Some evangelists have perhaps overlooked these principles in their haste to wax poetic about an asset in which they've invested large parts of their lives. They would rather describe why Bitcoin is great and how its price will increase—all the while assuming that listeners will be swept up in their enthusiasm. This spirit is common to all entrepreneurs, and anyone involved in Bitcoin in the early days fits into that category.

I know that I can sometimes speak fast and cover a lot of ground in my conference presentations as I try to win converts. So, I've tried to think of myself more as an educator, modeling my approach after the teachers I liked best at Lawrenceville and Stanford, and the communication styles of my favorite managers over the years.

They were clear, concise, and meticulous in how they shared information. They treated all questions respectfully, keeping in mind that sometimes people need extra time to grow comfortable with the material, and that a teacher's goal in the end is to ensure that everyone understands the material. They were willing to repeat information. So, I've kept these principles in mind in my interactions with people who harbor doubts about Bitcoin's security.

I repeat what has become a mantra: Bitcoin is more secure than any other financial platform. I show how there is safety in numbers and that the various hacks stemmed from issues with individuals and companies, rather than with Bitcoin itself. I remind my listeners that traditional institutions have their own gaps and have been victims of some of history's greatest cybercrimes, and that they endured nonetheless. This is a point that all Bitcoin evangelists have made to the media to dispel their doubts. As I've already said in this chapter, a hack of Goldman Sachs or a robbery at Bank of America doesn't mean the US dollar has been compromised.

Are more breaches of Bitcoin service providers likely? Yes. Could yet-to-imagine hacking schemes occur in the future? Absolutely.

As industries and movements evolve, so do the bad actors looking to grift off them. The Bitcoin industry undoubtedly has its share of people who are tracking it with the hope they one day might be able to steal from it.

But they face a steep climb. Bitcoin's vulnerability is nothing less than a fiction, a myth that will disappear as its popularity and participation grows.

FIVE OTHER MAJOR FEARS DECONSTRUCTED: FDIC, LOSS, REGULATION, MINING, AND GOVERNMENT

I understand that people have fears. Everyone does. It's part of being human to react strongly to stimuli that we believe can harm us. The different ways we react to these stimuli is also innately human. Why are some people afraid of heights while others embrace them?

For example, although I'm not anxious by nature, I'm also not crazy about bungee jumping or scary movies, and the occasional hairy spider leaves me squeamish, sometimes to the amusement of friends. Yet they have their own phobias that I don't understand, particularly because they, like me, are confident executives who have been unafraid to take chances in their careers.

Experts say that fear stems from an inability to control events that are immediately threatening, such as a missing guardrail on a hairpin turn or a great white shark heading for us in the surf. We get out of the way fast in these types of situations, understandably. But our response may also derive from the perception that a single incident might kick-start one or a series of events that can hurt us in the future. Scary films play on this deep-rooted emotional reaction. A new field of psychology research called neurocinematics studies how movie scenes affect our brains. "The audience is like a giant organ that you and I are playing," twentieth-century maestro of film fright Alfred Hitchcock reportedly once said. "At one moment we play this note, and get this reaction, and then we play that chord and they react."

Hitchcock and other terror masters understood the power of imagination. And while it can spur us to quick action, it can also paralyze us. Watch a YouTube video of riders on Six Flags' Lex Luthor: Drop of Doom holding their breath as they plummet 40 stories in five seconds, or note your reaction to Hitchcock's famous shower scene in *Psycho*, as Bernard Herrmann's violin-heavy score screeches in the background. I know respected speakers who still tense up when they go on stage at conferences, fearful that they won't remember their cues or that an audience might reject their presentation. "Fear is pain arising from the anticipation of evil," wrote Aristotle.

So why do people fear Bitcoin? It bears no resemblance to a horror flick, hair-raising ride, or life-threatening experience. It is simply a means of exchange, a tool that makes commerce easier and may one day transform personal finance and the daily transactions that are part of society's cloth. It endangers no person or thing, not even the fiat monetary system that some financial traditionalists fear it may usurp. Bitcoin will complement these systems for decades, maybe more—that is, unless Bitcoin proves itself more useful in all transactions. Then my guess is that even the most diehard traditionalists will accept it.

Some critics and more casual consumers have raised general concerns about Bitcoin's fragility, arguing that it may be a fad of which investors will tire or will end when it reveals a weakness or something better replaces it. As soon as the fad ends, demand will sink and the market will dry up. Investors will lose much of their holdings, and Bitcoin could even disappear entirely. These perceptions are ludicrous, of course, but they remain part of the ongoing Bitcoin dialogue. Too many people simply don't know that Bitcoin's sturdiness is one of its greatest strengths. It was engineered and designed to be this way. The steady growth in users underlines this point. There are a lot of smart people who are participating now, and this trend will not change. As for something better in the future, I'm always open to improvement. But it will take a lot to create a system with parts that fit more perfectly and that provides a better, more consumer-minded system of exchange and global digital store of value.

In the previous chapter, I explained why Bitcoin isn't really that volatile if you consider the big picture. Volatility probably is the number one fear that people have about Bitcoin. They are hesitant to buy bitcoin or are too quick to divest from the market because they fear the price could fall to penny stock levels or even evaporate completely at some point. How wrong they've been, and will be, as bitcoin's price heads north in the upcoming years.

But people fear accidents and criminality nearly as much as volatility. The more sordid episodes from Bitcoin's past—the hacks and loss of bitcoins that have occurred every year—still mark it as susceptible. They worry about regulatory foot dragging. If Bitcoin is such a boon to economic growth, why aren't regulators moving faster? And as social impact issues have played a bigger role in investment decisions, they have grown more concerned about Bitcoin's impact on the environment. Mining groups use a significant amount of electricity.

Bitcoin doubters and some supporters, as well, have other fears. Some of these fears simply underscore what they perceive as a lack of industry progress. They are less concerned with how far Bitcoin has come than why it hasn't done better, particularly in recent times. They are looking for quick payoffs or a landscape that would seem to guarantee profitability quickly. Such preferences are also part of human nature. Inculcating a long-term investment view is challenging when bitcoin's price news is the top story on the web pages of all major industry publications. But some fears also reflect a deep misunderstanding of Bitcoin. People have attached qualities to Bitcoin that it does not possess. They identify Bitcoin with price fluctuations, shady dealings, cyber hijinks, and extreme complexity, instead of deconstructing it so that they might judge Bitcoin on its own merits. The end result has been to hamper Bitcoin's wider use.

A 2018 survey by cryptocurrency lending platform CreditCoin found that 44 percent of consumers said that their biggest concern about bitcoin was the difficulty in purchasing it.[1] I agree very much. I think the second biggest hurdle for people is learning how to store their bitcoins. The study of 1,000 people also found that about two in three millennials, who now compose the largest demographic in the US population, worried about security. The younger age groups, who have grown up with technology, harbored the same concerns. A separate 2019 survey by Grayscale, the provider of cryptocurrency investment funds and CoinDesk sister company, found that of the nearly 65 percent of investors who didn't own bitcoin, almost 90 percent said their lack of interest resulted from not knowing enough about it.[2] Well, I hope they all get to read this book!

"Crypto is so complicated for 99% of the population," tech billionaire Mark Cuban said in a 2019 YouTube interview with *Wired* magazine.[3] "Do you put it in a device? Do you print it out? How do you keep from being hacked, and who's going to host it for you?"

Fearful of the mysterious harpooner Queequeg whom he encounters for the first time, Ishmael, the narrator of *Moby Dick*, famously says that "ignorance is the parent of fear." People overcome their terrors about something once they understand it, and that includes dissecting its counterarguments and concerns. Ishmael grows to admire Queequeg, tattoos, carry-on shrunken head, and all.

I believe that with time and effort, people will overcome their fears of Bitcoin, although as I've already written, it will take a willingness to plunge in. That includes looking critically at Bitcoin's faults. "Inaction breeds doubt and fear," wrote Dale Carnegie, an early twentieth-century forefather of self-help literature, in his *How to Win Friends and Influence People.* "Action breeds confidence and courage. If you want to conquer fear, do not sit home and think about it. Go out and get busy." This cannot be truer about Bitcoin. Go out and buy some bitcoin already.

Or as gonzo journalist Hunter Thompson wrote in his semi-autobiographical take on the counterculture, *Fear and Loathing in Las Vegas*: "Buy the ticket, take the ride."

In the ensuing paragraphs I'll consider five of the biggest fears people have about Bitcoin and why these fears are misplaced. But I encourage you to look beyond these. The more you're able to work out your deepest concerns, the more comfortable you'll be with Bitcoin, and the more likely to invest in it.

THERE'S NO FDIC OR EQUIVALENT INSURANCE FOR BITCOIN

The Franklin Roosevelt Administration created the Federal Deposit Insurance Corporation (FDIC) as part of the Banking Act of 1933, sometimes called the Glass-Steagall Act, named for the two lawmakers who introduced the legislation, Virginia Democratic Senator Carter Glass and Alabama Congressman Henry Steagall. Glass-Steagall prevented FDIC members, namely commercial banks, from trading stocks, buying non-investment-grade securities, or underwriting or distributing non-government securities. These now-banned speculative activities had doomed thousands of commercial banks in the late 1920s and led to the Great Depression. Glass-Steagall ensured that commercial banks would concentrate on their core loan and deposit businesses, with investment banks focusing on the securities market. Neither could take on businesses of the other.

The FDIC was a built-in safeguard for consumers who had lost their savings amid rampant bank failures. The FDIC generates income from its assessments of FDIC member banks and investments. Today, it provides up to $250,000 of protection per account. (That FDIC protection used to be just $100,000 not too long ago, which strongly suggests that even it knows how money loses its value over time.) Five board members, all appointed by the president and generally career bankers, oversee policy. It is the ultimate fiat monetary system insider organization, and it is indeed centralized.

Given Bitcoin's structure, why would it require the FDIC or any other organization—governmental or otherwise—to provide insurance? There is no central organization or group of organizations to potentially fail. As an analogy, just look at gold: There is no global gold organization to insure the value of gold. If you lose it, it's your loss! With Bitcoin, consumers can control every aspect of their transactions and have direct control of their digital bitcoin. If a consumer were to lose a bitcoin by forgetting the private key, or even in the unlikely event of wallet theft, how could an insurer correct the unfortunate event? Even if an agency could somehow provide insurance individually to every bitcoin holder in the world, it could not take back possession of the bitcoin. Remember, once a bitcoin transaction has been sent out and confirmed on the Bitcoin blockchain, it can never be recalled and there is no recourse. Similarly, if any of the 21 million bitcoins that Satoshi Nakamoto created is lost due to user error or loss of the private key, then it is forever inaccessible. The "lost" bitcoins are still part of the 21 million total on the Bitcoin blockchain, but it's inaccessible to you—effectively not yours anymore.

Ask the Mt. Gox account holders who are unlikely ever to see the return of any of the 650,000 bitcoins still missing. Or consider the case of Gerald Cotten, the Canadian entrepreneur who died unexpectedly at age 30 in 2019 of complications from Crohn's disease. He died without sharing the private keys to more than $140 million in bitcoin and other cryptocurrencies that investors stored on his Quadriga CX exchange. The aftermath was messy for investors. Some believed Quadriga was a scam, and at different points sent death threats to Cotten's wife and requested that his body be exhumed because they suspected that he faked his own death. As this book went to press, the matter was still unfolding in Canadian courts, but my guess is that it will never be fully resolved.

Compare Bitcoin's nature to gold. If you were to buy gold or gold jewelry somewhere and then accidentally dropped your purchase overboard into the ocean during a cruise vacation, it could be gone forever. My grandparents took a huge risk during their early years by smuggling gold out of the country on a ship. If someone had stolen the coat the gold was sewn into, the gold would likely have been irretrievable. Or if a curious immigration official had confiscated that gold, they would have had little if any recourse. The same is true with Bitcoin.

In each of these instances, a central organization could have no effect.

You could even say that the very existence of an FDIC organization is an argument for Bitcoin. The agency's purpose is to protect a system of which it plays an integral part. Why should the FDIC work to eliminate itself? Like virtually every regulatory body, the FDIC seeks to perpetuate itself. But for argument's sake, suppose that the FDIC didn't exist to protect consumers from bank failure and the loss of funds. I would suggest that the Federal Reserve would treat these events as it has other financial crises by printing more money. Such measures, as I've already written, represent one of our current monetary system's biggest failings, devaluing money in a seemingly endless spiral. Money printing, which leads to inflation and a loss of purchasing power by everyone who holds the currency, is essentially an unlawful blanket tax on the whole population. I despise that.

To be sure, you could reasonably insure a physical part of the Bitcoin ecosystem, such as a hardware or paper wallet, or find some way to protect assets you keep parked on an exchange. That would be your choice, and for small amounts, hardly worth the expense.

Remember that Bitcoin's biggest protection is that you are in control of the information (the private keys) that gives you full, exclusive access and ownership of your bitcoin. There's no third party to guard against. Keep your private keys safe and make proper and secure backups if possible, and even consider allowing your trusted family and friends to have access to your bitcoins. This way, if you ever become incapacitated, your bitcoins will still be around and accessible by someone. I've suggested a few approaches to security. You'll have to determine the system that works best for you. I can assure you that whatever you choose, it won't require a central government agency to protect your holdings.

YOU MIGHT LOSE YOUR BITCOIN

Everyone loses things.

Socks! (How many people have drawerfuls of single socks?) Books that they're two chapters away from completing. House keys. Even computer files or USB thumb drives that you occasionally store in the wrong place.

I don't mean to sound trite. Although I'm well organized, I've also occasionally misplaced an item or two. It's a frustrating experience. But losing things is also simply a by-product of life's daily bustle. We also forget important information. Human memory is fallible. Our brain cannot always process and remember all the things it must track. As much as I wish Bitcoin had magical properties that would make it unlosable, it has the same susceptibility to loss as any other item in someone's life. In most cases, the only difference is that the loss of a private key (or keys if you have more than one wallet or bitcoin account) may cost you a lot of money. Perhaps the value of bitcoin holdings is their biggest defense against loss.

After all, the more valuable something is, the more careful you'll be to secure it. We don't leave big amounts of cash or valuable jewelry lying around in the open. We're careful to build redundancy into how we keep our passwords to our online banking accounts. But nothing we do to secure any type of sensitive information is perfectly foolproof, including how we ensure that we will always have access to our bitcoin. Because we are human, there's always a possibility, albeit often remote, that we may forget what we did with something, or that even our well-intentioned backup systems will fail.

What we can do is reduce the likelihood of such a mass foul-up by thinking through our bitcoin storage methods meticulously. I've covered this issue to some extent in the previous sections of this chapter. You'll note again here the importance of choosing a storage method that is most comfortable for you. I myself have created a complicated system using various storage products and multiple locations. This somewhat intricate system works for me because of my engineering background and long experience with Bitcoin. You may choose a different less convoluted option and be equally safe and satisfied.

If you choose an online or exchange wallet, follow the provider's instruction carefully to use the service properly. Most importantly, understand the natural risks of third-party custody if you're storing your bitcoins on a custodial wallet or service provider. I humbly say that in my experience, the level of security is much lower than what these service providers claim.

If you decide to store your bitcoins yourself using a paper or hardware wallet, ensure you know where it is and build in redundancy, in case something happens to your main wallet. A backup is always recommended, assuming that you're sophisticated enough to know how to make a reliable backup that's also safe from theft. (Remember, the more copies you make, the more vulnerable your bitcoins are to theft.) Unfortunately, most new users will not have the skills necessary to make a safe and effective backup, and in so doing, they might actually worsen the security of the wallet through the well-intentioned process of backing it up. Despite all the potential difficulties, remember that fear of losing your bitcoin is no reason not to invest.

FUTURE CRACKDOWNS MAY HURT THE BITCOIN MARKET

I lived through the two of the most significant crackdowns in Bitcoin's short history, both in China. In December 2013, the same year I took over running the BTCChina exchange, and with Bitcoin activity booming throughout the country, the government over the course of three weeks determined that Bitcoin was not a currency and outlawed banks and payment processors from working with Bitcoin exchanges. By the end of the third week that month, bitcoin's price had declined by nearly 50 percent after cracking the $1,000 level in late November. The price drop continued the following years, and stayed low through 2016, falling below $300 on several occasions. I didn't know if the government's action would freeze mining and trading volume, which had been steadily increasing. China already dominated mining hash power and had arguably the world's most enthusiastic Bitcoin community at the time, which is why I saw so much potential in BTCChina and BTCC. What could it all mean? You can imagine my distress as the CEO of China's—and at one point the world's—largest Bitcoin exchange.

Four years later, in 2017, the Chinese government struck again, banning cryptocurrency exchanges altogether. The business press jumped on the news as Chinese mining and crypto trading activity had remained unmatched by any other country. By this time, I was already planning to accept an acquisition offer for BTCC, so the government's decision didn't affect me. I was more confident about Bitcoin's future than ever as trading volumes surged worldwide toward the end of 2017, and there were other signs of Bitcoin's acceptance. Even if the Chinese government tried to crush Bitcoin again for the second time, it wasn't going to die, but rather would continue to flourish globally.

The relentless crackdown may have had something to do with the price drop from over $20,000, the highest in bitcoin's history, to under $4,000 over the next four months. But then again, the decline may have been due to one or a combination of other factors. There's never a single correct answer.

More importantly, the Bitcoin community's reaction—or perhaps lack of reaction—following the Chinese hard stop and its 2013 and 2017 attempts to gain more control over Bitcoin demonstrated how it was ultimately unaffected by governmental or other intervention. It was a great real-world test for Bitcoin, to see if it was truly censorship resistant as it was designed and built to be. Even as China has maintained its iron grip on Bitcoin exchanges and bank interactions with Bitcoin within the country, trading and mining has reached new highs in China and worldwide. The mainstream press has grown increasingly interested in bitcoin's movements, even creating cryptocurrency/blockchain beats.

Of course, some countries like Bitcoin more than others. There are still governments, largely of authoritarian strains, such as Bolivia and Bahrain, that outlaw it completely, or others that outlaw any relationship between Bitcoin and banks, including Russia, Saudi Arabia, and Iran. They see their banking systems as an extension of their rule and fear losing control of the movement of currency.

But no attempt to rein in Bitcoin anywhere globally will dent its growth. Bitcoin operates above any governmental fray.

Trying to limit what it can do would be like trying to limit the air we breathe. The air we breathe is out in the open, available for everyone on earth. The same is true for Bitcoin.

BITCOIN MINING NETWORKS WILL BE TOO COSTLY AND HARMFUL TO THE ENVIRONMENT

Satoshi Nakamoto designed the Bitcoin system, but Bitcoin miners have been its builders, verifying the groups—or blocks—of Bitcoin transactions that are the foundation of its public decentralized blockchain platform. Without miners, there is no one to solve the mathematical equations that ensure that a transaction occurred and that no one used the same bitcoin for two different transactions. Miners are the creators of the public ledger that ensures that Bitcoin is accurate and incorruptible.

Due to its permissionless nature, bitcoin mining continues to use up a lot of electricity, more and more every year. The latest generation of mining gear are powerful, sophisticated computers dedicated entirely to the task of mining bitcoin. A decent-quality bitcoin mining rig typically costs more than $2,000, and some can run into six figures. Because mining has become competitive, many miners have joined forces and pooled together their hash power. To increase their chances of solving the block algorithm before another mining pool, and earning the so-called block reward, most bitcoin mining operations run nonstop, 24 hours a day. It is this block reward compensation that financially motivates miners to continue participating.

I mined my first bitcoin using rudimentary GPU graphics cards on a hand-built PC computer in the summer of 2011. Mining hadn't proven itself as a major way to make money, so there were fewer miners globally. But even my small rig—if one could even call it a rig—heated up my apartment room and more than doubled my usual monthly electricity bill.

As bitcoin mining has become more difficult, the mining costs have increased, albeit with an occasional blip when energy prices decline or some new source of electricity emerges. Low electricity prices in the mining hub of Sichuan, China, for example, kept mining costs from rising as was expected after the May 2020 halving, in which the bitcoin reward fell from 12.5 to 6.25 bitcoins. Still, in early 2020, researchers from TradeBlock predicted that mining a bitcoin would cost $12,000 to $15,000, depending on hash rates.[4] Is that enough reward to justify the investment? What if mining profits continue to climb as bitcoin's price increases, increasing the population of miners and energy needs?

After accounting for the fixed and variable costs to bitcoin mining, the margins are usually small. Even if bitcoin prices go higher, mining margins don't increase accordingly because mining hardware manufacturers end up increasing the prices for the machines, limiting the profitability of new miners. According to the Bitcoin Energy Consumption Index of the Digiconomist, which tracks digital energy trends, miners earned $3.59 billion in revenue but paid $3.48 billion—or about 97 percent of their income—for electricity.[5] Due to the free market nature of bitcoin mining, the overall mining industry revenues will always be higher than the costs, but not necessarily by a large margin.

But I would argue that this is a supply and demand issue, not unlike the historic landscape for other industries in their early years. There's only room for so many companies and practitioners, and gradually some fall away, unable to remain competitive. If some bitcoin miners feel they do not see a way to be profitable, then they will stop mining. The result will be that the overall mining difficulty will decline, making it slightly easier for the remaining miners still going at it. Digiconomist modeled that miners will one day spend only 60 percent of their revenue on power. I don't quite believe that, as increased competition will reduce the profitability of those miners. As long as

Bitcoin proves itself superior to the fiat monetary system, there will always be miners and enough energy to support them.

Bitcoin's overall potential stress on the power grid and effect on overall energy pricing are also a supply and demand issue. Some Bitcoin observers, including lawmakers, are concerned about how much energy Bitcoin uses and will need in the future. Indeed, according to Digiconomist, a single bitcoin transaction on the blockchain consumes about 684 kilowatts of energy, the same as the average US household uses in about 23 days.[6] Over a year, bitcoin transactions use roughly the same amount of energy as Colombia, a country with nearly 50 million people, twenty-ninth most in the world, and more than the Czech Republic and Switzerland. Bitcoin accounts for more than 13 percent of Germany's and Canada's energy consumption, more than 16 percent of France's, and 24 percent of the United Kingdom's.[7] A single Bitcoin transaction uses about six times as much energy as over 100,000 Visa transactions.

Amid heightened concerns about the environment, Bitcoin will have to work hard to convince people that it is not an environmental hazard. Digiconomist researchers say that Bitcoin's annual carbon footprint is about equal to Denmark's, and a single transaction generates as much carbon waste as about 790,000 Visa transactions or watching nearly 48,000 hours of YouTube online. This massive footprint reflects China's dominant mining position—the country accounts for approximately two-thirds of all global mining activity—and reliance on coal to produce electricity. China is the world's largest producer and consumer of coal-based energy, and not coincidentally, also the world's largest emitter of CO_2 emissions. But it has also been sensitive to heated criticism from other countries that it needs to do better environmentally, recognizing that this issue is increasingly important for economic growth as more consumers weigh social and environmental impact in their buying decisions. As China and other countries improve their environmental records, Bitcoin will limit its carbon impact.

GOVERNMENTS WILL NEVER ACCEPT BITCOIN

Some people just won't accept a movement, trend, or enterprise unless it has the blessing of a central authority. They equate such acceptance with legitimacy and look for guidance from the organizations they trust to set policy and pass legislation, even when they profess to dislike their leaders. This desire is part of a human urge for order, which I covered in Chapter 4. Government, even in its earliest forms, served as a stabilizing force socially, politically, and economically, establishing rules for interaction and determining when something might pose a threat. Monetary policy and the regulation of commerce has arguably been its most important responsibility, falling only behind defense.

So, it is not unexpected that people would look to governments for some acknowledgment that Bitcoin is a reasonable and safe store of value and means of exchange. But as I've mentioned, it is also completely unnecessary. Bitcoin doesn't need any endorsement. And it does not require any special set of rules. In fact, if the US Congress's multiple subcommittee sessions did not produce any new regulations, doesn't that imply that Bitcoin as it now exists is not a threat to individual users?

Naturally, it would be nice to have some clarity regarding taxation and to see national legislators get around to allowing a Bitcoin ETF and creating a few other minor rules. And in an ideal world, I would like to hear governments endorse Bitcoin's merits and perhaps even use bitcoin for some of their own dealings. All of this would draw the notice of investors and would be a boon to the bitcoin market.

But none of this needs to occur on any timeline, if at all. Bitcoin's merits are clear to anyone who studies it closely, regardless of what governments say. "Things done well and with a care, exempt themselves from fear," wrote William Shakespeare or his collaborator John Fletcher in *Henry the VIII*. Bitcoin was done well and carefully. There is nothing to fear.

A BETTER WAY OF DOING BUSINESS

Some of Bitcoin's doubters and the uninformed have likened it to play money or virtual Monopoly money. It's a facile argument that may have something to do with the word itself, which to some casual observers sounds like a Parker Brothers or Electronic Arts game. Even Bitcoin's gold ₿ logo evokes something vaguely fictional with its Ubuntu Bold Italic font. This script could hardly differ more from the formal Banknote Roman of US dollars that practically screams corporate. Note that Ubuntu Bold Italic first appeared only about a year after Bitcoin first launched, while Banknote Roman's origins extend back to nineteenth-century mechanized lettering.

Against the evidence, the skeptics and know-nothings say that similar to play money, you can't use bitcoin to purchase many things. Few brick-and-mortar retailers, e-commerce sites, and service organizations take bitcoin, they argue. Nor can you directly pay your utility bills or buy a house, stock, or a rare work of art with it. You would first have to sell your bitcoin and then convert it to regular money.

Skeptics also note bitcoin's lack of a physical existence. How can something denote real physical value if there's no coin or note you can hold? They compare it to virtual, make-believe currencies that are integral pieces of some video and arcade games, often serving as rewards that encourage participation. The currencies have no worth except to accumulate new characters, tools, or other features within the game's confines. As soon as someone stops playing, the virtual currency might as well not exist. These games, of course, fade from memory, replaced by the next cool thing.

All these arguments reflect a deep misunderstanding that I've highlighted in earlier chapters.

People don't know what to make of Bitcoin, so they concoct bogus comparisons that allow them to explain it away quickly. "It's no better than Monopoly money," is easier to explain than a more detailed counteranalysis that won't stand up to scrutiny. The Bitcoin as fictional currency argument reflects a fear that Bitcoin has substance—that it's all it's cracked up to be. In many cases, it mirrors how someone's personal experiences shape their opinions.

Bitcoin hasn't been part of their world, so they're not yet open to its possibilities. Their banks, credit cards, and other financial services have addressed their needs, so why praise an alternative system that operates outside this universe? And if they can't use it, how can bitcoin be valuable? Moreover, how can it help anyone's life if there's nowhere to spend it? These questions raise concerns about bitcoin's investment potential. If it possesses no utility, how can it be a good investment? Why would people want it? And if demand is slack, why should its price do anything but flounder?

But these questions are all based on false assumptions. The creation of Bitcoin coincides with the arrival of a new, more global economy and addresses crucial, longstanding social and economic issues that threaten to undermine this economy's growth. At the core, many people are unaware how many people do not have the ability to participate in current banking systems.

BANKED AND UNBANKED

If you live in an industrialized country or a big city in a developing economy, like Kuala Lumpur, Montevideo, Kampala, Dar es Salaam, or Abidjan where I grew up in the Ivory Coast, you probably have a bank and easy access to cash through branches and ATMs. For example, the United States has about 77,000[1] retail branches, or roughly 31 for every 100,000 people.[2] France and Japan have approximately 39 branches per similar capita, and Italy has 40 branches per similar capita.[3] Walk down a major boulevard in big cities in these countries and you can hardly travel a block without seeing a bank branch or ATM or both. Even in my US hometown of Las Vegas, hardly a banking mecca, I can reach a dozen or more branches and ATMs in under 10 minutes from the Strip.

Such convenience can make you oblivious to places that operate without it, and there are a lot of them. Recent technological advances in fintech and beyond have bypassed huge swathes of the world. Many people cannot deposit checks or cash, withdraw money, or move money conveniently. And for small business owners looking to expand, borrowing money is not possible.

Some people say that the global economy is a sign of progress, and to be sure, the number of people with access to banking services has increased. A 2018 World Bank financial inclusion report (Global Findex), a biannual measurement of consumer access to banking funded by the Bill & Melinda Gates Foundation, found that the percentage of the global population with banking accounts rose from 51 percent in 2011 to 69 percent in 2017, to a total of 3.8 billion people, an increase of 1.2 billion, a development that World Bank Group President Jim Yong Kim referred to as "great strides . . . in connecting people to formal financial services." The gains also reflected improvements in mobile technology.[4]

But this progress has been uneven among the six regions that the Findex measures. For example, 70 percent of the population in South Asia now have accounts, a 23 point increase from 2016 when the World Bank released its previous Findex. This spike resulted largely from initiatives in India, the world's most populated country, which has been modernizing its economy and pushing financial inclusion. The other five regions that the report targeted experienced smaller increases in bank accounts and less progress in expanding mobile banking.

More importantly, the report found that a whopping 1.7 billion people, roughly 31 percent of the global adult population, still do not have banking accounts. Just 52 percent of men and 35 percent of women in the Middle East and North Africa region have accounts. In Europe and Central Asia, which includes some of the world's most industrialized countries, only 65 percent of the adult population possesses accounts. And in Sub-Saharan Africa, as many as 95 million people who earn their living in agriculture receive their payments in cash.

Many of the rural outskirts of these countries have limited access to running water, electricity, and other utilities, and very little opportunity for traditional banking infrastructure or, in some cases, even for computer connectivity. Many of these communities lack electricity, clean water, and sanitation. About 940 million people globally don't have electricity, while over 660 million people live without access to safe water. In some cases, there is simply not enough population density to support a bank branch.

The gap in financial services has contributed to a vicious spiral in poverty, health, and environmental problems, and worsening mortality rates. The World Bank estimates that about 10 percent of the world's population, nearly 750 million people, live on less than $2 a day, and that the number is likely to rise in the aftermath of the COVID-19 pandemic.[5]

A widely distributed study by the National Center for Children in Poverty found that a third to nearly half of US adults who spent at least half their childhood living in moderate to high levels of poverty were poor in their early and middle adult years, and that even lesser poverty levels could doom children throughout their lives. The authors attributed this ongoing condition to a lack of educational, healthcare, and other resources crucial for development. "Children growing up in low-income families face many challenges that children from more advantaged families do not," the authors wrote, adding: "Because the negative effects of deprivation on human development tend to cumulate, individuals with greater exposure to poverty during childhood are likely to have more difficulty escaping poverty as adults."[6]

Researchers who study underserved communities see financial inclusion as a linchpin to creating individual opportunities and stimulating a community's economic growth. "In recent years, financial inclusion has been perceived as a dynamic tool for attaining multidimensional macroeconomic stability, sustainable and inclusive economic growth, employment generation, poverty reduction, and income equality for advanced and developing countries," the authors of an April 2020 paper on financial inclusion in the *Journal of Economic Structures* wrote. They added: "Despite decades of rapid progress in reducing poverty and boosting prosperity, a large portion of the world's poorer population still struggles to attain a minimum standard of living across developing regions, especially in Asia, Africa, and Latin America and the Caribbean."[7]

Among the report's six conclusions, the authors recommended that financial institutions partner with central banks, governments, and development groups to create financial infrastructures "and upgrade the financial services network in rural and urban areas," and that countries work "to boost financial literacy." While these are noble goals, they showcase the limitations of these organizations and their entrenched ways of looking at problems. Unfortunately, a significant amount of scholarship looks at inclusion and poverty with the same blinders, prescribing remedies based on traditional financial systems.

But this paper also hints at a solution that can be truly transformational innovation. The authors wrote that "financial institutions should cater innovative and need based formal financial services suited to financially excluded segments of the population as the demand for financial services varies due to differences in culture, customs, beliefs, and income levels" and that "policies should initiate necessary actions regarding specific socio-economic constraints, macroeconomic volatility, institutional inefficiencies, and financial system inefficiencies at country level to promote a more inclusive financial system."

Banks have tried hard to develop innovations to make banking more attainable. PayPal, Venmo, and other online payment services have addressed the problem of accessibility and transformed personal money management. More recently, nonfinancial services firms have entered the fray, launching payment initiatives that they will manage. Apple, Amazon, Facebook, and Google, among other tech, telecommunications, and service giants that are looking for new revenue streams, have started to recast themselves as one-stop shops able to accommodate an increasingly wide range of consumer needs. They are posing the question whether global, multifaceted brands that already infiltrate many people's lives are also best equipped to serve people's financial needs. This belief is probably what accounted for Facebook's decision to explore launching its Libra digital cryptocurrency. I give them credit for trying something new.

This same rationale has also drawn hoots of derision from consumer groups and legislators concerned that such efforts will amount to monopolies. They raise reasonable points, and the decentralist in me is skeptical they can succeed. Why would anyone want to allocate more responsibility, particularly for our financial affairs, to firms that already know so much about us through their sophisticated data collection? I see this as an understandable but wrongheaded probe by firms that have the size and technological ability to offer financial services, but are already too enmeshed in our lives. I think it's questionable at best whether they will be able to replace financial services firms.

THE MOST INNOVATIVE SYSTEM OF ALL

All of this leads us inevitably to Bitcoin. What new technological development is more innovative or on point in solving financial inclusiveness, and by extension the various problems that it creates? Digital banking and cryptocurrency represent the future.

The Global Findex report noted that about 66 percent of the world's unbanked people have mobile phones. And it found that much of the spike in accounts throughout the five regions resulted from the opening of mobile accounts and had nothing to do with brick-and-mortar retail banking. In Sub-Saharan Africa, while the percentage of people with banking accounts remained the same, the percentage of people with mobile accounts doubled. In the Caribbean and South American region, about one in five people make use of digital payment systems, while in the Pacific Rim, Europe, and central Asia, the government is using digital platforms to pay workers, which has forced workers to open mobile accounts. This shift offers particular benefits for women, who traditionally have been left out or only had a minor role in many underserved families' finances. "When the government deposits social welfare payments or other subsidies directly into women's digital bank accounts, the impact is amazing. Women gain decision-making power in their homes, and with more financial tools at their disposal they invest in their families' prosperity and help drive broad economic growth," said Melinda Gates, cochair of the Bill & Melinda Gates Foundation.

Mobile services have certainly made my life easier by allowing me to check balances and execute certain transactions when I'm not able to reach a bank or have access to a computer. An increasing number of people undoubtedly feel the same. A 2018 survey by Morning Consult for the American Bankers Association found that that 7 in 10 consumers used a bank's mobile app to manage their banking accounts and more than 90 percent of them rated their online experiences good or very good.[8] But I would add, with just a little snark, that their satisfaction, particularly among older consumers, comes from comparing online banking to earlier systems. Most consumers know little beyond the mobile-based platforms used by banks and payment service firms.

Mobile banking suffers from exactly the problems inherent in all aspects of banking. It builds in the same account management rules that create obstacles even as it aims to make you feel more secure about your assets. In a 2018 note based on its most recent Survey of Household Economics and Decisionmaking, the Federal Reserve found that nearly one in four consumers who used mobile banking apps for general reasons deemed them unsafe or very unsafe.[9] More than half who used them for specific purposes held the same view.

The concern extends to financial apps, in general, which have become more popular as a way to bring further efficiency to financial management. In 2019, a study by The Pew Charitable Trusts found that 30 percent of consumers did not make mobile payments because they were concerned about losing funds.[10] A separate 2018 survey by The Clearing House, a nearly 175-year-old trade group and payment systems provider, found that two in three consumers were very or extremely concerned about their data privacy and information sharing. Many of them were unaware that these apps shared personal data with other third parties, and nearly half said they would be less likely to use these apps had they known.[11]

The survey also cited a study by the consultancy AT Kearney that found that fewer than half the financial apps in existence, including Amazon and other large retailers, credit cards such as Visa and American Express, and payment services such as

PayPal, could not safeguard personal data. Only three in five consumers said that banking apps could do so. "The financial services ecosystem is built on trust between consumers and companies; failure to live up to consumers' expectations and keep their information safe puts that trust at risk," the Clearing House authors wrote. "There is a need for a concerted effort by all stakeholders—including banks, fintechs, data aggregators, regulators, and consumers—to ensure data security."[12]

Aren't these issues that Bitcoin was built to solve? I've mentioned my difficulties on more than one occasion in sending money to loved ones, including limits on the amounts, short-notice rules changes, and delays in completing transfers. I realize that I'm financially comfortable enough to tolerate these delays, but they are annoying. They are also unnecessary.

And imagine if my family desperately needed the transfers. More than one billion people—almost one-seventh of the world's population—depends on remittances that are often enabled by banks, pay platforms, and transfer services that may have their own storefronts or operate within other retail businesses. Such money is often crucial for families to buy food and pay bills. According to a UN report, about three in every four remittance dollars cover "essential things," including food and housing expenses. In crises, this money can also offset the loss of crops due to weather extremes and other emergencies. The remaining quarter, about $100 billion, often helps generate economic activity with its subsequent benefits to education, training, and job creation.

About half of remittances go to rural communities with the worst poverty rates, and totaled around $1 trillion in the last five years, an amount that is triple the foreign aid that relief and development groups funneled to the developing world over the same period. The UN believes this capital can eventually help achieve 7 of its 17 Achievable Development Goals, a 2015 initiative meant to address poverty, environmental, social, and other global problems.

Yet remittances can also be costly to send. Organizations that execute these transactions charge an average 7 percent of the amounts sent, and the average for Sub-Saharan Africa is 9 percent. Most remittances range from $200 to $300, so those fees take a sizable bite from the totals. These are huge service charges, all because some intermediary remittance and payment company is forcibly there in the middle, charging a toll for a simple task that can now be done practically for free using Bitcoin.

Could Bitcoin, which excludes any third-party intervention and requires only a mobile phone, be the alternative? Absolutely. Wouldn't it make the sending of remittances and other money both cheaper and easier? For sure. Then what's the downside? The existing incumbent businesses would lose out on this very profitable remittance business.

As long as the sender and receiver have digital wallets, transactions could take just minutes, all without relying on any central entities such as banks or payment companies. It would also improve on current systems in protecting personal data and assets from hacking.

Bitcoin would offer the same advantages for small businesses in the developing world to sell their products. They would avoid the massive payment processing fees that banks charge these enterprises, allowing them to reach markets miles and even continents away. Their ability to sell in places outside their own small geographic circle would likely help them prosper beyond what would have been previously feasible. They could save on fees and receive payments faster. All of this could reverse the downward spiral of worsening poverty that I outlined earlier in this chapter.

Some people have argued that completing bitcoin transactions takes too long as miners must verify blocks of data. The average time to confirm a transaction in 2020 was about nine minutes, which represented a three-minute improvement over the rate in 2019. Mining pools will quickly reject a transaction that is an attempted double spend or does not compute in some other way. Compare bitcoin's transaction rate to those of major credit cards, which can process millions of purchases in an hour. For example, Visa's platform can process about 65,000 transactions in a single minute.

Bitcoin's platform may never reach this speed, but I believe it will get faster without compromising its other advantages over credit and debit cards and other payment methods. Will society ever use bitcoin to pay for coffee? I wouldn't be surprised years into the future if that does happen. It would be a logical progression in civilization's payment systems. But whether bitcoin becomes a national or de facto global daily currency is not important at this point.

Consider Bitcoin an economic enabler. It is already helping some forward-thinking small businesses and will do so on an even larger scale in the future. It offers too many conveniences for entrepreneurs to pass up. Wise investors weigh the usefulness of a company's products or services before deciding to purchase its stock. The more useful the product or service, the more likely the company will attract customers, thrive financially, and generate higher stock prices. This is the path followed by virtually every successful company.

Bitcoin clearly is headed in the same direction as top-performing companies. It is being used more and more, and as this occurs, its price increases over time. Bitcoin is the soundest of investments.

HOW TO INVEST: BITCOIN'S WORLD OF GREAT RESOURCES

Let's assume if you've gotten this far in the book, you've decided to invest in bitcoin.

Congratulations.

You've overcome the doubters, the Bitcoin naysayers, the upholders of traditional monetary systems who've raised nearly every imaginable concern and smoke screen about digital currency.

You've passed the point where Bitcoin is an abstraction. You've taken the time to understand its logic and to review the resources for buying and holding it.

Most importantly, you've surmounted your fears.

Now you're ready to buy.

Ready, set . . . wait.

As is the case with any investment, you'll do better operating from a plan. Here I'll interject again that I am not an investment professional. Skilled financial managers spend years learning their craft and gathering experience that helps them advise clients correctly.

But as I've already said, investing depends largely on common sense, a quality that amateurs possess equally to professionals. Smart investors of all types start with some sort of blueprint that considers their stage in life and their near-time and long-term goals. Most importantly, they establish the level of risk they're willing to tolerate and the amount of money they want to allocate to various assets.

Then they create principles to guide their portfolio or to direct the individuals they hire to build and manage their portfolio according to agreed-upon principles. These are usually the most successful investors, and I'd like to think they represent a majority. "From the outset, every investor should form an investment strategy that serves as a framework to guide future decisions," according to the CFA Institute, the trade group of chartered financial analysts.[1]

THE FOUR MOST COMMON BITCOIN INVESTMENT MISTAKES

Yet there are still a lot of people who make mistakes in how they approach their investments. This is no different with bitcoin. Many bitcoin investors think short-term, act rashly, or choose wrongly, growing cautious when they should be bold or overreacting when caution is a better option. I have often witnessed these patterns in the questions that would-be and early bitcoin investors pose at conferences. Usually, they trail me and others whom they consider leaders of the Bitcoin movement following a presentation. They want to know the secret sauce of bitcoin investment success.

For this reason, in late 2017, I decided to pin what I think are the four most common bitcoin investment mistakes to my Twitter feed, believing these principles could guide the retail investor to a better Bitcoin experience. What I found over the years about inexperienced bitcoin investors was that:

- They were indecisive about buying bitcoin.
- Once they decided to, they didn't buy enough bitcoin.
- They sold too quickly after just a small gain.
- They sold their whole position out of panic when bitcoin prices dropped during a crash.

The end result is that these investors didn't benefit fully after committing intellectually to Bitcoin. They waded through the toughest part of becoming an investor but then missed opportunities to earn more on their investment because they didn't have enough patience. I accept that when investment conditions swirl, it's easy to opt for what is perceived as the safest route. But in my experience, bitcoin investors' biggest fault is lack of faith. They are like kids who swim comfortably in the deep end of a swimming pool but then become spooked when they think about where they are.

Let's evaluate the results of each mistake independently.

Mistake 1: Indecision to Buy Bitcoin

I regularly come across people who do all the prep work, decide on how much to invest, and then back off. Many of them approach me at conferences with stories about how they were ready to invest in bitcoin months or years earlier, but somehow didn't push forward and regretted their inaction. When I ask them why they didn't invest, they sheepishly say something that they wanted to wait for a better price. Then they usually ask me when they should invest. They seem to be asking for permission. They seem to be waiting for the perfect moment when prices are the lowest. (The irony is that if bitcoin prices did subsequently go down, they would be spooked and would back off, and not actually make the investment. Human nature!)

Let me tell you how I explain bitcoin investing during each of these encounters.

You don't need much time to invest—a purchase takes just minutes on most exchanges. And at this stage in Bitcoin's history, there is no bad timing. A day earlier or later won't make a big difference. It's not like anticipating a stock increase on news of a company's big deal where a delay can cost someone huge profits. Bitcoin doesn't correlate to traditional or financial news, and it isn't something anyone should be day-trading at this point or counting on for quick gains. It's too unpredictable. This type of technology needs time to ripen.

Forget about being picky on price. And don't worry if you can only buy part of a bitcoin. Once you've decided that bitcoin is a good investment, pop open your laptop or grab your smartphone or tablet and click buy. Over the long run, bitcoin's price is only going to increase significantly. And that's what you should care about—the long run. You'll land way ahead over time.

How many of you will put down this book right now and go buy some bitcoin? Don't wait and don't delay! Any waiting now will cause you to be more indecisive and lead to even more delay. It's what I call the vicious cycle of procrastination. Very few of you will have the strong will power to go out and buy bitcoin right now, as in *right now*. However, if you do go out and buy bitcoin while you're reading this chapter, please tell me in person next time you see me at a conference or other event. I'd love to meet you, as you'll be known as a member of my Chapter 11 Bitcoin Buyers Club—an exclusive group that took action and bought their first bitcoin while reading this chapter. Will you be a member?

Mistake 2: Not Buying Enough

It is laudable to weigh decisions carefully when money is involved. You don't shell out wads of cash or ring up huge credit card charges every time you visit the supermarket or some other retail store. You don't invest beyond what's reasonable, given your savings and income.

However, you also don't underspend when you need to spend more for items you need, or when making an investment that can lead to bigger long-term gains if you go in full force instead of in dribbles. Some of the most remorseful bitcoin investors I've met failed to dive in as fully as was within their means—in some cases as much as they had intended.

Consider my friend Stephen, an executive for a major international corporation, who bought his first bitcoin in 2015 after I'd encouraged him to investigate this new technology. Stephen was comfortable with technology. I respected how meticulously he approached things and I knew that he wouldn't jump into an investment just because we were friends, but rather would size it up from all angles. This was just the sort of convert I was seeking. I knew Bitcoin would be a good fit. Sure enough, Stephen did his due diligence, and I was pleased when he told me about his initial purchase in a text exchange.

Let me confess here, however, that I was also disappointed that Stephen didn't invest more. It was still Bitcoin winter, which would last through into 2016, as the industry rebounded from the hacking of the Mt. Gox exchange that had raised deep, fundamental concerns about Bitcoin. Prices had sunk under $300 from a 2014 high of near $1,000. It was a good time to scoop up multiple bitcoins inexpensively, before pricing recovered from its cybersecurity shock. For Stephen, an investment of even $5,000—a little more than 15 bitcoins—was well within his means.

Fast-forward four years and Stephen texted me that he had purchased 10 additional bitcoins—more than $50,000 worth based on its price at that point. This was after bitcoin had risen to its all-time high of over $20,000 in December 2017 before settling at a still respectable $5,000. I was excited to hear the news, particularly because Stephen had paid less attention to Bitcoin's price drop over the previous month and the I-told-you-so refrain of skeptics who saw it as proof of Bitcoin's flightiness. Instead, he had focused on its long-term potential. But Stephen was strangely less upbeat than he had been when he made his smaller 2015 investment. He wrote me that he wished he had purchased more bitcoin in 2015 instead of waiting until 2019.

Overall, I saw Stephen's experience as a win. He had ridden the ups and downs of bitcoin pricing to push to a new level of commitment. His original investment had multiplied by nearly 100-fold, and he operated in a world where, in a quiet way, he might have some influence over colleagues and others with whom he interacted. But Stephen's experience also reminded me of many other investors who complain about their timidity. They wind up buying less than they could have or should have and become regretful. As the twentieth-century novelist Kurt Vonnegut wrote, "Of all the words of mice and men, the saddest are 'it might have been'" (a variation of the poem "Maud Muller" by John Greenleaf Whittier).

Mistake 3: Not Waiting for Bigger Gains

If you were one of the few and the brave who discovered Bitcoin in June 2011 at the height of its first bubble, you could have purchased bitcoins for $31. That's an incredible bargain compared to today's pricing. But remember, at the beginning of 2011, bitcoin was selling for under a dollar. It did not reach the symbolically important threshold of equivalence with the dollar—one bitcoin equal to one US dollar—until February of that year.

Make no mistake, that was an important event psychologically. The milestone drew a few minor headlines in the news, and if you had been able to buy a few bitcoins at that price, you would have approached savant status, given how few people even knew about Bitcoin at the time. But you still would have been doing really well at $31.

If you had held those $31 bitcoins for two years, you would have multiplied your investment eight times. Bitcoin by April

2013 was selling at an all-time high of $266. That is not an unreasonable timeline for an investment to pay off at that level. Consider three of the world's highest-profile companies. If you'd acquired IBM two years after it went public, you would have had to wait 21 years for gains similar to bitcoin's; for Walmart, 7 years; and for Amazon, more than 15 years. Under normal circumstances, real estate, and certainly alternative investments (unless *Antiques Roadshow* determines that the portrait you just bought is a previously unknown Rembrandt) do not achieve these types of increases over two years.

Had you held your bitcoin through 2013, even after it topped $1,200 in November and held steady above $500 for most of 2014—still an 87 percent gain—you would have been much better off.

The scenario would have been much the same if you had bought in the $500 to $600 range in 2014 and held on until bitcoin surpassed the $1,000 mark again in January 2017—you would have doubled your investment. Or if you had bought at $1,000 and held until it reached $5,000 in September 2017—you would have realized a 400 percent increase on your investment in nine months.

In contrast, the best-performing US large company mutual fund that year, RidgeWorth Aggressive Growth, offered a 22 percent return to investors, according to the financial publication Kiplinger's annual top 10 rankings.[2] None of the nine other big company funds in the list bettered 16 percent yearly returns. Returns for US midsized and small company funds fell mostly in the teens or high single digits.

With one or two outliers, funds that focused on foreign companies, bonds, and alternative investments generated similar results. These performances came during a bull market in which stocks in the S&P 500 grew over 22 percent and the Dow Jones Industrial Average topped the 20,000 mark for the first time. A 2016 survey by Natixis Global Asset Management found that retail investors expected an 8.5 percent annual return on their portfolios, although financial managers said a 6 percent return was acceptable.[3]

Bitcoin's growth in less than a year shattered all those figures. And note that bitcoin was hardly finished; it reached $20,000 about two weeks before New Year's Day of 2018. But even if you had been one of the people fearful of missing out on the bitcoin tidal wave, you would have been wise to hold on. Bitcoin needed about three years to return to this same rarefied air. Nearly six months after the May 2020 halving, it hovered above $18,000. But should its price double or triple, or even go back down to under $10,000 in the next few years, you would be wise to hold on. Remember, HODL.

My favorite "wait for bigger gains" story involves my classmates from the China Europe International Business School, where I did my Global Executive MBA program from 2012 to 2014. Right after I became CEO of BTCChina, I had the opportunity to give a presentation about Bitcoin to my whole EMBA class of 60 students. It was June 2013, and that was the year when the term *Bitcoin* started to trickle into society more widely and the general public first started hearing about it. Bitcoin was only trading at around $100 at the time.

After giving that short presentation, my biggest regret was not thinking of the idea to forcefully insist every single classmate buy one bitcoin. It would have cost only about $6,000 for the whole class, for everyone to own one bitcoin. Instead, I only suggested that people should invest in bitcoin, and not surprisingly, only a few classmates listened to my advice.

Later that summer, my classmate Xiongbing confessed to me that he regretted not making the purchase in June. Prices had already gone up, but I told him it's not too late to invest in bitcoin, and I promptly helped him buy some at $120. He was a happy man.

And of course, 2013 was the year when bitcoin went on a FOMO (fear of missing out) rally, which propelled the price to $1,200 by November. Not only was I happy for my bitcoin investment, I was also happy for my many friends and CEIBS classmates who bought bitcoin that year, including Xiongbing. Unfortunately, unbeknownst to me, Xiongbing had already sold off his entire investment in October, when bitcoin hit $400. He had quickly tripled his investments in just a few months, so he decided to get out. I only found this out much later and was very sad to hear this story.

If only he had asked me for advice on when to sell, I would have made it clear to him: don't sell your bitcoin after just a small gain of two times or even five times your investment. Wait for the monster return of 100 times your investment. And if you do decide to sell, never sell your whole stash, as you should wait for the long-term gain of 1,000 times your investment. This could take 10 years, or even 20 years. If you think about it, it'll be worth the wait.

With all of the price volatility in 2014 and 2015, Xiongbing hesitated to get back in. For a long time, he actually could have bought back all of his bitcoins at an even lower price than what he had sold for. I constantly reminded him to buy back those bitcoins. But he didn't, maybe because he was spooked when the price dropped lower, or was waiting for an even lower price. Soon enough, bitcoin took off again in late 2016, and quickly rushed past its all-time high set in November 2013. The rest is history, and Xiongbing likely could not bring himself to buy back bitcoin at the high prices when I wrote this book.

As I have repeatedly told people who come to me looking for bitcoin investment advice, bitcoin's best days are ahead. Wait for gains of at least 100 times your investment price for at least some of your bitcoins. And even if you are inclined to sell then, be sure not to sell everything, and keep some until it reaches 1,000 times your initial investment. Yes, as long as you're patient enough, bitcoin really might increase to 1,000 times your original investment value. Do you believe me?

Mistake 4: Panic Selling

In September of 2017, the People's Bank of China asked all Bitcoin exchanges in China to shut down, allegedly over concerns that inexperienced retail investors could too easily lose their hard-earned savings by investing in cryptocurrencies, such as initial coin offering (ICO) tokens. (It was unfortunate that the government would lump bitcoin together with all of the other dubious ICO tokens, which are indeed quite risky and a prime candidate for fraud.) The truth was more likely that the government didn't like the lack of control it had over the new monetary system. The move shocked the global Bitcoin community, leading to a sharp decline in prices in mid September.

The drop followed a six-month run-up in prices during which I had convinced many of my employees at BTCC that it was a good time to buy again. I had made my usual strong arguments about Bitcoin's potential to transform society, and the importance of investing with long-term gains in mind. I told them that I anticipated their stake could increase 100 times or more in the years ahead. They just had to be patient and not get frightened by the price volatility. Easier said than done, of course.

They may have thought I'd randomly chosen 100 times as the potential growth multiplier for bitcoin. In any case, they clearly, didn't appreciate my message about staying with the investment. Instead, they let their concerns about the price falloff color their judgment. On the weekend after the exchange closure announcement, they told me with smiles that they'd sold their bitcoin, fearing for the worst now that China was going to take action against this nascent industry. (I later learned that many of my other friends also ended up selling their bitcoins at around the same time.)

They felt good because they had nearly tripled their investment. I was quiet, unwilling to spoil their good mood. They had made money, which I never oppose. But their actions amounted to a panic sell. Instead of riding through the bumps, which occur with every new investment class, they exited at the first sign of distress. Although they all worked at my company, BTCC, a globally recognized leader in the cryptocurrency space, they allowed worries about price volatility and bitcoin's staying power to scare them. By late 2020, their investment would have been worth nearly ten times what it was in September 2017. In bitcoin, panic selling rarely is a good strategy when viewed from the long term.

Let's contrast this situation with my actions following the coronavirus outbreak and shuttering of the economy. On February 12, 2020, bitcoin was flying comfortably at about $10,000. It had increased steadily from a year-beginning price of about $5,000. Experts were eagerly awaiting the effect of the next halving in early May, when the number of bitcoins released every 10 minutes left a smaller supply available to miners.

A month later, bitcoin's price dropped to $6,000, and in the following days it fell to just under $4,000, igniting a selling panic. This sell-off was totally unexpected, yet if you think about it, it wasn't surprising at all. People who had invested early in bitcoin saw their net worth cut by hundreds of thousands if not millions of dollars.

But rather than join the wildebeests galloping away from the Serengeti's crocodile-laden Grumeti River, I remained calm. I kept my faith in Bitcoin's future. So did other Bitcoin bulls. "This pandemic will be an inflection point for Bitcoin and the Metaverse," wrote my friend Cameron Winklevoss on his Twitter feed a few months later.

Indeed, I saw the decline as an opportunity—what goes down in a panic because of one-time macroeconomic conditions is bound to rise again—and I dived in and purchased some bitcoin at a good price. I'm not crowing because the price promptly increased a day later by almost a third and had regained its recent losses by the end of May. Nor do I claim to be a great investor. I've made many mistakes myself.

But I'm also sure that making investment decisions out of trepidation is never helpful. Bitcoin prices will be volatile, but you shouldn't let volatility guide your decisions. Don't panic sell.

ANOTHER IMPORTANT CAVEAT: Invest Within Your Means

So, I've covered what you shouldn't do. Now I'll add an important caveat that may seem obvious but bears mentioning because many investors make this mistake. While many investors err on the side of caution, as my four don'ts highlight, others are too aggressive. They become so enamored by the potential gains of an investment that they invest beyond their means. I call these investors "the overzealous," and while I respect enthusiasm, I also know the importance of staying within a budget.

Advisors traditionally recommended subtracting your age from 100 to determine how much of your portfolio should be devoted to stocks. But that advice has changed as people live longer and the world's economic complexity has prompted greater flexibility in asset allocation. A conservative portfolio might allocate 20 to 30 percent to equities with most of them blue chip companies unlikely to see huge price fluctuations. Fixed-income securities, including municipal and corporate bonds, which are less risky, should compose most of the remaining investments with cash and related products making up 5 to 15 percent. Ratchet up the ratio of equities to fixed-income securities to create a portfolio with higher risk but potentially greater returns.

A simpler investment philosophy is setting aside 10 to 15 percent of your monthly or yearly income for investments. The exact percentage you choose depends on your personality, age, and lifestyle. If you live in a pricey urban center with high expenses, like to go out frequently, or are simply a worrier who likes to have more cash at hand, you will likely fall toward the lower end. But if you're a planner looking to achieve specific goals and excel at staying on budget, you will save a higher amount.

Where does a bitcoin investment fit in?

You might approach it as an alternative investment, similar to precious metals, coins, artwork, or rare crafts. To be sure, some financial advisors see a 10 percent, even occasionally a 20 percent allocation in alternatives as reasonable, and chosen wisely, they can generate higher returns than other investments. (They can also be more volatile—sound familiar?)

I'm not asking anyone to go that far. Investing 1 to 2 percent of your total net wealth in bitcoin is all it takes. With a 1 or 2 percent investment, if bitcoin goes up 100 times, as I predict, then you will double or triple your net wealth. That amount will allow you to make a solid commitment without creating any undue stress or taking a bite out of your savings. If you're taking out a second mortgage, for example, or otherwise compromising your financial security, you're not proceeding the right way. Bitcoin, even when it's on an upswing, is not an excuse to run wild with your finances.

That said, if you have the resources and you're a confident investor not easily thrown by the occasional price contraction, you might consider going to 5 percent or even 10 percent of your total net wealth. Or if you like your initial experience—in some cases that may simply mean getting over initial investment jitters—you may want to add to your bitcoin as time goes on. My friend Stephen used disposable income that he might have spent on travel, food, or a new gadget. He wasn't concerned when bitcoin took a dive not long after his second purchase.

Base your decisions on what you believe is right at a particular moment. Don't be swayed by prevailing sentiment or vast sweeps of momentum. Don't follow the crowds because it seems safe. When bitcoin is soaring in price, when people are buying in droves, or buzzing about it at a conference, you can feel as if you're missing out on something. Remember, when you feel compelled to invest a certain amount at a certain time, you're more likely to make a decision outside your comfort zone. When you approach Bitcoin in a measured way, you'll make the most of your experience. Bitcoin is risky but no more so than a lot of other investments. Keep your risk tolerance foremost in mind as you wade in, but also remain flexible.

Stephen bought his bitcoin in two installments and still had regrets. To be sure, he could have made more money on his investment had he purchased all his bitcoin at the lower price in 2015. While I would have done things differently, Stephen wasn't wrong in his approach. Stephen wasn't comfortable initially purchasing more than one bitcoin. Cautious by nature, he needed to see more evidence of how bitcoin would behave. Would the public continue looking at it as an alternative to traditional monetary systems or lose interest? Or would bitcoin show some crack in its armor that had not previously been apparent? These were all reasonable concerns.

That said, his experience also underscores the variety of ways that someone can invest in bitcoin. I have repeatedly encouraged potential investors to do what's right for them, provided they are operating within their means and remain cognizant of their risk threshold. Part of what this means is that no one should start having regrets even if bitcoin's price craters for a while or fails to meet expectations for a particular time span; nor should they feel inclined to buy more if the price balloons.

INVESTMENT OPTIONS

Let's examine a few options, starting with the simplest, most direct way to invest.

Buying Bitcoin in Bulk on a One-Time Basis

This can be 1 bitcoin, 5, 10, or even just 0.1 BTC. The amount doesn't matter as long as you've met the criteria I've outlined above.

The all-at-once approach can work well for decisive, confident investors, those who act quickly once they've come to a decision and prefer not stretching out their actions over time or having to look back at what they've done. These investors can buy their bitcoin in one swoop and wait for the investment to grow.

Bitcoin buyers who make their investment in one swoop don't have to worry about whether the timing is right or that they've invested too little or too much. It's easy: buy it now and you can forget about it for a few years.

Everything has a downside, though. Note that practically speaking, by buying your bitcoin all at one time, you forgo a chance to buy again at a lower price in the near future. If you're operating on a tight budget, saving a few dollars here and there could be important.

Going all in also won't work for the more measured investor who prefers dipping a few toes in the water before going deeper. These investors generally like to see how an investment fares and invest incrementally. They're not being too cautious, but rather they know that the gradual approach is better for them.

Most bitcoin investors in my orbit have happily followed the incremental approach. While they're all successful professionals and experienced investors, and they've taken the time to learn about bitcoin, they've had reservations about its volatility (mistakenly). They've also had concerns about how wider macroeconomic conditions would affect bitcoin, and want to see how it fares before making an additional commitment. Buying a little at a time has worked better, given their temperaments.

I often recommend a staggered approach, with dollar cost averaging. Now let's consider different intervals.

Buying Weekly

Set a total amount you'd like to invest and buy equal amounts, in dollar terms, each week over a four- to six-week period. Establish a single day each week—every Monday, for example—to make your purchases. The weekly investments on a particular day will discipline your approach, and the spacing will give you time to watch the markets and adjust your position accordingly. One risk is that prices rise significantly and you feel locked into your original plan. So, it's important to remain flexible.

Buying Biweekly

Instead of setting a weekly bitcoin appointment, set a time to buy bitcoin in equal dollar amounts every two weeks over an eight- or ten-week period. The increments will still force you to stay strategically disciplined but offer a little more time between purchases to take stock of price trends, wider conditions, and your feelings about the market. If you start having doubts, you can maintain your position or skip a week, but if you feel increasingly bullish you can up the cadence of your investment or invest more in one or more weeks than originally planned.

Buying in Three Monthly Installments

By spacing your investments over a still longer stretch, you have even more time to evaluate what you've done, how the market has performed, and what you would like to do going forward. But as is the case with investing in any set rhythm, you should be flexible. Events can change dramatically. Witness the collapse in just six weeks of bitcoin's price from $20,000 in mid-December 2017 to under $7,000 in early February 2018, or its one-month, coronavirus-spurred tumble from over $10,000 to $3,600 and then subsequent rebound over the ensuing few weeks.

Random Investment

There's nothing wrong with buying irregularly. Make an initial investment, and then add to it when your circumstances permit and you feel the timing is right. I would strongly suggest that you make a sizable first purchase. Of course, what's sizable is in the eye of the investor. And I would be among the first to say that any start in Bitcoin is better than no start at all, so there's no harm in making a small first investment. As a Bitcoin evangelist, my primary goal is to raise participation. That said, if you're serious about investing in bitcoin, start strongly, and you'll have an easier time building momentum toward your larger goal.

How often should you buy randomly? This is another question that depends on the individual. (One of my favorite aspects of Bitcoin is that everyone can choose their own path.) I would avoid buying in small installments but instead invest in larger lumps—a few hundred dollars or a thousand instead of just $100. But that's my preference rather than a logical investment principle. However you spread out your purchases, remember that you're aiming to invest around 1 to 2 percent of your total net wealth in bitcoin—or even more, if that's within your capability.

FINAL ADVICE

I have a couple of last bits of advice that smart investors have followed for decades, regardless of the asset in which they're investing. Look for opportunities that others might overlook, and don't be afraid to take the direction opposite the crowds. Or as my entrepreneurial grandparents and parents instilled in me: have the courage of your convictions. They built successful businesses by going to places where Chinese nationals still rarely emigrate—South America and West Africa.

My grandparents thought of an ingenious way to ensure they had the means to fund their business—they snuck gold bars out of China in hidden compartments of their clothing. My grandfather, William Lee, never said much about the agonizing minutes of boarding the crowded streamliner to Hong Kong, which was then a British colony. Had some Chinese official stopped him, he undoubtedly would have faced punishment. Or as he arrived in Brazil, he might have lost all the wealth he owned except the clothing in his suitcases and on his back to a zealous or unscrupulous customs agent. Ultimately, my grandparents started businesses that offered products that were rarely manufactured in, let alone exported from the countries in which they settled.

Perhaps I inherited some of their boldness. I mined bitcoin in 2011, when hardly anyone outside the founding circle and some other technology adventurists had even heard of it.

Two years later, I left a comfortable corporate track that probably would have continued with higher-level promotions to buy into an unknown business in an unknown industry. And I continued adding to my bitcoin because I believed the price—less than $10 when I started—was bound to skyrocket. I refused to be cowed by its volatility, even as other investors, some of whom have already made strong gains on bitcoin, sold at least part of their holdings.

They were part of the crowd that reacted the same way many equities investors have traditionally reacted to price decreases. They followed what everyone was doing because if everyone else was doing it, then everyone must be right. They saw more comfort in crowds than in their own wisdom. And in the end, their decisions proved short-sighted. Lemmings usually wind up at the bottom of a cliff.

When bitcoin dropped in the pandemic-induced economic collapse, I saw the opportunity to buy more at a price that may never reappear. In the future, when there are new drops from panic selling, I'll likely make the same decision to buy the dip. And when bitcoin reaches levels at which I will achieve the profitability to which I believe every bitcoin owner should aspire—at least 100 times the initial investment—then I'll also be willing to sell and take profit, rather than following the hordes who jump in at every increase.

In *The Big Short*, a brilliant account of the subprime mortgage collapse of 2008, journalist Michael Lewis focuses on the few brave analysts and investors who foresaw events leading to what was then the biggest economic downturn since the Great Depression. While most of Wall Street saw seemingly endless blue skies ahead, this small group of contrarians understood the precarious foundation upon which some of the world's largest financial services companies had built fortunes. They had packaged subprime mortgages into bonds that would lose much of their value as high-risk homeowners defaulted on their mortgages.

Among them was Michael Burry, a physician–turned–fund manager, whom Lewis said "almost comically" outpaced stock indexes with his Scion Capital fund largely by finding gems in little-read financial documents and trusting his analyses. From 2001, Scion's founding year, to 2005, Burry's fund rose 242 percent, while the stock market index over that period dropped about 7 percent. "To his swelling audience," Lewis wrote, "it didn't seem to matter whether the stock market rose or fell: Burry found places to invest money shrewdly."[4]

Three years later, Burry bet big against the subprime mortgage industry after observing that housing prices in San Jose, where Scion had its headquarters, remained high even after the dot-com bubble burst. Burry recognized that the real estate market was being "driven by the irrational behavior of mortgage lenders who were extending easy credit." In 2007, Lewis wrote, Burry "made his investors $750 million" by speculating against banks' subprime lending.[5]

But what has fascinated me about Burry's story and others portrayed in *The Big Short* is that any of the smart financial services wizards who had been willing to read some of the documents produced by subprime lenders and bond issuers and followed through on the information could have drawn the same conclusions. They were smart enough and more experienced than Burry, who had taught himself investment fundamentals while he was in medical school less a decade earlier. In addition, Burry had zero knowledge of subprime lending. The information about it—albeit hard to come by—was no less available to anyone else taking an interest. Other investors could have made a similar investment if they'd been willing to take a chance.

Bitcoin is a less risky bet than Burry or any subprime contrarians made from 2005 to 2007. These contrarians bet against the world's largest financial services firms. An investment in Bitcoin requires merely an acknowledgment that there is a better way to store value, albeit digitally, given that traditional money's purchasing power is at risk because of excessive printing.

But perhaps there is a bigger lesson for the would-be bitcoin investor here: namely, that if you study an investment carefully and follow through logically with patience, it can pay off.

Study, buy, and then HODL.

BITCOIN IS ONLY GOING UP

Where is bitcoin headed? What's your price prediction? How high will it go?

These are three variations of the same question I'm asked more than any other at cryptocurrency conferences or in casual exchanges with people curious about Bitcoin. It's not a question I mind answering, but I also have mixed feelings because it doesn't permit much evangelizing about why I think bitcoin is a great investment. In fact, it's *the* investment of our lifetime!

I don't have time to discuss the central monetary system's ills in the few minutes that it takes me to leave a conference hall for my next obligation. It takes time to address fiat currency's steady loss in value and the arbitrary nature of central authority, the plight of the unbanked, and freedom of money. These are deep subjects. The querying audience members want short answers. They want a number that they can take home to buoy their confidence in this new phenomenon.

Bitcoin will reach X in one year, Y in another five years, and Z in 10 years.

I've been an investor for almost half my 46 years—stocks, real estate, of course gold, along with bitcoin—so I sympathize. I'm polite.

As a teaser, I'll state the obvious. I've been bullish about bitcoin—playfully predicting that the bitcoin price in US dollars will match the number of my Twitter followers, which was at about 100,000 at the time of publication. Time and knowledge have only sharpened my optimism, and pending some new, unexpected development, I expect my belief in bitcoin will continue to grow stronger. But I have never lost sight of what's truly important—not a numerical price target, but rather the issues underpinning its existence. Unless you're day-trading, which I definitely do not recommend doing for bitcoin, it's best to have conviction in its value, and more importantly, its potential.

I want people to invest in bitcoin because they believe in it, believe in the future of money, and not because they see big dollar signs in their futures. That's what people do when they play the lottery or gamble in casinos.

Bitcoin is neither a lottery nor a game of chance, despite what some skeptics say.

As I've tried to show throughout this book, there is a remarkable order to Bitcoin. The pieces fit together seamlessly to provide a needed service. It most resembles gold in that it has some unique features, and there is a limited supply that does not depend on any organization or individual for its value in the manner of stocks or bonds. Understanding Bitcoin's value was a short leap from the lessons I learned about gold as I grew up in the Ivory Coast. I want to encourage people to invest in bitcoin because they understand its truly unique features and its potential for changing the world, not because of a price prediction from me or some other expert.

Now understand that my prediction is based on subjective analysis, not some fancy algorithm that I plug into a computer. I read a lot, pay attention to current events, and trust my instincts. Nothing I do is beyond anyone else's abilities. The only difference between my approach and others is that I've been around Bitcoin longer than most people (a full 10 years now, since early 2011), and perhaps I have more patience.

But as I said from the start, I am not an investment advisor. I'm not trying to get anyone to follow a herd or to buy bitcoin out of FOMO (fear of missing out) investing. As I've said earlier, FOMO investors are desperate, and desperation leads to rushed, poor decisions. What I want is for investors to heed common-sense investment principles. I want them to look rationally at bitcoin's performance and potential.

Consider what Bitcoin has already accomplished and why it will be useful for years to come. Analyze its fundamentals the way Warren Buffett or some other famed investor would. And don't be cowed if not everyone agrees with you. There are plenty of people who will.

As of December 2020, according to Statista, more than 60 million Bitcoin wallets had been set up globally.[1] That's almost as many people as the populations of Spain and Argentina and more people than Canada. Statista found that about 5 percent of the US population—about 18 million people—held at least some fractional amounts of bitcoin. The global Bitcoin community? It's almost impossible to pinpoint. I don't think 5 percent of the global population own at least some bitcoin—yet. My sense is that the total is somewhere around 50 million, and given the global population of 7.7 billion, there's a lot of room for growth.

If you buy into my arguments, my hope is that you'll invest in bitcoin—as much as 1 or even 2 percent of your total net worth—and hold it long-term, for more than 10 years.

So, let me now satisfy those readers seeking a short answer and predict now that by 2040, one bitcoin will be worth at least $1,000,000. Actually, if the world's central banks continue to print as much money in the next two decades as they have in the last two decades, then bitcoin prices could easily be in the millions of dollars by then.

That's right: bitcoin will be worth no less than *a million dollars* in two decades.

Consumers and investors will consider it like gold in its ability to increase in value because of its unique features and limited supply, but it is actually more usable than gold due to its digital nature.

OTHER BITCOIN PREDICTIONS

Antivirus software developer and provocateur John McAfee also once famously maintained that bitcoin would reach $1 million by the end of 2020 and account for at least 5 percent of the world's transactions. "Let's get real, there are only 21 million bitcoins," McAfee told *Forbes* in a 2019 interview, "Seven million of which have been lost forever, and then, if Satoshi is dead, add a few more million."[2]

The mercurial McAfee subsequently retracted his prediction and has hedged about offering a new target. But his logic was not unreasonable. There are no shortage of other pundits, successful investors, and individuals intricately involved in Bitcoin's history and far less prone to outrageous statements who have made similar or bolder predictions.

Start with Hal Finney, who in 2009 theorized bitcoin reaching $10 million in an exchange with founder Satoshi Nakamoto. "As an amusing thought experiment, imagine that Bitcoin is successful and becomes the dominant payment system in use throughout the world," wrote Finney, a brilliant Cal Tech–trained computer engineer who died tragically of Lou Gehrig's disease just five years later at age 58. "Then the total value of the currency should be equal to the total value of all the wealth in the world. Current estimates of total worldwide household wealth that I have found range from $100 trillion to $300 trillion. With 20 million coins, that gives each coin a value of about $10 million." He added: "So the possibility of generating coins today with a few cents of compute time may be quite a good bet, with a payoff of something like 100 million to 1! Even if the odds of Bitcoin succeeding to this degree are slim, are they really 100 million to one against? Something to think about."[3]

In 2017, former hedge fund manager and bestselling author James Altucher also predicted that bitcoin would reach at least $1 million by 2020,[4] and in a 2019 interview with TheStreet.com, he said it could rise seven or eight times beyond that if bitcoin replaced some of fiat currency.[5] "How much paper currency is out there . . . it's about $200 trillion dollars out in the world, and there is only about $200 billion dollars of crypto currency, so that is 100,000% from here," Altucher said. So that could give bitcoin a price of $8 million, so $1 million is even a discount to where bitcoin could eventually go, according to Altucher.

Altucher, who founded the financial social network Stock-Pickr and was a seed investor in Salesforce, once condemned Bitcoin as a Ponzi scheme. "At first I thought bitcoin was a fad because I kept seeing day traders gamble and lose money on it," Altucher told *Business Insider* in a 2013 interview.[6]

But a conversation with AngelList founder Naval Ravikant prompted him to reconsider his position. Altucher and Ravikant recognized the same benefits that I had several years earlier. "It is not dependent on a government," he said in the interview, or "on complicated central bank operations to have the money transfer from one wallet to another." Altucher noted that every transfer of money at some level involves the central bank except for small cash transactions. "Nor is it dependent on 'In God We Trust,' a phrase that was first put on coins in 1862 to instill more 'faith' in a currency that was potentially in trouble due to war," Altucher noted. With Bitcoin, I now prefer the phrase "In Crypto We Trust."

Altucher came to see Bitcoin not only as a potential replacement for fiat currency, but "for all contract law" because of its underlying public distributed ledger technology. No longer would we need the layers of legal documentation—escrow, loan, and transfer statements—that are part of all major transactions. "In one swoop," Altucher continued, "any economy that takes up bitcoin as a currency will rewrite all contract law (eliminating the need for lawyers in 99% of situations), will eliminate the need for exchanges, and make international trade infinitely simpler." Maybe that's a bit exaggerated, but certainly savings can be had.

That year, he became the first author to sell a book, his popular self-help tome *Choose Yourself*, solely for bitcoin. (Naval Ravikant was the only person to pay in the cryptocurrency before the book became available on Amazon.)

PayPal director and crypto entrepreneur Wences Casares offered a similarly bullish prediction in an essay on the website kanaandkatana.com, a research platform run by Ikigai Asset Management. Casares pointed to the rapid adoption of crypto, which was adding about one million users a month each month at the time of his article. "In my (subjective) opinion those chances of succeeding are at least 50%. If Bitcoin does succeed, 1 bitcoin may be worth more than $1 million in seven to 10 years," he wrote, adding: "If bitcoin succeeds it will most likely not replace any national currency. It may be a supranational currency that exists on top of all national currencies. If Bitcoin succeeds it may be a global non-political standard of value and settlement."

Casares recommended that a smart $10 million portfolio should include about 1 percent crypto. "If bitcoin fails, this portfolio will lose at most $100,000 or 1% of its value over 3 to 5 years, which most portfolios can bear," he wrote. "But if bitcoin succeeds, in 7 to 10 years those $100,000 may be worth more than $25 million, more than twice the value of the entire initial portfolio."[7]

Perhaps even more telling, in an informal end-of-2019 poll on his Twitter feed, Australian financial analyst and bitcoin bull Mati Greenspan found that more than half of nearly 3,000 respondents also expected bitcoin to reach $1 million by the end of the 2020s.[8] Clearly, it's not just high-profile Bitcoin converts who see the digital currency's potential.

Other crypto observers and investors have not been quite so bullish but still forecast strong growth. In a 2019 interview with *Business Insider*, Morgan Creek Capital CEO Mark Yusko charted a steep, steady climb over the ensuing decade to $100,000 by the end of 2021, to $250,000 by 2025, and then to $500,000.[9] Yusko is no lightweight investor. He ran the giant endowments fund at his alma mater Notre Dame and then at the University of North Carolina earlier in his career. He was deeply skeptical of Bitcoin at one point.

He believes that Bitcoin offers a unique opportunity to address financial inequality that has become more pronounced with time. "The government and the elites want to have all the wealth, so they manufacture inflation and the wealth flows to the top," Yusko said. "And that's why we have the greatest wealth inequality in the history of mankind. Bitcoin helps solve that because now we can opt-out as an owner of assets from that fiat system."

Venture capital heavy hitter Tim Draper has steadfastly maintained that bitcoin would reach $250,000 by 2023. The widely respected Draper, an early investor in Skype, Tesla, and Baidu, was among the first major bitcoin investors when he famously bought 30,000 bitcoins for $19 million in 2014. He has touted Bitcoin's potential usefulness as a financial service and dismissed the dips in price as a growing pain. "The Internet started in the same way," he said in a 2019 interview with BlockTV.[10] "It came in big waves and then it kind of came crashing down. And then the next wave comes concentrated but much bigger. I suspect the same thing will go on here."

A number of other optimists have been more circumspect about their predictions or offered a wide range of price forecasts. In a June 18, 2017, tweet that is no longer available, Bitcoin Foundation board member Vinny Lingham said there was a 2.5 percent chance of a bitcoin being worth $100,000 and 0.25 percent chance of a $1 million valuation.[11] Bitcoin was trading under $3,000 that day. Lingham has offered other shorter-term predictions over the past four years, most recently predicting in a tweet that bitcoin would reach $33,000 to $55,000 over the ensuing 12 months.[12]

A range may be the best way to consider the pricing question. It builds in the unpredictability of events that could determine what level bitcoin reaches—high or low end—over the next two to four decades and how quickly. A pandemic, global economic crash, social and political upheaval, or environmental catastrophe could paralyze investors and delay the embrace of Bitcoin by years or more. Alternately, these same events could be a catalyst for people to abandon traditional money that's prone to inflation and devaluation and embrace Bitcoin as a better alternative.

Consider the possibility of a government crackdown. I've already said that governments will have difficulty stopping Bitcoin because it is more an idea than something physical that can be confiscated (like cash, bank accounts, or gold bars), and because of its easy accessibility worldwide. Governments would have to learn the private keys of everyone participating in the Bitcoin system, an impossibility, given that would require identifying everyone by their private keys. Case in point: When China banned exchanges in 2018, investors in the country merely shifted their business to overseas exchanges. No bitcoins were ever confiscated by China; that would have been entirely impossible.

That said, governments run by authoritarians eager to control monetary systems or responding to bank lobbyists could slow Bitcoin's progress by overregulating it or creating other hurdles that would ultimately impact bitcoin's price. How long or how deep the effect of these actions would be difficult to predict.

A growing Bitcoin derivatives market could also retard Bitcoin adoption and price gains. As is the case with oil and gas, gold, and certain commodities markets, speculation via purchases of futures and options instead of the foundational asset often drive price trends. This approach, if adapted to Bitcoin, would prevent miners and other investors from determining bitcoin's price.

On the other hand, developing economies where there are few if any banking services are likely to spur greater demand for bitcoin as small business owners buy and sell goods and services. International trade tensions, an extension of the nationalist political trends, are also likely to prompt companies to look outside traditional channels for ways to conduct their business. These issues will likely lead to a devaluation of the dollar and other powerful fiat currencies as countries look to limit the damage to their economies. The result would be an undermining of public trust in the institutions that control monetary policy. These events, should they occur, will lead to a tipping point in bitcoin's use, sending its price skyward.

REMEMBER: DON'T SWEAT THE VOLATILITY

That brings me to my next Bitcoin prediction.

Expect continued volatility. I know that the word spooks many people. Volatility suggests that an investment will never be trustworthy and that they should stand clear. As I explained earlier in Chapter 7, they are confusing volatility and riskiness. That's unfortunate. First let's clarify again that I'm not writing this book to force anyone into Bitcoin—or any other cryptocurrency. I've also been clear that I'm not an investment advisor.

Everyone must make their own decisions about what they're seeking in an investment. That includes the timeline by which they hope an investment grows to a certain level. More importantly, it also means the level of risk they're willing to tolerate. If you're a smart investor, you are undoubtedly mulling factors like your employment situation, age, and size of your family.

Skilled investment advisors are quick to say that investments take their own paths. They may start fast and lose steam; they may reverse directions quickly; or they may alternate ups and downs. Remember that Amazon's stock famously dropped into single digits before heading steadily upward to its early 2021 $3,000-plus per share and roughly $1.6 trillion valuation.

Many analysts considered Amazon a volatile investment in the days before the full power of internet buying became apparent, and they had a point. But smart investors looked at the long-range picture. They analyzed Amazon's potential, management, and operational efficiency. Amazon, as we can see more clearly now, was a great idea pushed forward by a visionary founder. Jeff Bezos also ran a tight ship, ensuring the company kept expenditures low without compromising its ability to grow.

Bitcoin's continued volatility will stem from a continued lack of understanding of its potential global value. Too many people will invest for the wrong reasons—FOMO or otherwise—and then overreact to every gust of wind casting the slightest doubt on Bitcoin's status. But it will also reflect the powerful forces resisting its widespread adoption.

Until the central banks, traditional financial services institutions, and political leaders sympathetic to their cause embrace Bitcoin, markets will remain turbulent. These groups will continue to create obstacles, unsettling many investors and leading to steep sell-offs that will create more of the huge dips we've already seen. But there will also be run-ups in price that reflect surges in confidence.

Volatility isn't necessarily a bad thing. It is simply where Bitcoin is in the early going of what will be a long, successful history.

Don't let the dips—or gains—affect your HODLing strategy. Pay closer attention to Bitcoin's overall growth trajectory. What you're seeing is merely the beginnings of a multidecade rally. Is there another investment that you could have had for fractions of cents (not dollars) in 2010 that is now worth upward of $10,000? Few investments over the previous decade have generated a greater percentage increase than bitcoin. And likewise, few investments in the next decade will outperform bitcoin.

I made more money investing in bitcoin in 2013 than many people who invested much earlier than I. How? Because I invested more in real dollar terms and held onto my bitcoin longer than many others who got in as early as 2010. I benefitted from the huge increase in price, whereas many early investors who didn't have as strong a conviction bought less, and sold too early. The same goes for you. Even if you're buying bitcoin now at over $10,000, which is much higher than the price I invested at first, you still have the opportunity to make millions, as long as you invest enough and hold it long enough to benefit from the huge price increase in the coming decade.

At a conference in Malta in early 2019 when bitcoin had entered a bear period dragging its price into the mid $3,000s, a few attendees asked if they had made a mistake by not selling a year earlier when prices were still near $10,000. My answer was that if they had bought their bitcoin in February 2017 when it hit $1,000 again, held it through its spike above $20,000 ten months later, and sold when the price was hovering in the mid $6,000 range, they would have made a sizable profit—more than they would have on most equities. Similarly, if their bitcoin climbs to $200,000 by 2021 and then sinks to $60,000 during another bear market, they will still be way up compared to today. Nothing to worry about!

Accept bitcoin's volatility and stay to play the long game. Your bitcoin will buy you a lot more than it previously would have. Remember that in May 2010, Laszlo Hanyecz paid 10,000 bitcoins for two pizzas. Eleven years later, those bitcoins were worth over $500 million.

At some point, probably not long after bitcoin reaches $1 million, it should start to stabilize. Of course, whether bitcoin reaches my $1 million target in 10, 20, or 50 years is not crucial in the long term. When some human endeavor reaches a milestone or breakthrough is not as important to anyone except to historians. Would it have mattered if the internet achieved mass adoption 10 or 15 years after its debut in the 1970s? Bitcoin will get there. Logic is in its favor.

LOSS OF VALUE

Bitcoin's biggest advantage is that the world's main currency measuring stick, the US dollar, is devaluing every single year. If the measuring stick is literally shrinking every year, then the item being measured (bitcoin) will naturally increase over time. Let's look at McDonald's burger prices at various intervals. What product is more indicative of American monetary trends than a hamburger? What product is more American than a hamburger?

A McDonald's hamburger cost just $0.15 in 1955 when the restaurant chain launched. By the 1980s, the same burger cost $0.50, and now it's already at around $1.10. A Big Mac was $0.60 in 1970, about three years after McDonald's introduced the iconic two all-beef patties, special sauce concoction that has fueled many a late-night high school student's metabolism. Today, it's at least $4. The cheapest McDonald's meal, which includes fries and a drink, has risen to over $5, and much more in certain high-cost cities. So have burgers and meals at other fast-food franchises. Money's purchasing power just isn't what it used to be.

Has McDonald's suddenly started using the finest sirloin beef? Increased the serving sizes? No and no. McDonald's beef patty has been a constant over decades, coming from the same suppliers and in the same roughly 1.8-ounce package. So, it's not as if the chain needs to spend more to prepare these items.

What's changed is the US dollar. Its buying power has shrunk. Just think of it as being a smaller US dollar now. This has all happened in the open, through a time scale of years and decades, but with nary an objection. And the people who have been most hurt are those with less earning power. Have you ever wondered why money's purchasing power shrinks every year? Is that a law of nature, or an intentional man-made phenomenon? I know it's the latter.

Meanwhile, bitcoin's value increases over time. Wow!

Bitcoin's second advantage is that governments and banks have increasingly restricted people's access to money via laws and regulations. This has become a source of frustration for many people. They are unable to execute even the most basic transactions without interference or extra costs. Today, as we enter the 2020s, it's mind-boggling that the banking sector still insists on holding our hands when we make our own monetary transactions.

I've made the point that money should be an inalienable property and right and that we should be able to control it as we would our arms and fingers. It belongs to us, as it is the fruits of our labor. Bitcoin's decentralized structure certainly gives people this ability, and this core feature is a major factor behind its rapidly gaining popularity. This momentum is likely to continue building as millennials and younger generations who are less technophobic and more suspicious of authority become a bigger part of the economy. Many of them are looking for more command of their lives.

A poll conducted by the Harris Group for the venture firm Blockchain Capital not long after the height of the 2019 crypto bear market found that the percentage of people in the 18-to-34 age group who described themselves as at least "somewhat familiar" with Bitcoin increased from 42 percent to 60 percent, since a similar Blockchain Capital report two years earlier.[13] The study also found that nearly 60 percent of individuals in this group held a positive outlook on Bitcoin as a financial innovation, and nearly half felt that people would use bitcoin in the next decade, while more than 40 percent said they would be likely to buy bitcoin over the next five years. Perhaps more telling was that nearly a third of millennials already preferred bitcoin over government bonds or stocks, and almost a quarter preferred it to real estate or gold.

Millennials compose the United States' largest demographic group. Their disposable income will surpass all other generations before 2030. A *Wall Street Journal*–commissioned study found that the Great Recession, which occurred when many millennials were in their twenties, shaped their investment behavior to be distrustful of many traditional investment options and to seek alternative assets.[14] A separate report by the investment group Adamant Capital found that millennials were comfortable with peer-to-peer protocols such as BitTorrent and open-source software.[15] "As the disposable income of Millennials continues to grow, we expect further tailwinds in terms of Bitcoin adoption and price appreciation," the report said.

The more control society places on money, the greater Bitcoin's value to society. Bitcoin is true freedom of money. That's why it's valuable today, and that's why it will be increasingly more valuable in the coming decade. There's no stopping freedom of money.

A third advantage is that people will find Bitcoin increasingly useful. This will be particularly true for small business operators, who have been relying on electronic fund and bank transfers, payment platforms, credit cards, and even cash for their various transactions. Cryptocurrency understandably at this point has accounted for a minute part of that total. But that's what gives it so much potential. There is a huge untapped market for it.

My own dealings in launching my new startup Ballet are telling. Early in Ballet's development of a credit card–sized Bitcoin cold wallet, an Argentinian-based group we were working with said that they preferred payments in bitcoin. US dollar bank transfers were too complicated, as many countries restrict foreign currency transactions and even limit people's ability to open a US dollar bank account (Argentina's traditional payment systems are particularly Byzantine). Around this time, a few of my remote employees made similar requests. Some accountants advised against payments in bitcoin because they thought it might alarm regulators and complicate tax filings. But I saw that once these issues were settled, bitcoin made payments easier and more efficient on a global level.

Bitcoin could be particularly important for unbanked and lightly banked areas. An African import-export business could accept bitcoin for shoes it has shipped from China; a South American farmer could buy seeds and equipment with bitcoin; or even a tech firm in some remote corner of the world could pay vendors providing IT support or marketing help in bitcoin.

Expect to see bitcoin's use increase in daily retail transactions as well. This doesn't mean we'll be using bitcoin in grocery stores and coffee shops. Bitcoin's growing presence in our daily lives will be gradual—a few businesses at a time. But the increase will occur.

And as Bitcoin becomes a bigger part of the business world, the public will become less wary. I've already noticed a dramatic shift in attitude. This change has been apparent in my audience's response to two questions that I've been posing at the beginning of my cryptocurrency conference presentations for several years: (1) Do you own any bitcoin? (2) How many of you got into bitcoin in the past year?

I've always received a healthy show of hands to my first question. Most people at crypto conferences own bitcoin, or they wouldn't be attending in the first place. But an increasing number of people, sometimes one-third of the audience, are now responding affirmatively to my second question. For me, this shows that Bitcoin is becoming more popular.

Some of my casual encounters show the same encouraging trend. In late 2019, a TSA agent at the Las Vegas McCarran Airport flagged one of my bags, in which I had stored some Ballet wallet cards. This didn't surprise me. The cards are made of stainless steel—purposely so they would hold up over time. I travel a great deal and routinely get stopped by airport security to x-ray my bags. As the agent respectfully unpacked my bag, he came across the cards and smiled. "I just purchased one of these Ballet wallets," he said. I was dumbfounded and pleasantly surprised, as we had only launched the cards a couple of weeks before.

But then I realized that more people are reading about Bitcoin on a daily basis. It has evolved from a mysterious sideshow that intimidated most people to daily part of many people's lives. It will continue on this road.

FIFTEEN PREDICTIONS FOR THE WORLD OF CRYPTOCURRENCY

There is no mystery why bitcoin pricing is the cryptocurrency world's leading topic.

Bitcoin was the trailblazer in digital money. The first to draw wider public awareness. To generate millionaires and multimillionaires. To spawn a cottage industry of exchanges and other support services. To attract the interest of government regulators and to threaten the pillars of the banking system.

Bitcoin is the crypto king—not Ethereum, Tether, XRP, Bitcoin Cash, Chainlink, Polkadot, Cardano, Litecoin, Bitcoin SV, EOS, Monero, TRON, Stellar, Tezos, Neo, Cosmos, NEM, Dai, IOTA, Dash, or other cryptocurrencies whose inventors say they have addressed Bitcoin's weaknesses, and with market caps now in the billions.

Bitcoin's market cap, which exceeded $1 trillion in early 2021, dwarfs all others. Just one cryptocurrency, Ethereum, had cracked $50 billion, and only about 75 others had market caps that exceeded $1 billion.

While I hold some other cryptocurrencies and investments, and I respect any crypto effort that builds momentum for digital money, I've built my portfolio around bitcoin. I'm a Bitcoin guy.

But I also believe it's important not to ignore the wider landscape. What happens outside Bitcoin politically, legally, socially, economically, and environmentally may affect its future—accelerating or slowing its acceptance, or even taking it in directions that are unexpected or counterintuitive.

For example, in early 2020 some crypto enthusiasts began thinking of bitcoin as a new safe haven during times of economic stress. They believed that because its price didn't depend on other units of value or the organizations creating monetary policy, bitcoin would be immune to events that traditionally affect stocks and other traditional assets. They noted a few occasions when equity markets slumped but cryptocurrency continued rising. They compared bitcoin to gold, the traditional safe haven asset, and predicted that it would draw new investors appreciative of its unique advantages in economic downturns.

The outbreak of the coronavirus possibly dispelled this belief—at least initially. When equity markets tumbled historically amid a global economic standstill, so did bitcoin, but just briefly. From February 20 to March 23, both the S&P 500 and bitcoin fell about 33 percent. Early 2020 momentum and the expectation of a major price boost from Bitcoin's first halving in four years seemed irrelevant, as bitcoin's price didn't appreciate significantly in mid-2020 as was expected by some people. The price increase finally occurred in the fall when bitcoin topped $20,000. Pinpointing the reasons for this late-year rise was difficult. Bitcoin pricing trends are always difficult to understand and predict. Blame bitcoin's price fluctuations on its youth.

"Bitcoin's narrative is changing, as is to be expected for such a young and complex innovation," eloquently wrote CoinDesk editor Noelle Acheson, in a March 2020 newsletter. "But so are the narratives that guide just about every other aspect of investing. A few years from now, when the new narratives have settled into some semblance of normality, we'll look back on this time and realize that the bigger story was in front of us all along."[1]

So, consider the following predictions as a starting point for your own considerations about how cryptocurrency will evolve outside of bitcoin pricing. Not that I'm bashful in what I see occurring. But I've also watched the industry long enough to be flexible in my thinking. You should do the same.

PREDICTION 1: Warren Buffett Will Come Around— or at Least Someone Will

Did I get your attention by including the Oracle of Omaha in the prediction?

I know, I know. Warren Buffett has sworn he'll never invest in bitcoin, and he has a reputation for integrity. "Cryptocurrencies basically have no value and they don't produce anything," Buffett told CNBC's Squawk Box in an interview following the 2020 release of his annual letter to shareholders, adding: "I don't have any cryptocurrency and . . . never will."[2]

And maybe Buffett will never come around. He's famous for telling people never to invest in something they don't understand or in which they don't believe. Who am I to question the wisdom of the world's first, second, or third richest person, depending on whether Wells Fargo, Apple, and a few other big Berkshire Hathaway holdings are soaring or skidding?

Not that smart investors aren't willing to change when they see an asset's advantages, and even the Oracle has changed his mind on more than one occasion. "We welcome change," Buffett said at Berkshire Hathaway 2019 annual meeting. "Change is a fact of life. . . . The key is to keep adapting with the way the world is changing and not be left behind."

It is worth noting that for many years, Buffett was hesitant to invest in tech stocks like Apple. I started investing in Apple stock in the early 2000s, way before it was fashionable to do so, and I predicted that one day Buffett will do the same. Years later, Buffett indeed changed his tune and started buying Apple shares and is now the single largest shareholder of Apple stock globally.

So even if Buffett never feels comfortable with Bitcoin, I predict some other famed investor who has been throwing darts at Bitcoin will buy in. They'll see Bitcoin's practical purposes for the unbanked and decipher its inner workings enough to understand that it's not a scam. They'll note the ease of acquiring bitcoin. Most of all, they'll watch bitcoin outperform other assets. Then they'll buy.

To be sure, the negativists won't fade entirely away. Every asset has its detractors, which I believe is positive. The naysayers are always the ones who ask questions, forcing an investment to prove itself and making it stronger, more creditable to a wider audience. Bitcoin's logic withstands the closest scrutiny. Its compelling narrative will win out in the end.

PREDICTION 2: Bitcoin Will Continue as the Leading Cryptocurrency

There are a lot of people touting different cryptocurrencies these days. Some people think that Ethereum offers the best user experience and is more capable due to its smart contract capabilities. Others favor stable coins tethered to fiat currencies because they offer at least the illusion of enhanced stability. Others are banking on tokens tied to specific projects that will achieve widespread success.

I appreciate the differing perspectives. Investing is a personal experience. Everyone knows what's best for them, and there is no one path to growing assets. Buffett made his $90-plus billion investing largely in big brand companies providing basic goods and services. Robert Smith, another Forbes billionaire, largely built Vista Equity Partners by snapping up software companies. Real estate mogul Donald Bren turned a small home building business into a giant enterprise, becoming the wealthiest person in Orange County, according to the *Los Angeles Times*.[3]

Similarly, there is a range of wildly successful portfolios each with its own mix of stocks, bonds, commodities, and alternative investments. So it is with digital currencies, with some people favoring certain coins and others choosing a different crypto investment strategy. Which approaches will thrive? That question is irrelevant as long as someone makes bitcoin the backbone of their crypto holdings.

Consider Bitcoin like the hero in an action suspense movie, challenged but unbowed and victorious in the end. It will distance itself in market cap and name recognition, asserting itself as the world's de facto reserve digital asset class. Bitcoin's price will soar to the levels that I predicted a chapter earlier—no less than $1 million by 2040, and most likely much higher.

PREDICTION 3: People Will Stop Lumping Other Cryptocurrencies with Bitcoin

"What's in a name?" Shakespeare wrote in *Romeo and Juliet*. Some people use the word cryptocurrency. Others use Bitcoin and cryptocurrency interchangeably. I'm glad that they're talking about it. But using Bitcoin to describe cryptocurrency underscores the confusion about what it is. Most people don't really know. So they use the catchier, more playful word *Bitcoin* instead of *cryptocurrency*, which sounds like something out of a spy manual.

Bitcoin is just one cryptocurrency. By a broad definition, there are about 1,500 as this book went to press. And these 1,500 different cryptocurrencies vary significantly in how they function and how they work, with some being more legitimate than others. Some are decent, but many others are just garbage, pardon my language. This is why some of these have earned the nickname "shitcoin." Bitcoin has become synonymous with cryptocurrency probably because it was the first to arrive and has the highest profile. But as the public gains greater insight into the crypto industry, people will use the term *Bitcoin* correctly. They will recognize how it differs from other cryptoassets, just as investors know the difference between Walmart and Macy's. This realization will mark a symbolic but important new beginning for Bitcoin and other cryptocurrencies—a new clarity that will make it easier for investors to see Bitcoin's advantages but without dismissing the future potential of other cryptocurrencies.

PREDICTION 4: Governments Will Work Out Their Regulatory Issues

Regulation has been one of the major obstacles to cryptocurrency adoption with governments struggling to develop rules and restrictions. They are unsure how to treat an entity that is so different from anything that preceded it and threatens tradition. Should they outlaw it until it's better understood as some detractors might favor? Or should they allow it to police itself? What's the right balance?

A number of authoritarian countries have come down hard on Bitcoin, eager to exert whatever control they can over the new phenomenon. A few of these governments have banned the acquisition of cryptocurrencies or the exchanges that enable these transactions.

In January 2020, the main financial regulatory agency of the Middle Eastern kingdom of Qatar, the Qatar Financial Centre Regulatory Authority (QFCRA), outlawed crypto's use. The move seemed like overkill, coming just two years after the country's central bank banned bitcoin trading. It also seemed counter to Qatar's ongoing fintech initiatives to upgrade financial services, including the development of blockchain platforms to facilitate and safeguard transactions. The QFCRA said crypto had raised security concerns. Did it? Or did Qatar have control issues?

In a rapid series of moves starting in 2017, China outlawed ICOs, exchanges, including my own BTCChina exchange, and cracked down on miners. In April 2018, police in the northern city of Tianjin confiscated 600 computers used for mining after an agency monitoring electricity usage reported a surge in power usage. The government even imposed travel and exit bans on executives from the prominent OKCoin and Huobi exchanges. China cited worries not only about fraud, but also about the industry's massive growth in China, which accounts for an estimated 60 percent of the world's hashing power and manufactures most of the world's mining equipment. In October 2020, executives from OKCoin were detained by the Chinese police, which subsequently caused a suspension of crypto withdrawals from its subsidiary, the global exchange OKEX. This trend in China is likely to continue for many years.

Although Russia has not regulated Bitcoin, the country does not permit bitcoin's use for payments, and as this book went to press, it was weighing a law that would allow the government to confiscate bitcoin. India's central bank, the Reserve Bank of India, tried to prevent trading of cryptocurrencies until its Supreme Court overturned the ban in early 2020, calling the regulation disproportional to the perceived threat that Bitcoin would bring to the country's banking system. The RBI had expressed concerns about security and other issues since 2013, noting in a public statement at that time that digital currencies lacked any foundational value or backing. It called Bitcoin's value a "matter of speculation," and warned that investors would be exposed to huge volatility. The bank also said that the legal standing of exchanges was not clear and could therefore create legal issues for investors.

In April 2018, Iran's Central Bank prohibited the country's banks, credit institutions, currency exchanges, and other institutions from conducting cryptocurrency transactions as part of a campaign to address money laundering and financing of terrorist activity. Bolivia, Ecuador, and Colombia have also outlawed the use and trading of bitcoin. These governments have fixated on bitcoin's threat to their fragile fiat currencies. Vietnam does not consider bitcoin a payment option, although it has not regulated it as an investment. What's the difference, anyway? The beauty of Bitcoin is that it is both an investment and a payment system, all fused together into one.

Yet even countries with full-fledged democracies and open economies have wrestled with regulation. In the United States, which has been largely receptive to Bitcoin, the SEC has yet to approve an Exchange Traded Fund (ETF) for Bitcoin. And agencies have yet to agree on whether Bitcoin should be a commodity or a security. Australia does not consider Bitcoin currency but taxes it as an investment for capital gains. In Canada, some banks won't allow bitcoin transactions on credit and debit cards.

I believe this will all work itself out before the end of this decade, or at least well before all remaining bitcoin is in circulation and as governments recognize Bitcoin's enormous, wide-reaching benefits. Equally important, I see all this hubbub as normal and positive. With so much government and regulatory attention on Bitcoin globally, it further validates that Bitcoin is very important and powerful. Otherwise, why would everyone care so much?

What I mean is that the government's involvement—even its missteps and some of the posturing by Bitcoin skeptics—validates Bitcoin's status as a legitimate form of exchange that merits attention. Note Bitcoin's scrutiny by not only the SEC but the CFTC, IRS, and Treasury Department. At times, I've felt they were fighting over which one of them would get to regulate it. In this regard, it has succeeded already in ways that other technology-based innovations had not at similar junctures in their evolution.

Certainly, none of the areas that my tech career has touched, such as online communities, cloud computing and storage, IP television, online videos, and e-commerce had the traction in terms of government involvement and regulation that crypto has achieved. Bitcoin truly has a special status.

PREDICTION 5: Some Bitcoin Bears Will Remain Bitcoin Bears—to Their Loss

There are three types of Bitcoin bears.

The most common bears are what I will call normal investors or cyclical bears. They approach Bitcoin as they have other investments. They use the best information available to decide what assets to acquire or sell, when to execute the transactions, and in what amounts. Depending on circumstances, they are bullish at times and bearish during other periods. That's exactly what's happened with Bitcoin, with consumers buying bitcoin when they felt strongly that the price would rise and unloading it when the market winds seemed less favorable.

The second group are bears-in-need-of-convincing. These bears struggle to overcome their preconceived notions about any alternative to the status quo. They raise reasonable questions and are unlikely to fully embrace Bitcoin. As I've said, Bitcoin isn't for everyone. But some of these bears are also able to put aside their prejudices when they hear a good counterargument.

Consider New York University business school professor Nouriel Roubini, also known as Dr. Doom for his dire but accurate predictions prior to the 2008 global recession and his harsh skepticism toward cryptocurrency. In a panel discussion with me, Tone Vays, and Brock Pierce at the 2019 CC Forum in London, Roubini repeated his criticisms that Bitcoin wasn't decentralized and that governments would suppress any monetary system that didn't identify the participants. He described crypto as "a populist backlash" affecting financial services and other industries, enabled by technology. "I'd take the US dollar over any one of your shitcoins," he told me at one particularly heated point in the dialogue. But I wasn't advocating for the shitcoins; I was advocating for Bitcoin. There's a huge difference!

While defending Bitcoin, I didn't entirely disagree with his observations about populism, which has been so apparent in the political movements sweeping the world. People have wanted to feel more listened to for years by the leaders of organizations—government and the private sector—that control our lives.

But what struck me was that Roubini only a few minutes earlier had seemed to soften his stance on Bitcoin, calling it "maybe a partial store of value." Those few grudging steps suggested that one of the world's highest-profile bears had not dismissed digital currency entirely. For me, it was a small sign of progress. One day, I hope that Bitcoin will convince him that it is indeed a legitimate store of value.

Then there are blanket bears, complete nonbelievers driven by irrational fear, unwilling or unable to consider the logical case for Bitcoin. They think cryptocurrency is unreal, funny money, a novelty that has caught a sizable part of the public's fascination but cannot thrive over time because it is so far removed from the only monetary system that they know. They see widespread adoption as an impossibility, requiring consumers to abandon their financial service providers en masse. For them, only the US dollar, the euro, the pound, or other widely used currencies are real. For them, gold, stock certificates, and real estate are real, but not bitcoin.

In Chapter 6, I wrote about my heated debate in early 2014 with popular Chinese business talk show host Larry Hsien Ping Lang. Lang had adopted the Chinese government's skepticism and had already decided to mock bitcoin no matter what I said.

At the time of my appearance, Bitcoin was hovering around the $700 range, more than five times what it had been just a year earlier. Meanwhile, BTCChina had just become the world's largest exchange, measured in the number and value of bitcoin transactions. But Lang would hear none of it. He dismissed my arguments about how Bitcoin, in addition to having a market price, also represents actual value even if the owner doesn't use it personally.

So, I decided to tease him about a hypothetical gift of 100 bitcoins, worth then upward of $70,000. He looked perplexed and refused. I had to ask forcefully, "Are you telling me if someone gave you 100 bitcoins, you wouldn't take it?"

Lang waved his hands profusely, as if Bitcoin were some evil monster trying to attack him, and said he wouldn't want to accept any bitcoins because, as he saw it, bitcoin was completely worthless despite clear evidence to the contrary. Lang's hand-waving gesture became a Bitcoin internet meme in China, mocking skeptics. I haven't run into Lang since our heated discussion, but I don't believe he's changed his mind.

Some Bitcoin nonbelievers will remain nonbelievers, the way some people refuse to invest in the stock market, the way some people hate gold, the way some people object to other types of investments, the way that some people believe it's best to keep your cash in a savings account, money market account, low-interest CD, or in flour jars on a kitchen counter. While this approach will protect them from the aftershocks of economic downturns or crises, it will also prevent them from achieving any significant growth in their investments.

If you become a bitcoin investor, you have to accept that some people will never join you. Don't let these people create doubts once you've made up your mind to invest in bitcoin. Robert Louis Stevenson, the Scottish novelist, who knew a thing or two about unfound treasures, wrote: "Most of our pocket wisdom is conceived for the use of mediocre people, to discourage them from ambitious attempts, and generally console them in their mediocrity."

PREDICTION 6: More Institutional Investors Will Participate

Many crypto observers believe that academic endowments, corporations, banks, mutual and hedge funds, and other institutional investors will drive Bitcoin's inevitable breakthrough. Understandably cautious by nature, these investors had been reluctant to commit to something so new and volatile.

But with time they've softened their stance, using the same deep analysis with which they dissect other investments to convince themselves of Bitcoin's potential. This has been one of Bitcoin's most promising trends because it signifies its acceptance among organizations that control some of the world's biggest pools of capital.

Why?

Compare these two numbers: 100,000 percent versus 179 percent.

If you'd invested in bitcoin in 2011, two years after its introduction, you would have achieved the former returns by 2020. The latter figure is what you would have gained over the same period by investing in the S&P 500. Many of the institutions and money managers may have gnashed their teeth about volatility and security issues—they receive their big fees to be worrywarts, understandably given how much they have at stake—but I predict they will come around to embrace bitcoin. When they do, their performance will undoubtedly improve as bitcoin continues to outpace major stock indexes.

Proof-of-Trend 1

A mid-2019 Fidelity Investments study[4] found that more than one in five institutional investors owned digital assets, a remarkable upswing given that hardly any of these groups held these assets in 2016. Nearly half of the more than 400 institutional investors surveyed felt there was room for digital assets in their portfolios.

They varied in approach with almost three in four favoring the purchase of investment products holding digital assets and about three in five preferring to buy digital assets directly or to purchase investment products holding digital asset companies.

"We've seen a maturation of interest in digital assets from early adopters, like crypto hedge funds, to traditional institutional investors like family offices and endowments," said Tom Jessop, president of Fidelity Digital Assets, which provides custody and trade execution services for digital assets to institutional investors. "More institutional investors are engaging with digital assets, either directly or through service providers, as the potential impact of blockchain technology on financial markets—new and old—becomes more readily apparent."

Jessop acknowledged that firms were still developing "their own investment theses," and that there was "more work to be done as it" related "to describing digital assets and blockchain technology in familiar terms." But he said that these companies had made progress in developing "custody, trading and financing infrastructure."

He added: "Institutional sentiment mirrors many of the positive developments we've seen in the underlying ecosystem . . . . The global regulatory environment remains cautiously constructive."

To be sure, Fidelity has been ahead of other financial powerhouses in embracing Bitcoin. Its forward-thinking CEO Abigail Johnson has pushed crypto initiatives since 2015 when she declared that it would play a big role in the future of finance. Fidelity's efforts have ranged from the small and quirky, the acceptance of bitcoin for payment in one of its cafeterias, to the big and bold, the creation of a stand-alone company to provide trading, advising, and other crypto services to institutional investors.

Proof-of-Trend 2

Consider 2018 data by the financial research group Autonomous Next, which identified 287 crypto hedge funds, up from just 20 in 2016. Noted Mike Novogratz, the billionaire hedge fund manager in a 2019 interview: "The institutionalization of this space is coming. It's coming pretty quick."

Proof-of-Trend 3

The digital currency investment group Grayscale reported that investors, almost three-quarters of whom are institutional investors, placed $607 million into its products in 2019.[5] That was more than the amount the company had raised in the previous five years. As this book went to press, the company had more than $27 billion[6] in cryptoassets under management.[7] "Institutional demand continues to be a long-term trend: Institutional investors continued to be the dominant driver of investment capital," Grayscale said in a Medium post capping its 2019 performance.[8]

Proof-of-Trend 4

Consider JPMorgan's and Goldman Sachs's development of their own digital coins. Don't confuse these efforts with Bitcoin. Having a central organization at the root of potential digital currencies defies one of Bitcoin's main tenets. But these efforts are a powerful acknowledgement of digital currency's potential, coming less than two years after JPMorgan Chase's CEO Jamie Dimon famously called Bitcoin "a fraud" at a conference for institutional investors.

"It's worse than tulip bulbs," Dimon said at the time, referring to the famous seventeenth-century speculative bubble that crashed the Dutch economy. "It won't end well." He added: "It's just not a real thing, eventually it will be closed."[9] Dimon undoubtedly does not feel the same way now.

Proof-of-Trend 5

Major college endowments have begun to invest in cryptocurrency. In 2018, Yale's endowment chief David Swensen, sometimes called the Warren Buffett of the endowment world, invested in Andreessen Horowitz's cryptocurrency fund and a second fund.[10] Yale's nearly $30 billion endowment fund at the time was the country's second largest behind Harvard, which has also devoted capital into crypto, along with MIT, Stanford, and the University of North Carolina. Now that they've begun, it's very likely these endowments will increase their holdings in cryptocurrency over the next decade.

As for institutional investors overall, I predict that bitcoin will account for as much as 10 percent of portfolios in the next several years. And this is also the case for companies. In September 2020, Nasdaq-listed MicroStrategy purchased $425 million in bitcoin to serve as its primary treasury reserve asset.[11] It was a bold move, and MicroStrategy was the first publicly traded company to make such a large commitment to bitcoin using its treasury reserves. That was soon followed up by Square Inc., which announced in October 2020 that it was buying $50 million worth of bitcoin.[12] And most notably, Tesla announced in February 2021 that it had purchased $1.5 billion worth of bitcoin. When a giant S&P 500 company like Tesla makes the move into bitcoin, every other company has to take notice. I predict that more and more public companies will start adding bitcoin to their balance sheet. Given that cash yields no meaningful return, and bitcoin offers a huge potential upside as an investment, companies will look to diversify their holdings into bitcoin. This will be a booming trend, and great for both Bitcoin and bitcoin investors worldwide.

PREDICTION 7: Bitcoin Futures Trading Will Expand

Bitcoin futures first appeared on cryptocurrency exchanges as an unregulated asset. As the price and public awareness soared, non-crypto exchanges took notice.

Did they see an opportunity to make money?

You bet.

In late 2017, the Chicago Board Options Exchange (CBOE) and then the Chicago Mercantile Exchange (CME) began offering regulated bitcoin futures trading. While the CBOE has since discontinued bitcoin futures, trading volume on the CME continues to rise. Futures trading offers the advantage of trading on bitcoin's performance without holding any of the currency. The presence of bitcoin on the longstanding CBOE and CME platforms was not only another small step in Bitcoin's legitimization in the public eye, but practically speaking, created a more transparent, liquid market. Those readers who have dabbled in futures trading know that it is a risky investment. It is speculative in nature, requiring steady resolve and an acceptance that not all of your bets will be profitable. But there's also a potentially big upside, and bitcoin with its huge swings presents great short-term opportunities for those people willing to take a chance.

Okay, so CBOE subsequently decided to exit this market less than 20 months later, saying that "it was assessing its approach" to digital asset derivatives for trading. CBOE's directors had concerns about bitcoin's place in the investment universe. And good luck forecasting correctly what bitcoin is going to do from one month to the next, at least for the time being. You don't need to hear again from me that you'd be better off HODLing. But I'm realistic, as asset classes mature, they invite different ways to profit. Futures trading is going to be a larger part of the Bitcoin world, and it is another sign of Bitcoin's maturation.

PREDICTION 8: Regulators Will Approve a Bitcoin ETF

Wherefore art the long-awaited Bitcoin ETF?

What's gotten in the way?

As these pages have already addressed, fear and bureaucracy mixed with a healthy dose of politics have created challenging obstacles. But the ETF will happen.

I give it a three-year timeline, probably less if regulators are able to turn away from issues stemming from the coronavirus-ravaged economy. Demand for the ETF has been growing, and government resistance has shown signs of weakening.

In rejecting the Winklevoss brothers' 2017 ETF proposal, the SEC said that it would not prevent "fraudulent and manipulative acts and practices."[13] The SEC also expressed concerns about fraud and the protection of investors' interests.

Their concerns echoed comments about investor protections in a January 2018 SEC letter.[14] In that 1,000-word document, the SEC posed questions about how ETFs would ensure the value of a cryptocurrency. "Would funds have the information necessary to adequately value cryptocurrencies or cryptocurrency-related products, given their volatility, the fragmentation and general lack of regulation of underlying cryptocurrency markets, and the nascent state and current trading volume in the cryptocurrency futures markets?" the SEC wrote. "How would funds develop and implement policies and procedures to value, and in many cases 'fair value,' cryptocurrency-related products?"

The SEC noted concerns about manipulation, custody, arbitrage (the buying and selling of the asset on different markets), and liquidity. Under a new liquidity rule, the SEC wrote, funds would have to maintain appropriate liquidity risk management, in which, among other things, they would have to classify their investments into one of four liquidity categories and limit their investments in illiquid securities to 15 percent of the fund's assets. The agency added: "What steps would funds investing in cryptocurrencies or cryptocurrency-related products take to assure that they would have sufficiently liquid assets to meet redemptions daily?"

But in referencing the Investment Company Act of 1940, the SEC sounded a more optimistic note. "As the Division with primary responsibility for regulatory policy regarding registered funds, we seek to foster innovation that benefits investors and preserves the important protections that Congress established in the 1940 Act," the agency wrote. "Over the years, dialogue between fund sponsors and the Division has facilitated the development of many new types of investment products that have expanded choice for investors. Exchange-traded funds and money market funds are notable examples."

It won't be long before the combined forces of a sound ETF proposal made by respected investors and a more receptive regulatory environment leads to a successful outcome. If anything, growing demand by the retail investment community for a product that provides the same advantages of traditional ETFs—lower risk, flexibility, and tax benefits—will eventually fuel the creation of a Bitcoin ETF. Or as I like to say: Where there's momentum, there are solutions.

PREDICTION 9: Everyone Will Use Bitcoin by 2050

So, you can't yet use bitcoin at a Rite Aid, Costco, or Cheesecake Factory; or buy a latte at your local coffee shop, let alone a car, or hundreds of other common items that we use daily. (You can purchase a gift card with bitcoin to use at Starbucks.) This scenario is unlikely to change soon. We're simply not far enough along in the Bitcoin journey to make it possible for people. And most importantly, this is not necessary. Bitcoin's success is not dependent on retail purchasing usage.

Most businesses are still too comfortable with what they know—credit and debit cards, and payment services like PayPal. They don't feel any curiosity, let alone urgency, to try something different. And then there are the fears. Some small businesses mistakenly worry about bitcoin transaction fees for transferring payments between wallets. From their perspective, using bitcoin for payment is more complicated and expensive than traditional methods. How ironic, given the amounts they're shelling out for paying and receiving money.

Some skeptics in the retail industry point to the relatively low number of people who use bitcoin to justify not diving in, which is a Catch-22 type argument. They won't accept bitcoin payments unless more people use bitcoin to pay. But more people won't pay in bitcoin if merchants won't accept it as payment.

But as I've already indicated, the number of people using bitcoin is not where people's focus should be; rather, they should be thinking about its potential usefulness outside of retail payments. It already has a solid enough foothold in developing countries where it has been facilitating commerce in areas that have few if any banking services. A few high-profile firms have also started using it to give their customers a new option.

No less than Microsoft started accepting bitcoin years ago. Telecommunications giant AT&T, BMW, and e-commerce platforms Etsy and Shopify were also early Bitcoin converts. Online retailer Overstock founder Patrick Byrne embraced Bitcoin so strongly that he wound up selling his stake in the company—about $90 million—to purchase cryptocurrencies, along with gold and silver.

By the end of 2019, more than 15,000 businesses were accepting bitcoin, doubling the total less than four years earlier. This mounting trend is worth watching. The baristas, pharmacists, dentists, and others will follow eventually as bitcoin becomes the de facto global standard, recognized by almost everyone. By then, $100 bills—and euro, yen, and franc equivalents—will be worth a lot less than today, or even completely worthless (except for rare bills that have special value as museum pieces or collectibles). Just remember, whatever paper currency you have, whether it's a US $100 dollar bill, a 500 euro note, or a 1,000 Swiss franc, the most value it will ever hold is today. Every month or year that passes by, it will be worth less and less. How tragic.

PREDICTION 10: China's Domination Won't Continue Forever

Ask people with even a passing interest in Bitcoin which country has dominated Bitcoin, and most of them are likely to say China.

It's an easy answer if you think in terms of where Bitcoin grew early on and how many people are involved.

As of the publication of this book, China is widely estimated to account for more than 65 percent of the world's mining hash power, and observers of the industry believe the country is home to the largest number of retail investors. They also tie most of bitcoin's significant price fluctuations to events in China.

A late 2013 price surge reflected a burgeoning Chinese middle-class fascination with the new investment opportunity combined with a willingness to invest in mining technology. Bitcoin had tickled a Chinese cultural funny bone for taking risks, a characteristic of the Chinese most commonly observed in the casinos of Macau.

Subsequently, a Chinese government clampdown amid fears that Bitcoin was enabling users—some with illegal intentions—to bypass traditional avenues of exchange sent prices tumbling. A decline in the Chinese renminbi in late 2016 spurred bitcoin investors to jump in, sending prices skyward. But the government's banning of ICOs and crypto exchanges in September 2017 led to a near 50 percent drop, albeit one that lasted only a few weeks. A late 2019 pronouncement by Chinese President Xi Jinping that endorsed blockchain technology led to a more than 30 percent increase that sent bitcoin prices over $10,000 again.

Now let me say something controversial: China has received too much credit for dictating bitcoin's movements. The rest of the world has been catching up and has more room for growth. To be sure, China's influence has been strong at times, but look at where much of the innovation in Bitcoin and other cryptocurrencies has occurred—in Europe, the United States, and other parts of the world.

Bitcoin is neutral and borderless; no country has a built-in advantage. Whatever advantage China once had is already waning. As time goes on, Bitcoin's benefits will be recognized by many people in countries other than China.

PREDICTION 11:
There Will Be More Women in Bitcoin

Men have dominated the Bitcoin ecosystem from its beginnings. Bitcoin's creator was likely a geeky man, and the cryptocurrency industry's early advocates came from the male-dominated tech and finance worlds. I think it's fair to say women have traditionally been more risk averse about personal finance and less likely to embrace any volatile asset. The website Coin Dance, which tracks cryptocurrency statistics, says that women compose just 12 percent of bitcoin holders. Women are scarce among the industry's investors and entrepreneurs.

But Bitcoin doesn't favor one gender over another anymore than it favors one country over others. It is a perfectly neutral asset. By Coin Dance's calculations, the number of women acquiring bitcoin has more than doubled since 2018. In a December 2019 survey, the crypto fund operator Grayscale found that 43 percent of investors interested in bitcoin are women, a 13 percent jump over the previous year.[15] According to an April 2020 CoinMarketCap survey, the number of women in the cryptocurrency industry rose more than 43 percent in the first quarter of 2020.[16] There is nothing inherently male about Bitcoin. Much of its future growth will come from women investors and entrepreneurs.

PREDICTION 12:
More People Will Appreciate a Permissionless System

If I were a Bitcoin outsider, permissionless isn't a term that would make me want to get more interested. It's another one of those abstract-sounding etymological creations that ring off the tongue, but its meaning isn't entirely clear.

What does it mean for Bitcoin to be permissionless? It means that, unlike many things in life, you do not need permission to participate in the Bitcoin ecosystem. You do not need permission to mine bitcoin, to send bitcoin, to receive bitcoin, to invest in bitcoin, nor to write software to improve bitcoin. The beauty is that Bitcoin is completely in the open, and no one can stop or prevent you from participating. Aside from gold, almost every other investment or asset class is permission-based. To buy real estate, you need the blessing of the county recorder to formalize the purchase. To invest in stocks and bonds, a broker evaluates your overall financial health before you're allowed to open an account. Even a car purchase has to be recorded by the state government, and the vehicle has to be formally registered with the Department of Motor Vehicles. Prior to Bitcoin, our life was full of examples of things needing permission.

What's wrong with a permissioned model? Technically, nothing is wrong, as it works quite well for the most part. However, Bitcoin offers an alternative. For the first time in human history, people can now use bitcoin to transfer money and value, of any amount, at any time, to anyone in the world, all without seeking anyone else's permission. Two parties can do it, without seeking a third party for approval or assistance. In addition, people can save bitcoins to preserve purchasing power—again, no permission is needed. Whenever permission is needed, then you're at the mercy of the third-party judge and jury, and there's a chance that they might disagree with you and not let you proceed. Bitcoin gives you an alternative, to make financial transactions without seeking permission, and that is what people find extremely valuable.

Permissionless systems fit within the current zeitgeist. Look at which direction the pendulum has swung for years in public attitudes toward regulation and the role of government. People are looking for less of it. Many of them have become wary of authority, believing the organizations that are supposed to make our lives easier frequently do the opposite. That includes those responsible for monetary policy and the financial institutions holding our money and enabling our transactions.

In the United States, the inept response to the coronavirus only reminded people of the inherent weaknesses of central systems. Where society needed quick action, there were delays. Where it needed a sense that monetary systems would be calm and stable, there was uncertainty because the people making decisions lacked judgment. In the calm after the storm, those problems haven't vanished.

Is there a better model than Bitcoin's permissionless approach? What could be more welcome than a system that removes central authority entirely?

A system that eliminates authority, that enables people to control their transactions almost completely, is tailor-made for the current mood. Bitcoin is the right answer at the right time. That's one of the big reasons there is so much room for growth.

Bitcoin sounds complicated, and some of the technological concepts are most easily understood by computer scientists and people with a more than passing knowledge of cryptography and distributed ledger platforms. But its root principles are readily understandable. You own the units of value—bitcoins, or the smallest fractional use, the Satoshi (0.00000001 of a bitcoin)—and can use them when and where you see fit by executing transactions without permission or any other involvement from an outside group.

In Chapter 4, I posed one of civilization's great ongoing questions: How much regulation do people need to live harmoniously while ensuring they can be productive? I have backed both Democrats and Republicans in the past, but now I lean Libertarian. I believe that I am the best arbiter of my affairs, economic or otherwise. And I believe that many people feel the same way.

Permissionless fits this part of human nature. It ensures that we have complete autonomy over our financial affairs. As Bitcoin sounds less strange, and spurs less fear, people will latch onto this core aspect of personal economic freedom.

PREDICTION 13:
Mining Will Continue to Be Robust

Some Bitcoin observers saw the May 2020 block reward halving as the beginning of a mining death knell. After all, why mine bitcoin for smaller payoffs? In this most recent halving, the block reward for solving the algorithm verifying a bitcoin transaction fell from 12.50 to 6.25 bitcoins.

Mining is time consuming, expensive given the cost of mining equipment and electricity, and also competitive as there is practically no barrier to entry due to its permissionless nature. While theoretically you could buy the latest mining rig, the reality is that all the newest equipment has long been paid for and reserved by large mining consortiums. So, consumers generally can't purchase a new generation of mining hardware until it gets resold on the secondary market, sometimes after it's been on the market for a long time. Also, you would be paying big-time for it without any guarantee of rewards. Future halvings, which occur roughly every four years, will further reduce the bitcoin rewards through year 2140, by which time all unmined bitcoin will have entered the market, bringing the total global circulation to 21 million bitcoins.

Why would any endeavor facing these conditions continue? Who would want to be part of an activity where you work harder and spend more, but have less likelihood of getting a reward, and, even if you do succeed, the reward will be smaller?

But don't be mistaken. Even though the reward as measured in bitcoin is smaller, the dollar value of it is increasing as bitcoin prices go up and up. So, from a US dollar perspective, Bitcoin mining has been a growing industry for the last decade and will continue so for a long time. The Bitcoin protocol cannot function without verification, and this fundamental part of the system will be even more important as bitcoin finds wider use. Consider the system similar to the postal service where you pay for stamps that ensure delivery. The cost of these stamps keeps the system running. No stamps, no delivery.

Similarly, if there are no miners, there can be no assurance that someone has enough bitcoin in their wallet to cover the cost of a product or service or that they're not trying to use the same bitcoin twice.

Mining will continue to be a vibrant part of the protocol. And look for mining hash power, the computing power that's behind the bitcoin mining network, to grow, focused particularly in places with low-cost electricity from renewable sources.

PREDICTION 14: Wallets and Exchanges Will Be Easier to Use

I almost hesitate to make this prediction because it's so obvious: Technology always improves with time.

So it will be with wallets and exchanges. They'll be faster, easier to use, and more secure. In a few instances, wallets will give people a more tangible sense of owning something, a physical presence.

This is what people have wanted, and the market has been responding and will continue responding. It is this principle that helped me turn BTCC into a juggernaut in the early Bitcoin days when Chinese consumers diving into bitcoin were looking for a faster, more efficient way to purchase bitcoin. I had noted in my time at Yahoo!, Walmart, and other firms that companies that don't address customer demands risk their very existence. Certainly, Yahoo! missed opportunities and is now an afterthought in the history of search engines and web portals.

At BTCC, the engineers I hired made a steady stream of improvements that addressed customer concerns and made our exchange arguably the world's most user-friendly. The best

Bitcoin-related businesses have done much the same, which is why they've survived while others haven't. The smart exchanges and wallets will keep tinkering, building better products, and keeping their eyes on consumer wants.

I sometimes think the evolution of technology in our society as a modern equivalent of Michelangelo hacking endlessly away at a piece of stone, bettering the creation with each stroke. With tech, each user experience, every exchange of information betters the product.

There's certainly room for better wallets and exchanges. Half my friends—many with advanced degrees and successful professional careers—still ask me to help them set up their electronic hardware wallets or need a step-by-step explainer on how they should use an exchange. There are still concerns (that I do not dismiss but respectfully answer) about wallet and exchange security. Nonetheless, we are further along than we were when I bought my first bitcoin.

Remember how slow website download times were even a decade after the internet had been around? We're at the equivalent in cryptocurrency.

One additional note: All this may come amid the expansion and contraction of companies providing these services. That's another characteristic of technology with companies entering a promising market beyond what the market can bear. Even as an industry succeeds, many, if not most firms fail or are bought out by stronger competitors.

I won't predict who will survive this next stage in Bitcoin, lest my mention be misconstrued as an endorsement. I suggest (as I discussed in the chapter on wallets and exchanges) that you look at the quality of services and other factors that seem best suited to your needs when you decide which wallet and exchange to use.

If you're curious, I'm trying to create the next generation of wallets that's super easy to use. My startup, Ballet, makes crypto easy by turning cold storage into a simple physical metal card.

At the same time, don't be surprised if a few other niche players catering to small parts of the market also find a foothold. Many of them will be locally based. Consider them the equivalent of boutique stores that know their customers particularly well and provide highly specified services.

PREDICTION 15: The US and Other Countries Will Create New Crypto Agencies

Where does bitcoin fit among investment categories?

Should agencies treat it like an equity to be governed by SEC rules in the same way stocks are regulated? Or should they group it with money and currencies? Or commodities like gold?

This unresolved issue has interfered with efforts to regulate Bitcoin. But in fairness, there is no easy answer.

It shares certain characteristics but is also different than anything already in existence.

Perhaps it's closest to gold in that it is an internationally recognized system of value and there is a limited supply. And I like the term *digital gold*. But Bitcoin is information based, not touchable like a gold coin or bar, and it trades every day, all day, and in amounts and at a speed that is beyond gold's capability.

People can trade stocks quickly, but stock performance depends on tangible events, leadership, and human decisions. In the end, stocks are an investment representation of a company, so each share of stock is implicitly backed by the performance of the underlying company, whereas Bitcoin is purposely not backed by anyone or anything else.

None of the current agencies, not even the US Commodity Futures Trading Commission, which has held multiple hearings about digital currency, can quite address the issues that Bitcoin raises. So, I predict that the United States and other smart countries will establish new agencies parallel to other financial services–related regulating agencies but focused on cryptocurrencies. These departments will appoint people with backgrounds in technology, security, and finance. They will stay abreast of trends and establish the ground rules for crypto trading, protect consumers, and perhaps most importantly demystify Bitcoin.

IT'S ONLY A MATTER OF TIME

I am a math and science guy at heart. I've always liked the care and thought required to solve problems. Mathematical analysis has informed my approach to business. I'm sure people who have reported to me would describe me as a methodical problem solver who fits pieces together until I have an airtight answer.

I highlight this part of my character to show that even if I am a Bitcoin evangelist inclined to make rosy predictions, I did not arrive at this point lightly or impulsively. My commitment to Bitcoin has come only by seeing Bitcoin prove itself repeatedly. Everything that I expected in regard to bitcoin's ever-widening use and price increases have occurred. In the time since I started writing the first pages of this book to the last words of this chapter, the price has risen over fivefold. To be sure, this line has not been straight, and there have been and will continue to be fallbacks in price, as well as in regulation and other issues that I highlighted here. But I am not concerned. Progress in any endeavor is often choppy.

So, when I encourage people to buy Bitcoin (within their means, of course), I do not make this recommendation lightly or impulsively. The logic behind the system is as airtight as the day that Satoshi Nakamoto released his paper. Even in my own 10-year journey in Bitcoin, I have never been more optimistic about Bitcoin's future. I have no doubt that Bitcoin eventually will be accepted as readily as any fiat currency and that its price will rise into six and seven figures. For me, the only question is how quickly.

ACKNOWLEDGMENTS

The great inventor Alexander Graham Bell famously said that "when one door closes, another opens." Bell's words now resonate with me as I look back to early 2018 when I sold BTCC and exited the cryptocurrency exchange business. After building China's first Bitcoin exchange into a crypto industry leader, I wasn't sure what my next move would be after the acquisition, but I knew that I wanted to continue to advocate for Bitcoin. I consider Bitcoin the world's greatest recent invention.

Throughout my 10 years in the industry, I would hear the same questions repeatedly from newcomers to cryptocurrency. These experiences were at the root of my decision to write this book. I felt that I could provide a service for consumer investors—and maybe a few professionals—by addressing all these questions and others I'd heard over the years in one document. So I owe an initial thanks to those who took the time at conferences to ask me all kinds of questions about Bitcoin. They forced me to think through issues and consider skeptics' concerns more deeply.

This project has required me to revisit events that I hadn't thought much about, if at all, for years. I tend to look ahead and not back, so I am appreciative of family and friends who helped me recall details that were a little fuzzy. They have provided steadfast support throughout my career, reinforcing my belief that few things in life are more powerful than having a nurturing community around you.

My agent, Eileen Cope, was enthusiastic about the project from our very first meeting. Her insightful comments sharpened the proposal, and she provided encouragement throughout the writing process. Much appreciation to Casey Ebro at McGraw Hill for seeing the promise of Bitcoin even during the lows of a prolonged bear market. Many thanks to James Rubin and Kevin Commins for their wise edits. This book would not have been possible without them.

Book writing is a time-intensive process. While I wrote *The Promise of Bitcoin*, I was also starting a new business. So I would like to thank my wife for encouraging my twin ventures with her usual patience and optimism. I'd also like to thank my mom and dad for instilling in me the qualities of hard work and a can-do attitude that they learned from their parents, and that seems to run throughout the Lee and Chu families. It is no accident that my grandparents built businesses in other parts of the world at a time when global travel was an arduous task. My parents built on that success. They taught me about the value of gold and money, and gave me the education and resources to explore my interest in technology. Given these lessons, my passion for Bitcoin is easy to understand.

Most importantly, I want to thank my brother, Charlie, for telling me in early 2011 about his then recent discovery of Bitcoin. I have fond memories of our early technical and philosophical discussions about Bitcoin: the decentralized peer-to-peer network, mining rewards via proof-of-work, what makes something valuable, the qualities of gold, and whether Bitcoin would ever surpass $100 million in total market value. We were such newbies back then! And for the success at BTCChina and BTCC that launched my Bitcoin career, I am eternally grateful to Linke Yang, Xiaoyu Huang, and Ron Cao, for believing in me.

Finally, I would like to thank Satoshi Nakamoto for his ingenious, transformational system, and his followers who have built it into what it is today. To these fellow evangelists, I say, "Keep going. We have only just begun."

NOTES

INTRODUCTION

1. https://bitcoin.org/bitcoin.pdf.

CHAPTER 1

1. Matt Soniak, "Was Manhattan Really Bought for $24?," *Mental Floss*, October 2, 2012, https://www.mentalfloss.com/article/12657/was-manhattan-really-bought-24.
2. Alison S. Brooks et al., "Long-Distance Stone Transport and Pigment Use in the Earliest Middle Stone Age," *Science* 360, no. 6384 (April 6, 2018): 90–94, https://science.sciencemag.org/content/360/6384/90.
3. "Barter Economies," Farming in the 1930s, LivingHistoryFarm.org, 2003, https://livinghistoryfarm.org/farminginthe30s/money_12.html.
4. Everett Millman, "The Importance of the Lydian Stater as the World's First Coin," *Ancient History Encyclopedia*, March 27, 2015, https://www.ancient.eu/article/797/the-importance-of-the-lydian-stater-as-the-worlds/.
5. Jennifer R. Davis, "Charlemagne's Portrait Coinage and Ideas of Rulership at the Carolingian Court," *Special Issue on Secular Art in the Middle Ages* (Spring 2014 Summer 2014), pp. 19–27, https://www.jstor.org/stable/23725947?seq=1.
6. Thomas Jefferson to John Taylor, 1816, *Online Library of Liberty*, https://oll.libertyfund.org/quotes/187
7. Scott Summer, "The Fed and the Great Recession," foreignaffairs.com, Volume 95, No. 3, (April/May 2016) https://www.foreignaffairs.com/articles/united-states/2016-04-18/fed-and-great-recession.
8. Ken Griffith, "A Quick History of Cryptocurrencies BBTC—Before Bitcoin" *Bitcoin Magazine*, April 16, 2014, https://bitcoinmagazine.com/articles/quick-history-cryptocurrencies-bbtc-bitcoin-1397682630.
9. http://vu.hn/bitcoin%20origins.html.

CHAPTER 2

1. "Hash rates," blockchain.com, accessed January 27, 2021, https://www.blockchain.com/pools?timespan=4days.
2. Jordan Tuwiner, "Bitcoin Mining in China," BuyBitcoinWorldwide.com, January 8, 2021; Electricity and coal costs: https://www.buybitcoinworldwide.com/mining/china/.

3. https://www.globalpetrolprices.com/China/electricity_prices.
4. Danny Palmer, "Mobile Malware Attacks Are Booming in 2019: These Are the Most Common threats," *ZDNet*, July 25, 2019, https://www.zdnet.com/article/mobile-malware-attacks-are-booming-in-2019-these-are-the-most-common-threats/.
5. Robert McMillan, "The Inside Story of Mt. Gox, Bitcoin's $460 Million Disaster," *Wired*, March 3, 2014, https://www.wired.com/2014/03/bitcoin-exchange/.
6. Paddy Baker, "Japan's High Court Rejects Former Mt Gox CEO's Conviction Appeal," *Coindesk*, June 12, 2020, https://www.coindesk.com/japans-high-court-rejects-mt-gox-ceo-appeal.

CHAPTER 3

1. "4th Lecture: Inflation," Mises Institute, https://mises.org/library/economic-policy-thoughts-today-and-tomorrow/html/c/49, accessed November 30, 2020.
2. Teddy Nykiel, "Banks Mine Big Data to Get to Know You Better, and Better," NerdWallet, March 6, 2015, https://www.nerdwallet.com/blog/banking/banks-big-data.
3. Matthew O'Brien, "Everything You Need to Know About the Cyprus Bank Disaster," *The Atlantic*, March 18, 2013, https://www.theatlantic.com/business/archive/2013/03/everything-you-need-to-know-about-the-cyprus-bank-disaster/274096/.
4. "Three People Die While Waiting in Queue to Exchange Rs 500 and Rs 1,000 Currency Notes," Huffington Post, November 11, 2016, https://web.archive.org/web/20161113002732/http://www.huffingtonpost.in/2016/11/11/73-year-old-dies-waiting-in-queue-to-exchange-discontinued-curre/.
5. "Venezuelan Bolivar—What Can It Buy You?," BBC.com, August 20, 2018, https://www.bbc.com/news/world-latin-america-45246409.
6. Anatoly Kurmanaev, "Venezuela's Collapse Is the Worst Outside of War in Decades, Economists Say," *New York Times*, May 17, 2019, https://www.nytimes.com/2019/05/17/world/americas/venezuela-economy.html.

CHAPTER 4

1. "Law in Ancient Egypt," University College London, 2003, https://www.ucl.ac.uk/museums-static/digitalegypt/administration/law.html.
2. "Coinbase's Written Testimony for the Subcommittee on Capital Markets, Securities, and Investment," Coinbase, March 13, 2018, https://blog.coinbase.com/coinbases-written-testimony-for-the-subcommittee-on-capital-markets-securities-and-investment-47f8a260ce41.
3. *United States of America v. Larry Dean Harmon*, Case 1:19-cr-00395-BAH, United States District Court for the District of Columbia, July 24, 2020, courtlistner.com, https://www.courtlistener.com/recap/gov.uscourts.dcd.213319/gov.uscourts.dcd.213319.59.0.pdf.

4. U.S. House Committee on Agriculture, "Cryptocurrencies - Oversight of New Assets in the Digital Age," written testimony of Daniel S. Gorfine, July 18, 2018, https://docs.house.gov/meetings/AG/AG00/20180718/108562/HHRG-115-AG00-Wstate-GorfineD-20180718.pdf.
5. U.S. House Committee on Financial Services, "Waters to Facebook: Today's Hearing Is Only the First Step in Our Oversight and Legislative Process," July 17, 2019, https://financialservices.house.gov/news/documentsingle.aspx?DocumentID=404104.
6. Coin Center, "Rep. Emmer Asks SEC About Token Utility," April 26, 2018, YouTube video, 3:30, https://www.youtube.com/watch?v=EO3qYW9DF-A.
7. Tom Emmer, 6th Congressional District of Minnesota, "Emmer Leads Bipartisan Blockchain Caucus Letter to the IRS Ahead of Tax Day Urging Virtual Currency," April 11, 2019, press release, Guidancehttps://emmer.house.gov/2019/4/emmer-leads-bipartisan-blockchain-caucus-letter-irs-ahead-tax-day-urging.
8. Internal Revenue Service, "IRS has begun sending letters to virtual currency owners advising them to pay back taxes, file amended returns; part of agency's larger efforts," July 26, 2019, https://www.irs.gov/newsroom/irs-has-begun-sending-letters-to-virtual-currency-owners-advising-them-to-pay-back-taxes-file-amended-returns-part-of-agencys-larger-efforts.
9. Internal Revenue Service, "IRS Announces the Identification and Selection of Five Large Business and International Compliance Campaigns," July 2, 2018, https://www.irs.gov/businesses/irs-lbi-compliance-campaigns-july-2-2018.
10. Financial Services Committee, "Committee on Financial Services Hearing: Examining Facebook's Proposed Cryptocurrency and Its Impact on Consumers, Investors, and the American Financial System," July 17, 2019, 6:55.31, webcast of hearing, https://financialservices.house.gov/calendar/eventsingle.aspx?EventID=404001#Wbcast03222017.
11. U.S. Senate Committee on Banking, Housing and Urban Affairs, "Crapo Statement at Hearing on Digital Currencies and Blockchain," July 30, 2019, https://www.banking.senate.gov/newsroom/majority/crapo-statement-at-hearing-on-digital-currencies-and-blockchain.
12. 4th Congressional District of Illinois, "Reps. García, Tlaib Introduce Bill to Protect Consumers from Market Manipulation," November 19, 2019, https://chuygarcia.house.gov/media/press-releases/reps-garc-tlaib-introduce-bill-protect-consumers-market-manipulation.
13. "Regulation of Cryptocurrency Around the World," The Law Library of Congress, Global Legal Research Center, June 2018, https://www.loc.gov/law/help/cryptocurrency/cryptocurrency-world-survey.pdf.
14. Cynthia Sewell, "Gov. Brad Little: Idaho Is Now Least-Regulated State in the Country," *Idaho Statesman*, December 4, 2019, https://www.idahostatesman.com/news/politics-government/state-politics/article238042974.html.

CHAPTER 5

1. "Venezuela: Inflation rate from 1985 to 2022," Statista, accessed January 27, 2021, https://www.statista.com/statistics/371895/inflation-rate-in-venezuela/.
2. United Nations Department of Economic and Social Affairs, "Remittances Matter: 8 Facts You Don't Know About the Money Migrants Send Back Home," UN.org, June 17, 2019, https://www.un.org/development/desa/en/news/population/remittances-matter.html.

CHAPTER 6

1. Ben Mezrich, *Bitcoin Billionaires*, (New York: Flatiron Books, 2019), 106–107.
2. "Prevalence of ATMs Drops Worldwide," *American Banker*, May 20, 2019, https://www.americanbanker.com/articles/prevalence-of-atms-drops-worldwide.
3. "Audience Profile," *CoinDesk*, https://downloads.coindesk.com/CoinDesk-Audience-One-Sheet-q3.pdf (accessed December 9, 2020).
4. Jamie Ballard, "79% of Americans Are Familiar with at Least One Kind of Cryptocurrency," yougov.com, September 6, 2018, https://today.yougov.com/topics/technology/articles-reports/2018/09/06/cryptocurrency-bitcoin-popular-americans.
5. "Largest Bitcoin Ownership Survey Reveals 6.2% of Americans Own Bitcoin, While 7.3% Are Planning to Buy Some," Crypto Radar, October 1, 2019, https://www.prnewswire.com/news-releases/largest-bitcoin-ownership-survey-reveals-6-2-of-americans-own-bitcoin-while-7-3-are-planning-to-buy-some-300928651.html.
6. "Congressman Thomas Massie: 'We can replace the FED with Bitcoin,'" bitcointalk.org, August 2, 2013, https://bitcointalk.org/index.php?topic=266612.0.
7. Tom Emmer, "Congressman Tom Emmer on Bitcoin and Decentralization," Pomp Podcast #352, August 3, 2020, https://www.youtube.com/watch?v=vxz1HFWWkPg.
8. Joon Ian Wong, "The Simple Formula for Becoming a Bitcoin Millionaire, According to One of Its Innovators," Quartz, May 23, 2017, https://qz.com/990088/how-to-become-a-bitcoin-millionaire-according-to-wences-casares-of-xapo/.
9. "Why Own Bitcoin," Xapo, June 17, 2017, https://blog.xapo.com/why-own-bitcoin/.
10. Matthew J. Belvedere, "Bitcoin Is Nearly Halfway to the $400 Billion Value Predicted by the Winklevoss Twins Four Years Ago," CNBC, November 12, 2013, https://www.cnbc.com/2013/11/12/the-winklevoss-brothers-bitcoin-worth-100-times-more.html.
11. David Abel, "Dorsey Still Making Weekly $10K Bitcoin Buy," altcoinbuzz.io, May 15, 2020, https://www.altcoinbuzz.io/cryptocurrency-news/finance-and-funding/dorsey-still-making-weekly-10k-bitcoin-buy/.
12. "What We're Building: Lightning Development Kit," Square Crypto, January 21, 2020, https://medium.com/@squarecrypto/what-were-building-lightning-development-kit-1ed58b0cab06.

13. Alexandra Frean, "Bitcoin Will Become the World's Single Currency, Tech Chief Says," *The Times of London*, March 21, 2018, https://www.thetimes.co.uk/article/bitcoin-will-become-the-worlds-single-currency-tech-chief-says-66slm0p6b.
14. William Suberg, "Billionaire Investor Tim Draper Quit Stocks for Bitcoin 6 Months Ago," *Cointelegraph*, February 25, 2020, https://cointelegraph.com/news/billionaire-investor-tim-draper-quit-stocks-for-bitcoin-6-months-ago.
15. Peter Edmonston, "Dear Investor: We're Stumped," *New York Times*, April 2, 2008, https://www.nytimes.com/2008/04/02/business/02HEDGE.html.
16. Kate Rooney, "Crypto Hedge Fund Known for Eye-Popping Early Returns Lost Nearly 50 Percent Last Month," CNBC, April 10, 2018, https://www.cnbc.com/2018/04/10/crypto-hedge-fund-known-for-returns-got-cut-nearly-in-half-last-month.html.
17. Marie Huillet, "Crypto Hedge Fund Pantera Capital Seals $130 Million for Third Crypto Venture Fund," February 22, 2019, *Cointelegraph*, https://cointelegraph.com/news/crypto-hedge-fund-pantera-capital-seals-130-million-for-third-crypto-venture-fund.
18. Pantera Capital, "Impact on Bitcoin: Pantera Blockchain Letter, April 2020," May 4, 2020, https://medium.com/@PanteraCapital/macro-impact-on-bitcoin-pantera-blockchain-letter-april-2020-1fdc792d4f33.
19. Grayscale Investments, "Grayscale® Ethereum Trust Announces Resumption of Private Placement," February 1, 2021, http://www.globenewswire.com/news-release/2021/02/01/2167368/0/en/Grayscale-Ethereum-Trust-Announces-Resumption-of-Private-Placement.html.
20. Ryan Browne, "Elon Musk says he's a supporter of bitcoin and thinks it will get 'broad acceptance' in finance," CNBC, February 1, 2021, https://www.cnbc.com/2021/02/01/elon-musk-on-clubhouse-i-am-a-supporter-of-bitcoin.html.
21. Reuters, "Time to Buy Bitcoin: Ex-Prudential CEO George Ball," August 14, 2020, video, 5:19, https://uk.reuters.com/video/watch/time-to-buy-bitcoin-ex-prudential-ceo-ge-id717403010?chan=9qsux198.
22. Joe McCarthy, "Bill Gates Says Digital Currencies Could Empower the Poorest," *Global Citizen*, December 13, 2018, https://www.globalcitizen.org/en/content/bill-gates-cryptocurrency-poverty/.
23. "Amazing dinner w/ Warren Buffett finally!" Facebook entry, February 6, 2020, https://www.facebook.com/justinsuntron/photos/a.560868230946888/1001675146866192/?type=3&%3Btheater.

CHAPTER 7

1. Ria Bhutoria, "The Institutional Investors Digital Asset Survey," Fidelity Digital Assets, June 2020, https://www.fidelitydigitalassets.com/bin-public/060_www_fidelity_com/documents/FDAS/institutional-investors-digital-asset-survey.pdf.

2. "I AM HODLING," BitcoinTalk.org, December 18, 2013, https://bitcointalk.org/index.php?topic=375643.0.
3. Paolo Tasca, Shaowen Liu, and Adam Hayes, "The Evolution of the Bitcoin Economy: Extracting and Analyzing the Network of Payment Relationships," July 1, 2016, https://papers.ssrn.com/sol3/papers.cfm?abstract_id=2808762.
4. Jamie Redman, "Close to 14,000 Google Scholar Articles Mentioned Bitcoin in 2019," December 25, 2019, https://news.bitcoin.com/close-to-14000-google-scholar-articles-mentioned-bitcoin-in-2019/.
5. Note that in 2019, nearly 14,000 research papers mentioned Bitcoin.
6. "Bitcoin Acceptance Growing in JAPAN," Business Insider Intelligence, April 7, 2017, https://www.businessinsider.com/bitcoin-acceptance-growing-in-japan-2017-4.

CHAPTER 8

1. Francesca Gino, "Banking Culture Encourages Dishonesty," *Scientific American*, December 30, 2014, https://www.scientificamerican.com/article/banking-culture-encourages-dishonesty/.
2. Malcolm Ritter, "Maybe Banking Culture Doesn't Always Make People Dishonest," phys.org, November 13, 2019, https://phys.org/news/2019-11-banking-culture-doesnt-people-dishonest.html.
3. Sheera Frenkel, Nathaniel Popper, Kate Conger, and David E. Sanger, "A Brazen Online Attack Targets V.I.P. Twitter Users in a Bitcoin Scam," *New York Times*, July 15, 2020, https://www.nytimes.com/2020/07/15/technology/twitter-hack-bill-gates-elon-musk.html?utm_source=newsletters&utm_medium=firstmover&utm_campaign=&clid=00Q1I00000KJy0CUAT.

CHAPTER 9

1. CreditCoin.com, "New Study Shows Complicated Purchasing Process Is Biggest Hurdle for Cryptocurrencies," June 29, 2018, https://www.prnewswire.com/news-releases/new-study-shows-complicated-purchasing-process-is-biggest-hurdle-for-cryptocurrencies-300674527.html.
2. Oliver Isaacs, "8 Reasons Why This Could Be the Time to Take Bitcoin Seriously," entrepreneur.com, May 22, 2020, https://www.entrepreneur.com/article/348168.
3. Mark Cuban, "Mark Cuban Answers Business Questions from Twitter," *Wired*, September 27, 2019, https://www.youtube.com/watch?v=DWBlN9o6Azc&%3Bt=2m18s.
4. "Analyzing Bitcoin Mining Profitability Following 'The Halving' and Its Indication for Price," February 7, 2020, https://tradeblock.com/blog/analyzing-bitcoin-mining-profitability-following-the-halving-and-its-indication-for-price.
5. "Bitcoin Energy Consumption Index," August 2020, https://digiconomist.net/bitcoin-energy-consumption/.
6. "Bitcoin Energy Consumption Index," Digiconomist, accessed January 28, 2021, https://digiconomist.net/bitcoin-energy-consumption/.

7. "Bitcoin Energy Consumption Index," Digiconomist, accessed January 28, 2021, https://digiconomist.net/bitcoin-energy-consumption/.

CHAPTER 10

1. "Number of FDIC-insured commercial bank branches in the United States from 2000 to 2019," Accessed February 13, 2021, Statista, https://www.statista.com/statistics/193041/number-of-fdic-insured-us-commercial-bank-branches/.
2. "Number of Bank Branches for United States," Economic Research Federal Reserve Bank of St. Louis, Accessed February 13, 2021, https://fred.stlouisfed.org/series/DDAI02USA643NWDB.
3. Commercial Bank Branches (per 100,000 people)—Italy, World Bank, Accessed February 13, 2021, https://data.worldbank.org/indicator/FB.CBK.BRCH.P5?locations=IT.
4. "Financial Inclusion on the Rise, But Gaps Remain, Global Findex Database Shows," The World Bank, April 19, 2018, //www.worldank.org/en/news/press-release/2018/04/19/financial-inclusion-on-the-rise-but-gaps-remain-global-findex-database-shows.
5. "Decline of Global Extreme Poverty Continues but Has Slowed: World Bank," World Bank, September 19, 2018, https://www.worldbank.org/en/news/press-release/2018/09/19/decline-of-global-extreme-poverty-continues-but-has-slowed-world-bank.
6. "Childhood and Intergenerational Poverty: The Long-Term Consequences of Growing Up Poor," National Center for Children in Poverty, November 2009, https://www.nccp.org/publication/childhood-and-intergenerational-poverty/.
7. "Does Financial Inclusion Reduce Poverty and Income Inequality in Developing Countries? A Panel Data Analysis," *Journal of Economic Structures* 9, Article number: 37 (April 28, 2020), https://journalofeconomicstructures.springeropen.com/articles/10.1186/s40008-020-00214-4.
8. "ABA Survey Finds Online, Mobile Most Popular Banking Channels," *ABA Banking Journal*, October 16, 2018, https://bankingjournal.aba.com/2018/10/aba-survey-finds-online-mobile-most-popular-banking-channels/.
9. "Mobile Banking: A Closer Look at Survey Measures," Federal Reserve, March 27, 2018, https://www.federalreserve.gov/econres/notes/feds-notes/mobile-banking-a-closer-look-at-survey-measures-20180327.htm.
10. "Are Americans Embracing Mobile Payments?" The Pew Charitable Trusts, October 3, 2019, https://www.pewtrusts.org/en/research-and-analysis/issue-briefs/2019/10/are-americans-embracing-mobile-payments.
11. "As Fintech Apps Become More Popular, Consumer Privacy Concerns Persist, Survey Finds," The Clearing House, August 22, 2018, https://www.theclearinghouse.org/payment-systems/articles/2018/08/data-privacy-08-21-2018.
12. "As Fintech Apps Become More Popular."

CHAPTER 11

1. "CFA Institute Cautions Investors On 12 Common Mistakes," CFA Institute, 2006, http://www.loveless-wealth.com/our-blog/63-article1.html.
2. https://www.kiplinger.com/tool/investing/T041-S001-top-performing-mutual-funds/index.php?table_select=Alts.
3. Natixis Global Asset Management, "Investors Expect Returns 44% Higher Than What Financial Advisors Say Is Realistic, According to Natixis Survey," September 9, 2016, https://www.businesswire.com/news/home/20160929005214/en/Investors-Expect-Returns-44-Higher-Than-What-Financial-Advisors-Say-is-Realistic-According-to-Natixis-Survey.
4. Michael Lewis, *The Big Short* (New York: W.W. Norton & Company, 2016), 44.
5. Lewis, *Big Short*, 246.

CHAPTER 12

1. Raynor de Best, "Unique Cryptocurrency Wallets Created on Blockchain.com as of December 9, 2020," Statista, December 10, 2020, https://www.statista.com/statistics/647374/worldwide-blockchain-wallet-users.
2. Benjamin Pirus, "McAfee Explains Rationale for Why He Still Sees 1 Million Bitcoin By 2020," *Forbes*, September 30, 2019, https://www.forbes.com/sites/benjaminpirus/2019/09/30/mcafee-explains-rationale-for-why-he-still-sees-1-million-bitcoin-by-2020/?sh=4b12dd366f92.
3. Hal Finney, "Re: Bitcoin v0.1 released," email exchange with Satoshi Nakamoto, January 1, 2009, https://www.mail-archive.com/cryptography@metzdowd.com/msg10152.html.
4. Evelyn Cheng, "James Altucher predicts bitcoin will reach $1 million by 2020," CNBC, November 29, 2017, https://www.cnbc.com/2017/11/29/james-altucher-predicts-bitcoin-will-reach-1-million-by-2020.html.
5. Shawn Elias, "Bitcoin at $1 Million Is Not Out of the Question, Says James Altucher," *TheStreet*, June 24, 2019, https://www.thestreet.com/video/bitcoin-1-million-not-out-of-question-james-altucher-14977130.
6. Dylan Love, "This Guy Is Selling His Book Exclusively Via Bitcoin," *Business Insider*, May 13, 2013, https://www.businessinsider.com/james-altucher-choose-yourself-bitcoin-2013-5.
7. Wences Casares, "The Case for a Small Allocation to Bitcoin," March 1, 2019, kanaandkatana.com, https://www.kanaandkatana.com/valuation-depot-contents/2019/4/11/the-case-for-a-small-allocation-to-bitcoin.
8. Mati Greenspan (@Mati Greenspan), "Where Will Bitcoin Be in 10 years?," Twitter, December 29, 2019, https://twitter.com/MatiGreenspan/status/1211200910669570049.
9. Christopher Competiello, "Bitcoin Price Could Hit $500,000 in 10 Years," *Business Insider*, December 11, 2019, https://www.businessinsider.com/bitcoin-price-could-hit-500000-10-years-gold-mark-yusko-2019-12.

10. BlockTV (@BlockTVNews), "Bitcoin to hit $250,000 by 2022? @TimDraper thinks that is a conservative prediction," Twitter, September 13, 2019, https://twitter.com/blocktvnews/status/1172528836652752896.
11. William Suberg, "Chance of $1Mln Bitcoin 0.25%: Vinny Lingham," *Cointelegraph*, June 19, 2017, https://cointelegraph.com/news/chance-of-1mln-bitcoin-025-vinnie-lingham.
12. @VinnyLingham, "I haven't been this bullish on #Bitcoin since 2016," Twitter, October 7, 2020, https://twitter.com/vinnylingham/status/1313944105743863808?s=21.
13. Spencer Bogart, "Bitcoin Is a Demographic Mega-Trend: Data Analysis," Blockchain Capital, April 30, 2020, https://blockchain.capital/bitcoin-is-a-demographic-mega-trend-data-analysis.
14. Maitane Sardon, "A Guarded Generation: How Millennials View Money and Investing," *Wall Street Journal*, March 13, 2020, https://www.wsj.com/articles/the-recession-left-millennials-loaded-with-debtand-cynical-11583956727.
15. Adamant Capital, "Bitcoin in Heavy Accumulation," April 18, 2019, https://docsend.com/view/jwr8qwx.

CHAPTER 13

1. Noelle Acheson, "Bitcoin, Bonds and Gold: Why Markets Are Upended in a Time of Fear," *CoinDesk*, March 9, 2020, https://www.coindesk.com/bitcoin-bonds-and-gold-why-markets-are-upended-in-a-time-of-fear.
2. Jessica Bursztynsky, Warren Buffett: Cryptocurrency 'has no value'—'I don't" own any and never will," *CNBC*, February 24, 2020, https://www.cnbc.com/2020/02/24/warren-buffett-cryptocurrency-has-no-value.html.
3. "The West 100," August 313, 2006, https://www.latimes.com/archives/la-xpm-2006-aug-13-tm-toppower33-story.html.
4. Aaron Hanken, "More than 20% of institutional investors already own digital assets, Fidelity survey finds," *Market Watch*, May 2, 2019, https://www.marketwatch.com/story/more-than-20-of-institutional-investors-already-own-digital-assets-fidelity-survey-finds-2019-05-02.
5. "Digital Asset Investment Report," Grayscale, 2019, https://grayscale.co/wp-content/uploads/2020/01/Grayscale-Digital-Asset-Investment-Report-2019-January-2020.pdf.
6. Grayscale Investments, "Grayscale® Ethereum Trust Announces Resumption of Private Placement," February 1, 2021, http://www.globenewswire.com/news-release/2021/02/01/2167368/0/en/Grayscale-Ethereum-Trust-Announces-Resumption-of-Private-Placement.html.
7. Grayscale (@Grayscale), "Total AUM: $10.4 billion," November 17, 2020, https://twitter.com/Grayscale/status/1328815176154492929?s=20.
8. "Grayscale's Record 2019," Grayscale Investments, January 16, 2020, https://medium.com/grayscale-investments/grayscales-record-2019-8040fd43957.

9. Akin Oyedele, "Jamie Dimon: Bitcoin Is a Fraud That's 'worse than tulip bulbs,'" Business Insider, September 12, 2017, https://www.businessinsider.com/bitcoin-price-worse-than-tulip-bulbs-2017-9.
10. Kate Rooney and Ari Levy, "The Most Influential Endowment ManagerJust Jumped into Crypto with Bets on Two Silicon Valley Funds," CNBC, October 5, 2018, https://www.cnbc.com/2018/10/05/yale-investment-chief-david-swensen-jumps-into-crypto-with-bets-on-two-silicon-valley-funds.html.
11. Kevin Helms, "Nasdaq-Listed Microstrategy Raises Bitcoin Holdings to $425 Million After Second Purchase," bitcoin.com, September 15, 2020, https://news.bitcoin.com/nasdaq-microstrategy-bitcoin-425-million/.
12. Square, "Square, Inc. Invests $50 Million in Bitcoin," (Media Release October 8, 2020), https://squareup.com/us/en/press/2020-bitcoin-investment.
13. Daniel Roberts, "Report: 43% of investors interested in bitcoin are women," Yahoo! Finance, December 11, 2019, https://finance.yahoo.com/news/report-43-of-investors-interested-in-bitcoin-are-women-192156926.html.
14. Dalia Blass, "Staff Letter: Engaging on Fund Innovation and Cryptocurrency-related Holdings," U.S. Securities and Exchange Commission, https://www.sec.gov/divisions/investment/noaction/2018/cryptocurrency-011818.htm.
15. Nathaniel Popper, "SEC Rejects Winklevoss Brothers' Bid to Create Bitcoin EFT," *New York Times*, March 10, 2017, https://www.nytimes.com/2017/03/10/business/dealbook/winkelvoss-brothers-bid-to-create-a-bitcoin-etf-is-rejected.html.
16. Ryan Browne, "Bitcoin Had a Wild Weekend, Briefly Topping $10,000, After China's Xi Sang Blockchain's Praises," CNBC, https://www.cnbc.com/2019/10/28/bitcoin-btc-price-climbs-as-chinas-xi-jinping-embraces-blockchain.html.

INDEX

ABOUT THE AUTHOR

Bobby C. Lee is the founder and CEO of Ballet, a startup that provides user-friendly physical wallets for storing cryptocurrency. His first startup was BTCChina, China's first bitcoin exchange. He exited the business after its successful acquisition in January 2018. Lee serves on the board of the Bitcoin Foundation, a nonprofit organization that has built wider awareness of Bitcoin.

Lee is among the most recognizable figures in the cryptocurrency industry. He is frequently interviewed on digital currencies by leading news outlets, including Bloomberg, *Business Insider*, CoinDesk, CNBC, *Forbes*, Reuters, the BBC, *The Economist*, *Financial Times*, *New York Times*, *Wall Street Journal*, and *Washington Post*, among others. He speaks regularly on the subject at conferences, business organizations, and academic institutions.

Before founding BTCChina, Lee was vice president of technology at Walmart. Lee started his tech career in Silicon Valley as a software engineer at Yahoo!, where he led the development of the earliest online communities.

Lee has bachelor's and master's degrees in computer science from Stanford University.

Visit www.bobbylee.com and follow him on Twitter @bobbyclee